83.54
ZAC

Studies in Immigration and Cultur[e]

Royden Loewen, series editor

Wapiti regional library

REWRITING *the*
BREAK EVENT

Mennonites & Migration in Canadian Literature

J M C P L
DISCARDED

ROBERT ZACHARIAS

UMP
University of Manitoba Press

University of Manitoba Press
Winnipeg, Manitoba
Canada R3T 2M5
uofmpress.ca

© Robert Zacharias 2013

Printed in Canada
Text printed on chlorine-free, 100% post-consumer recycled paper

16 15 14 13   1 2 3 4 5

All rights reserved. No part of this publication may be reproduced or transmitted in
any form or by any means, or stored in a database and retrieval system in Canada,
without the prior written permission of the University of Manitoba Press, or, in the case
of photocopying or any other reprographic copying, a licence from Access Copyright
(Canadian Copyright Licensing Agency). For an Access Copyright licence,
visit www.accesscopyright.ca, or call 1-800-893-5777.

Cover and interior design by Jessica Koroscil
Cover image by Jessica Koroscil

Library and Archives Canada Cataloguing in Publication

Zacharias, Robert, 1977–
Rewriting the break event : Mennonites and migration in
Canadian literature / Robert Zacharias.

(Studies in immigration and culture series, 1914-1459 ; 8)
Includes bibliographical references and index.
Issued in print and electronic formats.
ISBN 978-0-88755-747-7 (pbk.)
ISBN 978-0-88755-448-3 (PDF e-book)
ISBN 978-0-88755-450-6 (epub e-book)

1. Canadian fiction (English)–Mennonite authors–History and criticism.
2. Mennonites–In literature. 3. Emigration and immigration in literature.
I. Title. II. Series: Studies in immigration and culture ; 8

PS8191.M45Z32 2013   C813'.5409921289771   C2013-903501-X
                                                    C2013-903502-8

The University of Manitoba Press gratefully acknowledges the financial
support for its publication program provided by the Government of Canada
through the Canada Book Fund, the Canada Council for the Arts, the Manitoba
Department of Culture, Heritage, Tourism, the Manitoba Arts Council,
and the Manitoba Book Publishing Tax Credit.

FSC
www.fsc.org
MIX
Paper from
responsible sources
FSC® C016245

Contents

Write it again, tell it again.

—*Rudy Wiebe, "Walking Where His Feet Can Walk"*

Preface

Rewriting the Break

The striking image on the cover of this book is Jessica Koroscil's rendering of the Chortitza Oak, sometimes referred to as the "800-year-old oak tree." The massive tree, which still stands in the city of Zaporizhia, Ukraine, was reportedly the original meeting place for the first Mennonites who arrived in the area in the late eighteenth century. Over the next 140 years, the Mennonite colonies in the area grew into a network of villages so cohesive and prosperous that some historians have described it as a "Mennonite Commonwealth." In the aftermath of the Russian Revolution, however, the colonies suffered a dramatic and violent collapse. For those Mennonites who managed to flee to Canada, the Chortitza Oak would take on an important symbolic role in connecting them with their former homeland. It has been featured prominently in artistic and historical accounts of this period, and as the imprint for the first Mennonite publishing house in Canada. Saplings grown from its acorns have been planted at key sites across the country, commemorating a remarkable period in Russian Mennonite history.

Today, the great oak of Chortitza is nearly dead. Its enormous trunk, like most of its many limbs, is stripped of its bark. With its thick branches amputated, the tree has been reduced to a sparse tangle of impressive stumps. It squats at the centre of a small circular park, where a ring of massive metal poles, anchored in concrete around the tree's base, towers above it. A series of metal cords and thick ropes are strung through levers and woven around its branches, holding the limbs aloft. A single limb remains alive, green against the odds.

The Chortitza Oak has become a highlight of the heritage tours that regularly bring North American Mennonites to the former colonies as tourists. It is not, however, being preserved for any connection to the Mennonites' past. The tree—which sprouted from the ground before the Protestant Reformation, and thus before Anabaptism itself—was also an important site for the Cossacks, who had long met beneath its branches before being cleared from the area just prior to the Mennonites' arrival. Today, the oak is being maintained as a symbol of Ukrainian nationalism.

Trees are common enough as genealogical symbols, but it is the Chortitza Oak as it now stands—propped up as artifice in service of another people's past, a single branch stubbornly clinging to life—that most aptly reflects the way that cultural memories are constructed and sustained. The novels examined in this study rewrite the story of the Mennonites in Russia, and I like to think they function much like the wires and ropes wrapped around the limbs of the Chortitza Oak, enabling it to bloom against the weight of history.

Acknowledgements

Over the several years that I have worked on this project, I have had the good fortune of working with a host of generous scholars. I owe a tremendous debt of gratitude to Smaro Kamboureli and TransCanada Institute, as well as the larger School of English and Theatre Studies at the University of Guelph, where I completed an early draft of the book as my PhD dissertation. As my first reader, Smaro was a most rigorous and generous editor—a rare combination, indeed—and a model academic mentor; it was a privilege and pleasure to be a part of TransCanada Institute. From Guelph I moved on to the Centre for Diaspora and Transnational Studies at the University of Toronto, and I want to thank director Ato Quayson, who encouraged me to carve out the time and intellectual space needed to complete this work.

Thanks go to Paul Tiessen, Karen Racine, and Ric Knowles for their timely and valuable feedback on earlier drafts of this project, as well as to Daniel Coleman and Jade Ferguson, whose productive questions quietly nudged the work into deeper waters. I also want to thank both Di Brandt and Royden Loewen, for their warm encouragement and some timely words when I was contemplating a turn towards Mennonite studies. And, in particular, I want to thank Hildi Froese Tiessen, whose generous support of my work continues to be a source of tremendous encouragement to me.

Glenn Bergen and the team at the University of Manitoba Press showed keen interest in pursuing this book and offered steady and timely support through its completion, and for this I remain most grateful. Special thanks, too, go to Jessica Koroscil for her beautiful reconceptualization of the Chortitza Oak as cover art, and to Dallas Harrison for his attentive copyediting. I also gratefully acknowledge the generous financial support I have received over the years, including a number of Social Sciences and Humanities Research Council of Canada scholarships and fellowships that enabled my graduate and postdoctoral work. Versions of each of the chapters in this study were presented at various conferences, and an early version of the introduction and chapter 5 was published as "'What else have we to remember?': Mennonite Canadian Literature and the Strains of Diaspora," in the collection *Embracing Otherness: Canadian Minority Discourses in Transcultural Perspective*, edited by Eugenia Sojka and Tomasz Sikora.

Thanks, finally, to my family. To my parents, for their ongoing interest and support, and for their help with the Low German I never managed to learn. To my partner in life, Arvelle: thank you for your unfailing support, patience, and encouragement, and for making this project possible even as our three beautiful children—Adiah, Samuel, and Talia—were born over the four years that I took to complete the book. It's for you, of course.

—Toronto / Guelph, 2013

REWRITING *the*
BREAK EVENT

Introduction

On Rewriting Migration in Canadian Literature

"Is this the beginning?" So begins John Weier's experimental *Steppe: A Novel* (1995). *Steppe* tells the story of a young Mennonite Canadian man struggling to come to terms with the stories that his father has told him of life in the once-prosperous Mennonite colonies of southern Russia (present-day Ukraine). The novel opens with a page from the young man's journal that, as an introduction to the concerns of this study, is worth quoting in its entirety:

> Is this the beginning? A story should have a beginning. Something must be planted, born. Is this how the words started, where the world began? My father's story. The things he told and told and told.
>
> *Listen,* … he said. Father talked in the truck on the way to the factory, a ton of peaches loaded up behind.
>
> *When I was young,* … he said. We were driving on a Michigan highway.
>
> *In Russland* … Around the tree on Christmas Eve, coloured lights and candles. Father's stories. I loved my father's stories. Words slide through my sleep, pictures drift around me. Everywhere, my father's memories. This is my inheritance. His stories passed on, man to boy. People talk about the male line. This is how it is, and was, father to son. (Is that really true?) (1.1)

By invoking the famous first line of Genesis as a question, *Steppe*'s open-ing sentence signals the novel's larger examination of the ways in which the history of what scholars refer to as the "Mennonite Commonwealth" in Ukraine—from the great heights of its prosperity at the turn of the twentieth century to its dramatic collapse in the aftermath of the Russian Revolution—has come to function as a mythological beginning, or origin story, for the Russian Mennonite community in Canada. The narrator's subsequent ques-tion—"Is this how the words started, where the world began?"—reinforces this initial gesture by invoking and inverting a second biblical beginning, the enigmatic declaration that opens the Gospel of John: "In the beginning was the Word, and the Word was with God, and the Word was God. [...] Through him all things were made" (1:13). Playing on the similarity between "word" and "world," Weier emphasizes how the process of narrative representation is central to the construction of origins, how the structure of his Mennonite "world" is intricately connected to "the word" of his "father's story." By begin-ning, repeatedly, "in the beginning," *Steppe* not only suggests that the story of the Mennonite Commonwealth has taken on the status of a supplementary scripture for Canada's Russian Mennonites—as if its retelling has become as central to the identity of this deeply religious community as the biblical narrative itself—he also quietly begins the project of pulling that story apart.

Weier's narrator, an everyman character who is left without a name, is deeply suspicious of his father's nostalgia. Determined to better under-stand his heritage, he undertakes a research project on the history of the Mennonites in Ukraine, gathering a collection of documents that becomes the novel's patchwork content. Rather than simply replace his father's memories with a revised version of the Russian Mennonite story, the narrator restricts his commentary on his research to short journal and diary entries, which are interspersed between paragraphs from Mennonite and Ukrainian history texts, pieces of fairy tales and scraps of found diaries, snippets of academic lectures, and anecdotes from the trip that he ultimately takes to Ukraine. The novel is presented as an archive, with each of the more than 100 entries collated not by conventional pagination but filed in one of five sections. The first entry, for example, is presented as *1.1 Journal: September 3, 1992*, the second as *1.2 Father Remembers*. As a kaleidoscopic text in which a host of competing and often contradictory perspectives on the Mennonite experience in Russia meld into a portrait of a conflicted community, Weier's novel structurally parallels the larger body of Mennonite Canadian literature, which itself has compulsively "told and told and told" the story of the rise and fall of the Mennonite Commonwealth, along with the subsequent mass migration of over 20,000 Russian Mennonites to Canada. *Rewriting the Break Event* is a study of this repeated narrative, and of the many stories it tells.

Although Russian Mennonites began arriving in Canada en masse nearly 150 years ago, in the 1870s, much of their recent literature has been characterized by clear tropes of migration, displacement, and homelessness, themes that have arisen in large part through a preoccupation with the 1920s Russian experience. This study begins by theorizing what is at stake in a methodology that focuses on the repeated narrativization of key historical experiences in migrant communities, or what I am calling the "narrative strains" of a community's "break event." As I detail below, this formulation plays on historian Hayden White's suggestion that narrative itself always "strains" to project an artificial coherency and completeness onto its subject (11), and draws on sociologist Robin Cohen's suggestion that diasporic communities often mythologize a seminal dispersal history, or "break event," as a means of affirming communal identity across national and generational boundaries (57).[1] Given that, as Herb Wyile notes in *Speculative Fictions*, "historical novels are historically situated representations with contemporary motivations and concerns" (257), the various literary strains in which a key displacement is imagined can be read as recording the deep contestation over how a migrant community understands not only its past, but also its present and future. In this study, I build on Harry Loewen's widely repeated argument that the 1920s migration narrative marks the "birth" of Mennonite literature in Canada to read the collapse of the Mennonite colonies in Ukraine as a break event for Canada's Russian Mennonite community. Without suggesting that they are in any way exhaustive or prescriptive, I isolate and examine four strains of emphasis among the many novels that return to this history as a way of negotiating the shifting contours of Mennonite identity in Canada: the theo-pedagogical narrative, the ethnic narrative, the trauma narrative, and the meta-narrative.

In its most immediate use, the title "Mennonite" is a religious designation referring to the roughly 1.5 million baptized adult members of Mennonite churches around the globe. Along with institutions like the Mennonite World Conference, the five volumes of the recently completed Global Mennonite History Project reflect a faith-based collective identity that spans the world: *Africa: Anabaptist Songs in African Hearts* (2003); *Latin America: Mission and Migration* (2010); *Asia: Churches Engage Asian Traditions* (2011);

Europe: Testing Faith and Tradition (2011); and *North America: Seeking Places of Peace* (2012). Given the much narrower focus of this study, however, my use of the term "Mennonite" primarily refers to the community of approximately 200,000 "Russian Mennonites" in Canada today who can trace their history back through the former Mennonite colonies in present-day Ukraine. This includes both the "Russländer" Mennonites, whose families participated in the 1920s migration to Canada, and the "Kanadier" Mennonites, whose forebears emigrated out of Russia in the 1870s. This type of critical shorthand, which uses a general, faith-based term such as "Mennonite" to refer to a very particular heritage and history, reflects the conventions of the larger literary and critical discourses of Mennonite writing in Canada. Although such conventions are understandable, they are not without their problems, and part of my project here will be to unpack their histories and implications.[2] In fact, as I discuss at some length later in this study, the title "Mennonite" itself is complex and contested, crossed and confused by a host of parallel (and sometimes conflicting) histories—as is the term "Mennonite literature." Readers requiring a more detailed introduction to Canada's Russian Mennonite community might want to turn first to Chapter 1 of this study, where I gloss their long history of migration and the roots of their complex Dutch/ Germanic heritage, offer an overview of the rise and fall of the Mennonite colonies in southern Russia, and provide a brief account of its representation in Mennonite Canadian writing.

Rewriting the Break Event is, first and foremost, a critical consideration of the rewriting of the so-called Russian experience across Mennonite novels in Canada. As a result of this narrow focus, I make no effort to survey the larger body of Mennonite Canadian writing, though I do spend some time on the concept and history of "Mennonite Canadian literature" itself. I make little mention of Swiss Mennonite writing, I touch only briefly on the various writings that reflect the earlier (or later) immigrations of Russian Mennonites to Canada, and I have almost nothing to say about work by Mennonites that does not directly invite a conversation about Mennonite identity through its focus. In the same way, as this is an examination of the relationship among narrative, novels, and communal identity, I make only passing reference to the substantial and important body of Mennonite poetry and drama. Nonetheless, understanding the rewriting of the Russian experience in Mennonite Canadian novels requires a careful attention not only to novels that explicitly engage this history but also to the larger contexts into which these novels have emerged as part of a distinct body of literature. Chapters 2 through 5 offer close and comparative readings of individual novels within the Russian Mennonite context, and Chapter 1 offers a survey of Russian Mennonite history and its representation in Mennonite literature in Canada, along with a discussion of the form and function of Mennonite literary criticism to date.

This lengthy, two-part introduction adopts a much wider critical perspective, using Mennonite Canadian literature as a case study for a discussion about reading migration fiction in Canada. In Part 1, I outline a methodology to enable a careful reading of the rewriting of a given break event. Although the relationship between literature and communal identity is well established, I suggest that a focus on rewriting as a site of communal debate demands a reconsideration of the function of narrative specifically within the context of repetition, where it is complicated by questions of referentiality, difference, and temporality. In Part 2, I examine the institutional, political, and critical contexts in which the rewritings of the Russian experience have emerged, and how their circulation as part of something called "Canadian literature" in general, and "Mennonite Canadian literature" in particular, has worked to facilitate, restrict, or otherwise shape their forms. This second part calls attention to the perhaps obvious but rarely discussed fact that "Mennonite Canadian literature" is not a literary construct but a critical one. Far from a transparent descriptor of a clearly bounded collection of texts, it is better understood as a critical frame of emphasis with its own history and its own set of assumptions. Although the larger study is focused on a particular selection of Mennonite Canadian literature, this introduction works to establish a critical methodology that may hold significant implications for the study of migration or diasporic literatures in Canada more generally—a point to which I will return at some length in the Conclusion.

Part 1

"The Tragic Curve of All Mennonites": Narrating the Break Event

Recent diaspora scholarship has begun to grapple with the ways in which specific historical experiences of traumatic dispersal often come to function as originary narratives that authorize particular versions of non-national imagined communities. In his influential study *Global Diasporas* (1997, 2008), for example, Cohen notes that many diasporic communities are marked by

The "Mennonite Commonwealth": the former Mennonite colonies of Chortitza and Molotschna in southern Russia (present-day Ukraine). Inset: Mennonite migration patterns following the Russian Revolution.

what he calls their "catastrophic origins" (1), or the "unambiguously grisly episodes in their history that led to their original or further dispersion" (27). Naming these key historical moments a community's "decisive 'break event'" (54), Cohen offers the history of the Jewish people and the destruction of the temple in 586 BC as his primary example of how such events become mythologized in a collective memory. Noting that Jewish history includes a host of migrations spurred by a variety of motives, Cohen concedes that the community's history is "much more diverse and more complex than the catastrophic tradition allows" (2), and he even suggests that the Babylonian experience has been "unduly emphasized in [its] folk memory" (27). Nonetheless, he argues that the Jewish diaspora is widely "assumed to have been galvanized by [this] single cataclysmic event" (35), and he points out that "Babylon subsequently became a codeword among Jews for the afflictions, isolation and insecurity of living in a foreign place" (3). Cohen goes on to suggest that the memory of a single break event often comes to hold a dominant position in what he calls "victim diasporas," concluding that each community is lent a "particular colouring" by its "scarring historical event—Babylon for the Jews, slavery for the Africans, famine for the Irish, genocide for the Armenians and the formation of the state of Israel for the Palestinians" (28).

For other scholars working on diaspora, the break event lends a community something more than a "particular colouring." In her essay "Defining Diaspora, Refining a Discourse," for example, Kim D. Butler argues for a closer consideration of the various originary causes or "conditions" of dispersal, suggesting that they are "akin to the traumas of childhood; they mark the diasporan group and inform the direction of its development" (203). Given that "the dispersal itself stands out as a fundamental basis of understanding a given diaspora" (199), Butler argues that scholars ought to "emphasize the seminal dispersal because it tends to characterize the diaspora" (204), especially when the dispersal in question is "a massive relocation caused by a discrete crisis" (210). In a more concrete study, Astrid Wonneberger suggests that the popular history of the potato famine offers "a collective memory of a common origin" for Irish identity in the United States (126). Through extensive interviews with self-identified Irish Americans, Wonneberger found the famine to be such a dominant event in the community's history that many of her interviewees simply assumed that it was the motivation behind their families' immigration to North America. According to Wonneberger, few of her interview subjects offered any evidence in support of the claim, and many claimed the famine as part of their personal migration history even when there was clear and convincing evidence to the contrary. Much as Cohen and Butler have suggested, Wonneberger's study concludes that "the diaspora constructs its own catastrophic origin," which comes to function as "an ethnic marker all people of Irish descent could identify with, if they wish" (126).

Where the writings of Cohen, Butler, and Wonneberger constitute socio-logical engagements with diasporas, Vijay Mishra makes a similar argument while being attuned to their literary and psychoanalytic aspects.[3] Even as he argues for a move "beyond a purely heuristic desire for a neat taxonomy" (442), Mishra, too, insists that scholars ought to focus on the idea of an origi-nary dispersal. Drawing on Jacques Lacan and Slavoj Žižek, he emphasizes the "construction of desire [that takes place] around a particularly traumatic event," and argues that the "fantasy of the homeland is then linked, in the case of diaspora, to that recollected moment when diasporic subjects feel they were wrenched from their mother(father)land" (423). Offering slavery, indentured labour, the Holocaust, and the Ukrainian famine as examples of "wrenching" diasporic events, Mishra suggests that "the 'real' nature of the disruption is not the point at issue [; …] what is clear is that the moment of 'rupture' is transformed into a trauma around an absence that because it can-not be fully symbolized becomes part of the fantasy itself" (423). Importantly, Mishra goes on to suggest that the historical facts of dispersal are a necessary but insufficient focus for scholars, who, he argues, must also attend to "the complex procedures by which diasporas renegotiate their perceived moment of trauma and how, in the artistic domain, the trauma works itself out" (442). As the language of trauma, crisis, and catastrophe suggests, many of these originary events are deeply violent, a fact that helps to explain not only the dispersal itself but also the power that the memories of such events hold for the larger community.[4]

The central argument of this study is that it is worth pausing over the literary rewritings of such break events, which, in returning to the same conceptual and historical ground over and again, serve as cultural palimpsests for how a given migrant community renegotiates its larger collective history. Although I am drawing the vocabulary of the break event from diaspora studies, part of my argument will be that the framing concepts for critical engagement with migrant communities are themselves part of the matter up for debate in the retellings of a migration narrative.[5] I want to suggest that terms such as "diaspora," "immigrant," "nomad," "refugee," "expatri-ate," and "exile" are as much categories of literary and critical representation as they are sociological terms of classification. In the case of the Russian Mennonite 1920s migration narrative, for example, some rewritings stress the community's connection to the past Commonwealth, presenting Canada's Mennonites as a community in exile from its homeland; others focus on the community's adaptation to and struggles in Canada, positioning Mennonites as immigrants; still others present Mennonites as a diaspora, emphasizing the transnational network that connects members of the community across both time and space, while looking back to Ukraine as a lost homeland. All, however, implicitly underscore the ongoing importance of the migration narrative for the contemporary community. Although I recognize that the term "migration" is not entirely neutral, I am adopting it here as a more comprehensive term, of which the various concepts in the critical lexicon of displacement can be understood to constitute more specific forms. The juxtaposition of competing, contrasting, or contradictory literary representations of the same event does more than simply lay bare the central concerns of a given community; it also helps to reveal the politics inherent in the critical vocabulary employed to discuss such literature.

In much the same way, the critical vocabulary that we adopt often betrays our assumptions about the cultural identity of a given community, framing our discussions in terms that anticipate our conclusions. For reasons that I hope will become clear as this study progresses, I have adopted the term "community" as my primary framing concept for Mennonites in Canada. Like "migration," "community" is not an entirely neutral term, but, unlike "ethnic" or "religious" group or "nation," "community" does not immediately signal a clear set of assumptions regarding the key defining features of the group. Intentional ambiguity is rarely a solution to problems of definition, but it is useful in the context of this study in that it allows me to explore the diversity of ways in which a single community can be imagined. Furthermore, the language that I am deploying here—of the construction of Mennonite identity as a process of imagining a community—signals my indebtedness to Benedict Anderson's analysis of nations as imagined communities. Mennonite identity has, at times, been imagined in national or political terms (as I discuss in Chapter 3), but while I draw on Anderson's work to establish the connection between narrative and group identity below, I want to stress that I intend my use of "community" to be understood as an umbrella concept that encompasses its ethnic, religious, nationalist, or other manifestations. Again, the point here is not to foreclose the possibility that the Mennonite community might be best understood as grounded in particular conceptual terrain but to stress that such a question is part of the debate that unfolds across the literature.

It is hardly surprising that for the Russländer, or the 1920s migrants and their descendants, the Russian experience has taken a primary position in their larger understanding of Mennonite history and identity. "The destruction of the Mennonite Commonwealth," reports anthropologist James Urry, became "the foundation for a new marking of the past by Mennonite refugees from the Soviet Union" ("Memory" 39). As Urry goes on to note, however, the impact of this history as a "foundation for a new marking of the past" would quickly spread beyond the Russländer tradition, as it took on a central role in the construction of Mennonite Canadian identity more generally.[6] Part of my argument here will be that the literary tradition has played an important role in this process. As Sarah Klassen writes in a review of a novel returning to this period, this difficult era has "produced a prolific harvest of stories that Mennonites have been telling ever since" (57). Indeed, as I trace at length in Chapter 1, the Russian experience not only occasioned an unprecedented burst of literary output among Canadian Mennonites, it has maintained a place at the forefront of the negotiation of Mennonite cultural identity in Canada by virtue of an ongoing, prominent presence in this growing body of literature.

Just as Cohen recognizes that Jewish history is "much more diverse and more complex than the catastrophic tradition allows" (2), so too Mennonites have a long and varied history beyond the events of the 1920s on which their artists and authors have drawn. Although less reflective of a single dramatic moment, for example, life in the rural Mennonite villages scattered across the Canadian Prairies has been a key focus for Mennonite authors, explored in important novels such as David Bergen's *A Year of Lesser* (1996) and *The Age of Hope* (2012), Miriam Toews's *A Complicated Kindness* (2004), Sandra Birdsell's *Night Travellers* (1982) and *Children of the Day* (2005), Armin Wiebe's *The Salvation of Yasch Siemens* (1984), and Rudy Wiebe's *Peace Shall Destroy Many* (1962), as well as in poetry by Di Brandt and Patrick Friesen. There is also a small collection of texts focusing on the nearly 8,000 Mennonites who migrated from Russia to Canada following World War II, which includes Barbara Claassen Smucker's novel *Henry's Red Sea* (1955)[7] and Connie Braun's *The Steppes Are the Colour of Sepia* (2008). Perhaps most prominently, the martyrdoms of the sixteenth-century Anabaptists have offered poets a powerful reservoir of images and tropes. Kirsten Eve Beachy's recent edited collection, *Tongue Screws and Testimonies: Poems, Stories, and Essays Inspired by the Martyrs Mirror* (2010), offers an exemplary illustration of the impact of this history on the Mennonite writing community and on the enduring role of the *Martyrs Mirror* in negotiating Mennonite identity. The collection draws together Mennonite writing from both the United States and Canada to form an anthology of reflections on (and occasionally rewritings of) van Braght's text.[8] In gathering a wide range of contemporary perspectives on a seminal period and key text in Mennonite history, *Tongue Screws and Testimonies* can be understood as operating in parallel to the novels of this study, offering a collection of "rewritings" of a history that serves as an alternative break event for a larger North American community of Mennonite writers and scholars. Nonetheless, I take as my focus the many novels whose narratives return to the Russian experience of the 1920s because of this history's prevalence in the larger body of Mennonite Canadian literature, and because of the way in which scholars have emphasized its role in the beginning, or "birth," of Mennonite literature in Canada. In fact, while I focus on the repetition of this history across literary texts for much of this study, it is the repetition of this claim by critics—the interpretation of this literary repetition as constituting an origin for a larger Mennonite identity—that is of most interest to me in the Introduction and first chapter.

In a process that I will trace at some length in Chapter 1, the collapse of the Mennonite Commonwealth in Russia has come to function as a break event for a wider Mennonite Canadian identity. Novelist and critic Al Reimer offers a compelling account of this process in a personal essay entitled "Coming in out of the Cold." As a Kanadier himself (and so a descendant of those Mennonites who had migrated to Canada from Russia in the 1870s), Reimer writes that early in his life he had no interest in his Mennonite heritage. He considered his Kanadier history to be "utterly devoid of drama or glamour" (257), and he felt the Mennonites' Russian story "wasn't really mine" (258). Upon his arrival in Ukraine on a research trip, however, he reports being unexpectedly overwhelmed by both "a terrible personal loss" and an "aching sense of coming home" (261). Reimer suggests that he had finally found "the ancestral home that had lain buried within me all my life" (261). He describes being embraced by a Mennonite woman in Ukraine who mistook him for a long-lost relative, and he recalls approvingly that when he tried to correct her error she "simply laughed and said it made no difference" (262). As a result of what he calls the "ethnic vision that had come to me so unexpectedly," Reimer explains that he adopted the history of the 1920s collapse of the Commonwealth as his own on the logic that "the tragic curve of Russian-Mennonite experience […] is, after all, the tragic curve of all Mennonites" (263). Reimer would go on to write *My Harp Is Turned to*

Mourning (1985), one of the most prominent literary reconstructions of the Mennonites' experience in Russia.

Reimer's expansion of the Russian experience as the story of "all Mennonites" is likely to surprise or even frustrate some readers who have direct, personal connections to this history. Whether or not such a claim is accurate in a sociological sense, however, an examination of the literary history of Mennonites in Canada suggests that Reimer might well be right: because of its many rewritings, the story of the rise and dramatic fall of the Mennonite Commonwealth in Russia has transcended the particularities of its history and has taken on the role of a larger collective myth. That is, Reimer's claim is accurate to the extent that when a past displacement reaches a certain prominence in a community's collective memory—through cultural production, memorialization, historical studies, and so on—it begins to overshadow the complexity of a community's larger migration history and comes to function as an originary myth for the community as a whole. To be clear, recognizing the mythological function of this narrative is not to suggest that it is somehow false. The question to be asked of such narratives is not simply whether they are historically accurate, but what function they have come to play in the larger community. After all, when Weier's narrator closes his opening journal entry with the question "[i]s that really true?" he is referring not only to the details of his father's story but also to the (gendered) role of the communal story as his "inheritance" (1.1).

Narrative and Communal Identity

The argument that there is a tight reciprocal relationship between literature and the formation of collective identity has become a critical truism over the past two decades. This study assumes, with several key reservations, Benedict Anderson's argument in *Imagined Communities* (1991) regarding the prominent role that novels can play in binding communities over time and space. Although its value now lies nearly as firmly in the critiques that it has sustained as in its original arguments, Anderson's study is a classic of the humanities in the sense articulated by Jonathan Culler: in retrospect, its central thesis regarding the nation as an imagined and culturally constructed artifice has become so ubiquitous that it now seems nearly self-evident (20). According to Anderson's well-known account, the advent of print capitalism in the eighteenth century occasioned a widespread shift from a vertical, messianic conception of time (in which the majority of people understood

themselves to be part of divinely ordained, eternal, hierarchical communities) to a horizontal, secular conception of time (in which people began to
understand themselves as participants in a coterminous, communal experience with secular, rather than religious, parameters). Anderson argues that it
was this new conception of a distinct community moving forward in what he
calls, drawing on Walter Benjamin, "homogeneous, empty time"—a complex
and wide-ranging "meanwhile" that Anderson sees as both modelled on and
enabled by the narrative structure of early novels and newspapers—that
facilitated the dramatic rise of nationalism in that century (24). He goes on to
suggest that the process of narration central to the novel as a genre, of select-
ing and setting events in sequence, and drawing meaning from that process,
has been a key element enabling the construction of imagined national identities. Pointing out that those elements of a communal past that "can not be
'remembered,' must be narrated" (204), he suggests that the "heroic pasts" of
nations are carefully constructed narratives that string reified historical moments into a teleological story that binds community members through their
shared investment in the glory and sacrifices of a mythic past.

Anderson's study continues to be a foundational text for contemporary
scholarship on narrative and national identity, but *Imagined Communities*
has been subject to a number of substantive critiques. Most significant, in
the context of this study, are the concerns that critics have raised regarding
Anderson's claim of the universality of the "homogeneous, empty time" of the
nation. As Partha Chatterjee argues, the deeply imperial nature of eighteenth-
century nationalism means that, even where its mode of temporality was
operative around the globe, the so-called empty time of the nation-state was
hardly homogeneous, being experienced unevenly across the heterogeneous
communities that occupied the various strata of colonial rule. Moreover, as
both Chatterjee and Homi Bhabha have made clear, the "emptiness" that
Anderson ascribes to the temporality of the modern nation-state is a dream of
universality challenged by the varied realities of lives lived beyond, and under,
its authority.[9] The temporality of the historical nation-state is not empty at all,
then, but filled with a collection of assumptions central to its political claims
about the relationship between communities and geography, about the power
of capital to structure the rhythms of daily life, about the nature of modernity
and the sacred, and so on. Because these differences are unable to be fully sub-
sumed under a larger homogeneous time, Bhabha argues that the pedagogical
dream of a unified nation requires them to be continually reconfigured into

a patchwork national temporality: the "scraps, patches and rags of daily life must be repeatedly turned into the signs of a coherent national culture," he writes. "In the production of the nation as narration there is a split between the continuist, accumulative temporality of the pedagogical, and the repetitious, recursive strategy of the performative" (209). In Bhabha's reading, the claims of homogeneity and emptiness made for the nation's model of time are fatally undermined by the haphazard and conflicted process of its production.

Since, as Anderson points out (6), all communities larger than those enabled by face-to-face contact are, by definition and of necessity, imagined (which is not the same as saying that they are imaginary in their effects), the novels that help to both structure and reflect a community's self-imagination can be understood as vital sites for an examination of communal identity. While Culler has warned that critics interested in the construction of particular nations will be on shaky ground if they shift Anderson's claim about "the form of the novel as a condition of possibility of imagining the nation to the content of novels as representations of the nation" (38), Bhabha's reminder that it is the "scraps, patches and rags of daily life" that are reconfigured into a single, pedagogical narrative encourages precisely this shift. That is, a turn to particular novels is defensible as a critical investigation into the shape of a given imagined community precisely because, contrary to Anderson's thesis, the novel as a genre is not homogeneous enough to define its effects as the result of an empty or even consistent temporality, much less a static and coherent communal identity. Although it would be a mistake to assume that any single text accurately and fully reflects (or even impacts) the community as a whole, a consideration of a larger set of texts as reflecting a range of the community's engagements with its past, and particularly those texts that directly address the community's key historical narratives, can productively be read as part of its negotiation of a larger cultural identity. What I find in my reading of the strains of the Russian Mennonites' 1920s migration narrative leads me to affirm Anderson's insight into the tight relationship between the novel as a narrative form and the construction of imaginary communities but not to accept the correlative that this relationship is based upon a single, empty experience of time.

The fact that Anderson's study engages with narrative and temporality exclusively at the level of the nation-state might suggest that it is a strange fit for an examination of Mennonite identity. However, even if we accept that Anderson's insights should be restricted to the construction of national communities, the nation-state is not as far removed from Mennonite identity as one might initially assume. Nationalist sentiments are clear enough in many of the discussions of the Mennonite colonies of Ukraine as a "state-within-a-state" or "Commonwealth," for example, and, though rare, even the prospect of a separate Mennonite nation-state has been broached from time to time. As I discuss further in Chapter 3, Arnold Dyck wrote repeatedly of a *Mennostaat,* or Mennonite nation-state, in both his fiction and his personal correspondence. Similarly, James Urry's article "A *Mennostaat* for the *Mennovolk?* Mennonite Immigrant Fantasies in Canada in the 1930s" reveals the elaborate and well-documented political aspirations of the Manitoba Mennonite J.J. Hildebrand during the 1930s. According to Urry, Hildebrand proposed that "Mennonites establish a separate political and economic community in a distinct territory where they could control all aspects of their affairs and exclude outsiders, particularly groups which threatened their continued 'racial' purity" (66). Hildebrand's plans for a Mennonite nation-state, which circulated in various German-language venues in Canada, included a state language (High and Low German), a separate currency (the *Menno Gulden*), and a flag (a dove set against a background of blue, green, and white). According to Urry, Hildebrand's racialized vision of a Mennonite state was "clearly based upon his experiences of the prerevolutionary Russian Mennonite Commonwealth" (68) and heavily indebted to the rhetoric of National Socialism in Germany. What is more, far from being an easily dismissible aberration, as Urry notes, Hildebrand's proposals "drew on established Mennonite experience of peoplehood" and "fed on a belief that as a cultural as well as a religious people Mennonites should control and dominate their own community institutions" (76).

However, I see no reason to assume that the relationship between novels and communal identity should be understood as necessarily restricted to the formation of nation-states. Anderson's thesis is built upon his insight into a relationship between the parallel emergence of the modern nation-state and the novel in the eighteenth century, but as I will attempt to demonstrate in the chapters that follow, the form of the novel, broadly defined as an extended fictional narrative written in prose, is complex and flexible enough to reflect alternative modes of temporality and divergent forms of community. Taking seriously Anderson's claim that "[c]ommunities are to be distinguished, not by their falsity/genuineness, but by the style in which they are imagined" (7), I find that the "style" of a given community's imaginative form—including not only its particular concerns or political structure but also, as I explore throughout this study, its dominant temporal structures of thought—is a matter of significant debate that can be productively traced across the strains of its narrative representation. In fact, critics working on communal memory more generally have consistently stressed the function of narrative as being central to the construction of identity at a variety of scales. None has done so more consistently, or prominently, than philosopher Paul Ricoeur, who writes that "[o]n the deepest level [...] it is through the narrative function that memory is incorporated into the formation of identity" (*Memory* 84–85). Ricoeur argues that it is only through the process of narration that the notion of identity becomes tenable at all. "Narrative identity," he insists, "rests on a temporal structure that conforms to the model of dynamic identity" and thus is able to construct and reflect a dynamic conception of the self that remains the "same" over time only to the extent that it can weave together its "different states" into a coherent (if fragile) identity (*Time* 2: 246). For Ricoeur, *all* identity is, unavoidably, narrative identity: "Individual and community are constituted in their identity by taking up narratives that become for them their actual history" (*Time* 2: 247). Although Anderson touches only briefly on the formal qualities of narrative in relation to the nation-state in his *Imagined Communities,* Ricoeur identifies narrative as the constituent element of the very possibility of identity itself.

Although it might seem that we are drifting far from our original focus on Mennonite literature or on the repetition of key narratives of migration, the structure and function of narrative—along with its relationship to temporality that I will explore further shortly—will prove to be at the heart of this study. Recent work in narrative theory has questioned the structuralist assertion of the autonomy and stability of texts that would allow a quasi-scientific analysis of a narrative's constituent parts. Nonetheless, critics as varied as Suzanne Fleischman, Hayden White, Gerald Prince, and José Ángel García Landa all continue to emphasize how narrative, as a representation of a series of events over time, unavoidably selects some events and passes over others, imposing an order onto experience that does not exist outside the structure of narrative itself. When, in a 2008 article, Prince sought a definition that would not conflict with any "widely held views about the nature of narratives," he settled on describing narrative as the "logically consistent representation of at least two asynchronous events" (19). His emphasis on asynchronicity affirms both Anderson's focus on the form of temporality constructed by the narratives of early novels and Ricoeur's insistence that narrative identity "rests on a temporal structure." Importantly, Prince's suggestion that narrative aims to represent these events over time in a "logically consistent" manner, rather than, say, in list form, underlines what is at stake in what we might call the ordering power of narrative. The purpose of the "configurational operation of narrativization," writes Fleischman, is to "impose a particular order and coherence on the events and to render their configuration meaningful" (95, 96). Or, in White's memorable turn of phrase, "narrative strains for the effect of having filled in all the gaps, of [...] an image of continuity, coherency, and meaning" (11).

Although I take from Anderson the significance of the narrative form and an attendant concern with temporality in the construction of communal identity, I am equally interested in the way in which the contents of specific narratives work to structure the community that they imagine. That is, where Anderson focuses on the role of the media—on how newspapers and novels create imagined communities out of their shared audiences—this study narrows the critical focus to the process of narration through which such communities are subject to revision, including the role of content: on how a single historical story, told repeatedly, works to inform and potentially transform the community to which it refers. If it is true, as Ricoeur argues, that the construction of any coherent identity is necessarily the product of the narrative form, then the debate about the particular shape and scope of a given community—its central concerns, its core beliefs, its key histories, and the possibilities for its future—can be read as being undertaken by the contents of narratives themselves.

Rewriting a Usable Past

Scholars interested in Mennonite writing have long recognized narrative and literature as being central to the construction and maintenance of a communal Mennonite identity. It was, after all, a deep faith in the ultimate authority of Christian scripture that brought together their forebears, the sixteenth-century religious dissenters collectively referred to as Anabaptists. This focus on the pre-eminence of scripture resulted in an emphasis on basic education and literacy skills throughout Mennonite history, even leading to an active (if perhaps not exactly vibrant) text culture in the Mennonites' later years in Russia, along with a nascent literary community even among the early Mennonite settlers in Canada.[10] In addition to the Bible, which retains a central position in the larger Mennonite community, other key texts have played important roles in building and sustaining a collective Mennonite identity. Chief among these secondary texts is Thieleman J. van Braght's monumental collection of Anabaptist martyr stories, the *Martyrs Mirror* (1660). I will return to the important role that the *Martyrs Mirror* has played in Mennonite literature in Chapter 2 as part of my discussion of theo-pedagogical narratives. Here, however, I want to note that, in addition to the spiritual import that this text has held for Mennonites over the centuries, it can be understood, as Victor G. Doerksen has suggested, as "[t]he original Mennonite literature" ("From" 199). As such, the *Martyrs Mirror* has served to affirm and extend the community's collective investment in print narrative beyond the covers of the Bible itself. John S. Oyer and Robert S. Kreider suggest that the *Martyrs Mirror* illustrates how the Mennonite Christian identity has been "[e]ncompassed by the caring wings of story" (7), a claim that can be understood as being reflected, and affirmed, by Beachy's *Tongue Screws and Testimonies.*

In 1942, Harold S. Bender's brief but influential essay "The Anabaptist Vision" further cemented the role of narrative in the maintenance of Mennonite communal identity. Widely understood as a fashioning of what Albert Keim calls a "useable past" for the Mennonites in North America (327), the search for "the true essence of Anabaptism" led Bender to draw what he called "a clear line of demarcation" between the Mennonites' "true" Anabaptist forebears and those whom he deemed heretical. More recently, his selective methodology has been heavily critiqued by scholars of Anabaptist history; however, if van Braght's collection of martyr stories can be understood as extending the Anabaptist faith in texts beyond scripture, then it is Bender's vision of Mennonite history—short, selective, carefully constructed, and widely disseminated—that best exemplifies the impact of the ordering power of narrative in modern Mennonite history.

Over the past thirty years, scholarship on Mennonite literature in North America has quietly positioned literary authors as the heirs to this tradition. In fact, one of the earliest critical discussions of Mennonite fiction establishes a direct and self-conscious connection between narrative, literature, and the maintenance of a Mennonite communal identity. Writing in 1978, the American John L. Ruth laments the lack of literature produced by North American Mennonites and calls for a renewed interest in what he calls "our heritage—our story" (39). As the first extended study of Mennonite literature in North America, Ruth's *Mennonite Identity and Literary Art* has been widely influential in Canadian Mennonite criticism, cited (albeit often as a foil) by critics such as Hildi Froese Tiessen, Harry Loewen, Al Reimer, and Magdalene Redekop. In the collection's opening essay—"Where Is the Story?"—Ruth notes what he calls "the recent phenomenon of the Black story *Roots*" and "the sugar-coated Jewish *Fiddler on the Roof*" as evidence that, in order "to have identity, we must have some access to our past, and if we are speaking of group identity, we mean group-past" (10). Accordingly, Ruth positions narrative as the primary means of enabling Mennonites to imagine a communal identity: "Access to a meaningful past is mediated via story—information connected in a pattern that snags our attention by narrative, has a focus, carries a theme, resonates atavistically with our depths" (10). Although Ruth positions much of his argument in the context of the Swiss American Mennonites, he argues for a fundamental continuity between the Swiss and Russian Mennonite traditions on the grounds of a shared theological tradition as well as this shared commitment to narrative. "The basic challenge to the artist who has the imagination to see the story is the same," he writes. "To bring together in that imagination both the sadness and the victory of the covenant-experience, both the failures and the faith, in such a way the over-arching Salvation-story in which it participates may be grasped" (70). Identifying the 1920s Russian experience as one of the larger "culture of stories" that North American Mennonites should be telling, Ruth commends its potential as a literary subject, noting its "classic and powerful social confrontations, ironies, divergent impulses, personalities and social upheaval" (20).

Ruth is not alone in insisting on the importance of literary narratives in the construction of a contemporary Mennonite community. Al Reimer, for example, has insisted that a "people without its own literature, whatever its other social and cultural achievements, is not fully conscious of itself, has not probed its own depths, and remains culturally primitive, complacently provincial" ("Russian-Mennonite Experience" 221). Douglas Reimer has argued at length that Mennonite literature in Canada is functioning to "reterritorialize" a new form of Mennonite identity. Sara Wenger Shenk argues that Mennonites "must become more intentional in identifying and orienting our lives around a specific set of 'determinative stories'" (338). Mennonite self-identity, she insists, "is rooted in story, unfolded through story, and changed through story" (341). The writer Katie Funk Wiebe affirms Shenk's equation. "I am a Mennonite," she writes, "because someone told me a story and told me that it was also my story" (336). Two recent essays specifically consider narrative within the context of Russian Mennonite history. In "Miriam Toews' *A Complicated Kindness:* Restorying the Russian Mennonite Diaspora," Natasha G. Wiebe identifies "three interconnected stories of diaspora" within Toews's award-winning novel (35). Wiebe identifies the 1920s migration history as "a dominant narrative of the Canadian Mennonite scholarly and literary community," which Mennonite critics and authors adapt to "re-present community and personal histories and to establish their identities as Mennonites" (34).[11] In "Silence, Memory, and Imagination as Story: Canadian Mennonite Life Writing," Connie T. Braun draws on the work of Paul Ricoeur to argue for the importance of narrative in the context of Mennonite life writing. Reading work by Rudy Wiebe and Sandra Birdsell alongside Anne Michaels's *Fugitive Pieces* (1996), Braun argues for the importance of attending to the role of silence and memory in narratives that "give voice to the experience of suffering" in the Mennonites' past. "Narration," she declares, "guarantees our future." Although Mennonites are certainly not unique in their commitment to narrative and the retelling of their communal stories as a way of maintaining a distinct cultural identity, they do appear particularly self-conscious about the process.

There are no more than 200,000 Mennonites clustered throughout Canada, but the literary culture that has sprung up among this relatively small community is so surprisingly vibrant that it is sometimes referred to as the "Mennonite miracle"[12]: novelists such as Rudy Wiebe, Sandra Birdsell, Miriam Toews, and David Bergen; poets such as Di Brandt and Patrick Friesen; and playwrights such as Vern Thiessen have enjoyed tremendous popular and critical success, and have won many of Canada's most prestigious literary awards. There are other venues for the construction and maintenance of a communal identity, of course, including other areas of the arts that contribute to a larger cultural memory. The Mennonite craft and choral traditions, in particular, have played important roles in the maintenance of a distinct Mennonite identity, and monuments to the Mennonite presence in Russia are being placed at important locations across southern Ukraine. Historians can argue in great detail about the reasons for the Commonwealth's rise and fall, and theologians can debate at length whether its parameters were justifiable within Anabaptist principles. But part of my argument here is that in Canada, where the novels, poems, and plays written by Mennonites have been remarkably successful, literature is particularly well suited as the site of a larger debate or negotiation of identity. In fact, Hildi Froese Tiessen has recently suggested that today the voices of Mennonite creative writers are "possibly more widely listened to than those of any other thinkers to whom the Mennonite community might lay claim" ("Critical Thought" 238). Elsewhere she goes further, stating confidently that literary authors have become the dominant forces shaping "the new cultural memory of the Mennonites" ("Mennonite/s" 48). Others seem to agree. In the recently released Global Mennonite History volume on Mennonites in North America, for example, Royden Loewen (the current chair of Mennonite studies at the University of Winnipeg and the editor of *Journal of Mennonite Studies*) and Steven M. Nolt take note of the success of Mennonite literature in Canada, flatly announcing that, "[a]lthough many Mennonites chafed at the way they were depicted in these best-selling novels and poetry, these writers nevertheless often became the arbiters of Mennonite identity within the nation" (285). To be clear, Mennonite literature is certainly not always *about* Mennonite identity, even when individual texts make use of Mennonite names and places; one of the challenges currently facing critics of Mennonite literature is to consider what it might mean to complicate "identity" as the field's central concern.[13] Accordingly, in this study I am concerned strictly with works that explicitly seek to comment on Mennonite history and identity, and to take seriously the complexities of the influential debate that has arisen between them.

Time, Temporality, and the Strain of Repetition

What J. Hillis Miller writes about individual novels in *Fiction and Repetition*— that "what is said two or more times may not be true, but the reader is fairly safe in assuming that it is significant" (2)—holds true across a body of literature, as well. It may seem obvious that the repetition of a key narrative of migration both reflects and affirms the event's importance, but the process of repetition is itself complex, and its function cannot be overlooked in the meaning constructed by the narrative. For example, there is a sense in which *any* piece of writing is always, by definition, a form of repetition.[14] Structuralism demonstrated that, inasmuch as language can only signify through the acceptance of agreed upon signs and pre-established concepts, writers are always already appealing to, or repeating, a recognized construct. Every text, Roland Barthes famously declared, is but a "tissue of quotations drawn from the innumerable centres of culture" ("Death" 1468). Within any single novel, repetition functions through the recurrence of particular scenes, tropes, or phrases that gather significance with each appearance. Alternatively, one could expand that focus to show how, at the level of archetypes and mythological patterns, narratives will always, beneath their superficial variations, repeat one of a number of limited stories.[15] Janice Kulyk Keefer, for example, has suggested that Sandra Birdsell's *The Russländer* can be understood as a retelling of "the oldest story in the world: paradise lost," while Al Reimer has drawn a comparison between the 1920s migration and what he calls the "garden story" (*Mennonite Literary Voices* 16). While I consider several of these forms of repetition throughout my study, my focus here will be primarily on repetition in and across novels taking a shared historical event as their central focus.

Miller's study is useful in that it suggests two broad approaches to repetition that, while somewhat reductionist, offer a starting point for considering how repetition functions within the narrative strains of a break event. Arguing that Western ideas of repetition can be split between Platonic and Nietzschean traditions, Miller suggests that the former can be understood as theories grounding repetition "in a solid archetypal model" in which "the validity of the mimetic copy is established by its truth of correspondence to what it copies" (6). The latter, in contrast, "posits a world based on difference," in which repetitions are "ungrounded doublings which arise from differential interrelations among elements" (6). Here Miller shifts a little too quickly between repetition as representation (how a novel seeks to "repeat" the world by representation) and repetition as reiteration (what happens when a given trope, term, or image is repeated), but this distinction turns out to be largely superficial: in the Platonic tradition even reiteration is assumed to point to a transcendent plane, while in the Nietzschean tradition even the "original" subject of representation turns out to be the product of difference and repetition itself. In much the same way, the distinction between these two models of repetition is less clear than Miller initially implies. The mimetic claim of a novel such as Janice L. Dick's *Out of the Storm* (2004), for example, might be to represent the past "as it really was," but such a claim to truth can be understood as being always already destabilized by the differential assumptions that underpin such claims of referentiality. Weier's *Steppe*, on the other hand, might attempt to expose the unavoidable fictiveness of historical narratives, but it does so by uncovering shards of forgotten or forbidden histories, arguably appealing to the generalized authority of the very construct that it seeks to question. "[E]ach form of repetition," Miller concedes, "inevitably calls up the other as its shadow companion" (16).

To the extent that this study assumes that it is possible to isolate a collection of texts that recount the last days of the Mennonite colonies in Russia and the dispersal of Mennonites around the globe, it might appear to work within the Platonic tradition. Indeed, it seems to assume that, in some important way, *Texts C and D* are the same as, or able to repeat, *Text B* because they all represent the "same" historical event, with the validity of their representations at least partially established by their correspondence to the history that they purport to represent. The novels that I will examine here are bound together as a set of texts by their shared historical referents, which include a common repository of highly specific historical details, such as key individuals (Mennonite leader B.B. Janz or the anarchist leader Nestor Makhno) and key events (the massacre at Eichenfeld or the mass flight out of Moscow in 1929). This might appear as the normative model of repetition, a repetition that, at least according to Miller, marks the fundamental assumption "that underlies concepts of imitation in literature" (6). Yet, to the extent that I seek to locate the significance of these repetitions in their differences rather than in their similarities, the study is also deeply indebted to the Nietzschean tradition. That is, these texts are worth gathering together not because they succeed in repeating a shared past but precisely because they fail to do so. Their departures from their predecessors make it possible to talk of different texts (i.e., of *rewritings* rather than simple *replications*) and reveal the competing motives animating their reorganizations of the history that they simultaneously reflect and construct. Each retelling, each strain of the larger narrative, affirms the importance of the Mennonites' dispersal history while rewriting it in significant ways.

 We can gain a better sense of what is at stake in this process of repetition by turning back to Ricoeur's work on narrative identity. In the second volume of *Time and Narrative,* Ricoeur suggests that the process of change through repetition demonstrates the fragility of narrative identity, even as it constitutes the necessary condition for both the maintenance of identity and meaningful communal dialogue. Writing in terms that clearly resonate with the focus of this study, Ricoeur suggests that this process of change through repetition reveals the instability of the presumably secure historical events themselves. "Just as it is possible to compose several plots on the subject of the same incidents (which, thus, should not really be called the same events)," he writes, "so it is always possible to weave different, even opposed, plots about our lives" (248). I will return to this question of the stability of the historical referent in

Chapter 1. For now, I want to underscore that, if Ricoeur is correct that the narrative foundation of identity means that identity is always being secured and threatened by the unending process of repetition, then the rewriting of a break event can be understood as simply the most prominent example of a process constantly at work in the community. "Narrative identity continues to make and unmake itself," he continues, "thus becom[ing] the name of a problem at least as much as it is that of a solution" (249). What is more, Ricoeur argues elsewhere that the "selective function" of narrative—akin to but not synonymous with what I earlier called the "ordering power of narrative"—can be understood as the site or process through which memory is most open to ideology (*Memory* 85). As a result, he goes on to argue, narrative is at its most politically powerful in its repetition, in its function of "recalling, replying to, retorting, even of revoking heritages." "The creative power of repetition," he insists, "is contained entirely in this power of opening up the past again to the future" (*Memory* 380). It is these different interpretations of the past, the products of the "creative power of repetition," that I am referring to as the "strains" of the break event, welcoming many of the word's multiple meanings.[16] And it is in the function of narrative repetition as a politically powerful act that I am drawn to the rewritings of the Mennonites' 1920s migration narrative.

I will undertake a much more thorough consideration of what is at stake in particular examples of repetition throughout this study. In Chapters 2 and 3, for example, I will focus on novels that ground their narratives in a mimetic model of repetition, while in Chapter 5 I will consider a novel that assumes a differential mode of repetition as part of its destabilization of more conventional narratives. A third approach, implied in the psychoanalytic language used by Butler and Mishra in their discussions of diasporas and violence, is to consider the repeated narration of a break event as manifesting a Freudian repetition compulsion, as members of the migrant community attempt to gain mastery over an overwhelmingly traumatic experience by rewriting it. As I will explore further in Chapter 4, a Freudian reading can offer compelling insights into the relationship among trauma, narrative, and community, yet, as I will argue, it is also problematic for at least two reasons: first, it risks uncritically collapsing the differences between how individuals and communities experience trauma; second, as Smaro Kamboureli cautions, it risks "further pathologizing the diasporic subject" (personal interview).

As is suggested by Ricoeur's argument that the creativity of repetition resides in its "power of opening up the past again to the future" (*Memory* 380), the structure of repetition, be it Platonic, Nietzschean, or Freudian, is inextricably bound up with questions of time. For reasons of focus and space, I will not examine the relationship between the novel as a genre and the concept of time as a philosophical construct. Instead, I want to emphasize and explore how the particular representation of temporality in individual novels is integral to their conceptualization of the communities that they both reflect and construct. For the purposes of this study, I will use the word *time*, in its most general and abstract sense, to refer to the ostensibly universal, empty, clock-and-calendar structure that maps the movement of days, months, years, and so on, and the word *temporality* to refer to the human experience or representation of time.[17] It can be difficult to maintain a strict division between time and temporality, but when critics such as Anderson or Bhabha debate whether time is empty or not they are less interested in the metaphysics of time than they are in the political and ethical significance of how time is imagined and experienced, and it is time in this latter sense, properly understood as temporality, that interests me here. As such, questions such as *what is the nature of time?* and *how does the linguistic structure of narrative construct time?* will be set aside to make room for questions more immediately applicable to my project, such as *how does a given novel represent time?* and *how does its temporality reflect or support its larger re-presentation of the Mennonite experience in Ukraine?* These questions, as we will see, turn out to be quite complex themselves.

Keeping in mind how deeply invested both narrative and repetition are in questions of time, I want to return, briefly, to Anderson's suggestion that "thinking the nation" involves homogeneous, empty time. Because, as I will explore at length below, Mennonite Canadian literature as a body of literature was explicitly framed in its emergence by its relation to the nationalizing project of Canadian literature as an institution—hence Mennonite *Canadian literature*—it, too, is caught up in the larger temporal assumptions of the nation-state. Indeed, where it was once critically fashionable to argue that the ascendance of globalization heralded the imminent death of the nation, it has become clear that such pronouncements were hopelessly premature: despite the rise of transnational culture in an era of global capital, even the most non-national of literary narratives continues to circulate in institutional and critical contexts that remain, in many important ways, stubbornly national in their structure. As such, it remains important to attend to the ways in which the institutionalization of national literatures has worked to shape the construction, and continues to inform the negotiation, of non-national imagined communities, and to wrestle with the ways in which a national framework continues to inform such work. At the same time, however, understanding how individual novels imagine the Mennonite experience in Russia requires us, contra Anderson, to recognize the ways in which these novels often interrogate the conceit of a nationalizing temporality.

In an important recent essay, Daniel Coleman calls attention to what he names the "multiple, contemporaneous chronotopes" that are masked by the temporal assumptions of a national literature (231). Drawing on Bakhtin's concept of the chronotope as "the mental maps or images we have of space and time," by which "we humans picture ourselves in a meaningful sequence that adds up to something, that is heading somewhere, and that makes sense of the bewildering happenstance of our daily round" (231), Coleman identifies four of the many chronotopes that he suggests are operative in Canada: Imperial Time; Nation-Based Postcolonial Time; Diasporic Displacement Time; and Indigenous Concentric Time. Importantly, Coleman directly (if briefly) positions Mennonites among those cultural communities whose understanding of time and space opposes the dominant chronotope of the Canadian nation. In fact, the Mennonites' experience in Russia is the first example that he offers as part of his description of a diasporic chronotope that troubles nation-based time: "The successive waves of immigration throughout the twentieth century have given rise to what we might call the chronotope of Diasporic Displacement," he writes. "In this chronotope, cultural groups retain their image of themselves in time by reference to the trauma of displacement, whether it be Mennonites recalling the purges in Russia, Jews recalling the pogroms and Holocaust, Caribbean people recalling the displacements of slavery and colonialism, or Somalis fleeing the breakdown of civil government in their original homeland" (233). Coleman astutely recognizes that the Mennonite experience in Russia has impacted the community's understanding of time and space, but his description of a "Diasporic Displacement" chronotope in the singular shows him to be moving perhaps a bit too quickly. As I will demonstrate throughout this study, even where a communal identity is being negotiated explicitly in reference to a single historical displacement (which would thus, in Coleman's terms, seem to suggest a common investment in a diasporic chronotope), the structure of temporality is itself subject to the ongoing negotiation of identity. That is, the process of struggle or competition that Coleman rightly identifies as occurring at the level of the nation-state, where there is a dominant model of time and space contested by multiple, contemporaneous chronotopes, is a process that can also be traced, through its rewriting, as occurring at the level of any particular community within the nation. It is in this sense that questions of time and temporality, called into our discussion by way of narrative and repetition, will prove important throughout this study.

Among Canada's Russian Mennonites, no cultural object holds a more immediate and tangible connection to the Commonwealth years than the hand-painted Kroeger clocks popular among Mennonites in Russia. There are prominent displays of Kroeger clocks in places such as the Steinbach Mennonite Heritage Museum, for example, and in 2012, Arthur Kroeger's beautifully illustrated and exhaustively detailed coffee table book, *Kroeger Clocks*, became a local bestseller.[18] The easily recognizable Kroeger clocks have large, flat tin or wooden faces and work on a simple but elegant pendulum-and-weight system. Two long chains with brass weights hang well over a metre below the clock face, behind a large, swinging pendulum. Although clockmaking became a focus for Mennonites during their time in Prussia, it was in Russia that the Kroeger name became synonymous with their production and where their use became widespread as the necessary technology in an increasingly industrialized community.[19] According to the *Global Anabaptist Mennonite Encyclopedia Online,* these clocks "could be found in nearly every Mennonite home in Russia" (Krahn and Beck). Many of the Mennonites who fled the Russian colonies took their Kroeger clocks with them, and today the clocks are treasured as both family and community heirlooms. Given that the Kroeger clocks, as Reimer writes in his introduction to Kroeger's book, have become "cultural icons of the Mennonite past" ("Foreword" xix), it is not surprising to come across them at key moments throughout the novels that I consider in this study. In some, the swinging pendulum lulls children to sleep (Dyck, *Lost* 23–24) or provides comfort to frightened teenagers (Birdsell, *Russländer* 252). In others, they tick conspicuously during moments of crisis, as if to insist on the endurance of the Mennonite spirit (Smucker, *Days of Terror* 68–69) or dramatically stop to mark the exact moment of an estate's collapse (Wiebe, *Blue Mountains* 20). Although Mennonite Canadian literature as a body may participate in the temporal assumptions of a national literature, then, what we find in reading across the rewriting of a break event is that even the form of temporality is contested in the literary negotiation of a collective identity.

I want to close this section by returning to the possibilities of a repeated story as it is described in Ruth's early study of Mennonite literature and identity. If the primary question that his study asks—"Where is the story of our people, if one is there?"—is of interest to us, then his next question is just as important: "[A]nd from what point of view can it be seen?" (18). In the final pages of his book, Ruth poses a series of questions that is worth quoting at length. Although it is asked in reference to Mennonite writing more generally, it is astute in its anticipation of the kaleidoscopic portrait of Mennonite history that has been presented in the narrative strains of the Mennonite experience in Russia:

> What version of the truth of the group's experience is most valid? The version of the person who has become disgusted with the tradition's short-comings, and found it a threat to his self-realization? […] Possibly, but what of others of like sensitivity who find it an unintimidating and coherent spiritual home, for all its idiosyncratic imperfections? Is their version not also to the point? Are we likely to be given authentic insight into our heritage from interpretations by suburban, socially and professionally upward-mobile Mennonites who find the peculiarities of their tradition embarrassing? […] From graduates of Fundamentalist seminaries whose criterions of orthodoxy do not focus on issues the Schleitheim Confession found basic? From political leaders who view minority groups primarily as potential elements in voting blocs? (64–65)

As noted earlier, Ruth argues that each narrative of Mennonite history, properly told, becomes a chapter in the "over-arching Salvation-story in which it participates" (70). While Ruth's argument is complex and more nuanced than many critics have allowed—as Reimer insists, Ruth is "most emphatically not calling for mere literary apologists or religious propagandists" (*Literary Voices* 59)—the understanding of Mennonite art put forth in his study is one that ultimately offers a spiritual service to the community. Accordingly, the questions above are largely rhetorical for Ruth. In the context of this study, however, these are questions of a different order. They evince the very competition, or debate, that occurs around the repetition of key narratives and of the various sections of the community with vested interests in the shape of the retelling. I take from Ruth's study his valuable insistence on the deep connection that can exist among narrative, literature, and the maintenance of a Mennonite communal identity. In Chapter 2, I will draw further on his study to help unpack theo-pedagogical writings of the 1920s history. However, his claim that the many narratives about the Mennonites' different historical experiences ultimately ought to tell a single overarching story stands as the opposite of what I have found in reading about the Russian experience across Mennonite Canadian literature, where it becomes clear that even novels recounting the same history tell profoundly different stories.[20]

Before moving on, I want to briefly address the perhaps unusually wide range of voices with which my study engages. As I am interested in both the structure of these individual novels and their function within a wider Mennonite Canadian community, I draw not only on established literary critics publishing in peer-reviewed venues, but also on less scholarly sources, such as book reviews in non-academic Mennonite magazines, as well as commentaries or editorial pieces in Mennonite newspapers. While these latter voices come from very different discursive sites than the former—a fawning review in *Mennonite Brethren Herald* is often writing of a different order than a critical essay in *Canadian Literature*—they nonetheless play a key role in the construction of a communal identity, often reaching a wide audience and directly shaping the reception of the literary works in question. In much the same way, it is important to recognize that novels distributed by major publishers, such as Rudy Wiebe's *Blue Mountains of China* (1970), which was published by McClelland and Stewart, have a different reach than those released by a small press like Reimer's *My Harp Is Turned to Mourning*, which was published by Hyperion. In addition, *Blue Mountains* has garnered a sizeable body of critical responses, while *My Harp* has yet to receive critical treatment in the larger critical venues for Canadian literature. However, the difference between the reach of these novels' publishers, and the length of their critical commentaries, should not be mistaken as fully determining the quality of the novels, nor the scope and nature of their respective interventions into the communal narrative.[21] For example, though I have not found a single review of Reimer's novel in a venue that does not have an obvious connection to the Mennonite community, within the community itself, its publication was, unmistakably, a major event. The novel was widely reviewed, largely to gushing praise, in a host of Mennonite newspapers, periodicals and journals, and even church bulletins. In fact, it was reviewed multiple times in many of these venues, including at least twice in the *Journal of Mennonite Studies* and the *Mennonite Reporter*, as well as in the *Mennonite Mirror* (the latter of which adopted the novel's cover as its own cover image for an issue). The absence of Reimer's novel from the larger venues of Canadian criticism, juxtaposed with its prominence within Mennonite venues, ought to remind us that in questions of cultural identity, the discourses of Mennonite literature and Canadian literature may be overlapping, but they are not identical. As it turns out, untangling the two is a tricky but necessary step in understanding the rewriting of Commonwealth's collapse. In the following section, I consider the history of Mennonite Canadian writing as a body of literature in Canada in order to show how the rewriting—and, importantly, the rereading—of the collapse of the Mennonite Commonwealth has been shaped by the institutional, political, and critical contexts of its emergence. Placed within its historical context, the growth of literature by Mennonites in Canada, while certainly remarkable, is perhaps something less than the "miracle" for which it has been taken.

Part 2

Literature by Mennonites in Canada/Mennonite Canadian Literature

In *Walker in the Fog*, American critic Jeff Gundy makes a distinction between "Mennonite literature" and "Mennonites writing," suggesting that the former is best understood as literature that actively seeks to "promote Anabaptist faith and practice," whereas the latter is simply writing by Mennonites, work that "is sometimes deeply celebratory of this or that aspect of Mennonite identity, sometimes just as deeply critical, sometimes thoroughly ambivalent" (33). Gundy's term "Mennonite writing" is an adaptation of the critical term "Mennonite/s Writing," which has been used in the title of an ongoing series of international conferences and, occasionally, in the critical literature.[22] Increasingly, the term is used to reflect a broad, non-national framework for Mennonite literature, one that engages writing by Swiss, Russian, and other Mennonite groups living in both Canada and the United States. Although promising, this international discourse has remained widely undertheorized; in practice, it has been plagued by the vagaries of the nationalized literary genealogies that it has attempted to bring together. Before we can meaningfully move forward with an international or continental understanding of Mennonite writing, we must first understand the ways in which the discourses of Canadian and American Mennonite literature have been shaped by their divergent national contexts—including their differing socio-political histories, divergent migration histories, and often conflicting engagements with faith, race, and ethnicity.

I will return to what I see as the limitations of Gundy's distinction between "Mennonite literature" and "Mennonite writing" in Chapter 2 of my study, but here I want to draw on his valuable attention to critical terminology to explore a similar distinction that will be crucial to my project: the difference between literature by Mennonites in Canada and Mennonite Canadian literature. Although Russian and Swiss Mennonites have been writing literature in Canada since at least the mid-1920s, the emergence of what we have come to refer to as "Mennonite Canadian literature" as a distinct body of texts has a much more recent history, and its parameters are surprisingly narrow. Hildi Froese Tiessen has called for Mennonite critics to begin to "document our imaginative *becoming* as a community within the multicultural framework of this country" ("Critical Thought" 245), and it is an invitation that I attempt to take up here in order to understand the role of something called "Mennonite Canadian literature" in the various strains of the Mennonites' 1920s migration narrative.

When, in 1988, E.F. Dyck sought to document the emergence of a distinctly Mennonite literature in Winnipeg for *Books in Canada*, he expressed his anxieties about the terms in which it was to be understood. "If the Mennonites are an *ethnic* group then their writing is *ethnic writing*—and what that is is only slowly revealing itself or being invented," he wrote. "Is it a facet of Canadian postmodernism? An aspect of regional literature? A manifestation of our vertical-mosaic-not-melting-pot-identity? Or a barely distinguishable subset of 'immigrant literature'?" (20). Twenty-five years later, the participation of Mennonite Canadian literature in what Dyck speculated as the "invention" of ethnic writing in Canada has often been forgotten, and its implications have largely been left unexplored.[23]

The dehistoricization of Mennonite Canadian literature as a body of literature, indicated by the way in which the title often circulates as a transparent reference to literary writing by Mennonites in Canada, has enabled critics to mistake its emergence following the institutionalization of Canadian literature and through the federal government's nascent multicultural policies as fortuitous rather than formative. In her introduction to *Acts of Concealment* (1992), for example, Tiessen notes that Mennonite literature has benefited from the "celebration of our cultural diversity" in Canada (14), but she suggests that it is nonetheless "an interesting coincidence that Mennonite writing in Canada should flourish at a time when notions of difference, otherness, marginality are predominant in literary discourse" ("Introduction"

19). Similarly, Al Reimer points out that "Canadian literature as a whole
[...] did not gain real momentum until after World War II, at the very time
when Mennonite cultural and linguistic assimilation was taking place," which
meant that "Mennonite writers in the Canadian West have had the enormous
advantage of helping to establish a Western Canadian literary identity merely
by writing out of their own Mennonite experience and exploiting their sense
of ethnic difference" (*Mennonite Literary Voices* 21). Although Reimer is right
to say that the discourse of ethnicity was key to the rise of Mennonite literature in Canada, exactly who benefits from this discourse is somewhat less
clear than he implies. What is more, while Tiessen is careful to avoid the term
"ethnicity" in her 1992 discussion of Mennonite identity—she suggests that
the term is "no longer acceptable in literary criticism" because of its implicit
"exclusionary cultural politics" ("Introduction" 13)—I want to argue that,
precisely as a result of the position of Mennonite writing in the larger history
of Canadian multiculturalism, those exclusionary politics are deeply embedded in the discourse of what we know as Mennonite Canadian literature
today.

Although this is not the place to recount the full history of the institutionalization of Canadian literature or its relationship to Canadian
multiculturalism—a topic that has been well covered by others[24]—it is worth
underscoring the ways in which the politics that shaped the institution of
Canadian literature remain implicit in its contemporary form. Canada has a
lengthy history of government intervention into the nation's cultural production, with the 1951 *Report of the Royal Commission on National Development in
the Arts, Letters, and Sciences* (better known as the Massey Report) commonly
identified as both the founding document in, and the exemplary illustration
of, the federal government's efforts to construct a national culture in the
service of the Canadian state.[25] Commissioned in the wake of World War II
and implemented during the Cold War, the Massey Report positions culture
as a "front" in the ongoing fight for Canadian sovereignty, suggesting that the
country's "military defences" and its "cultural defences [...]" cannot be separated" (275). Noting the growing influence of American culture on Canadians,
the report openly worries that, without an investment in Canadian culture,
the sovereignty of the country is in danger. "We are now spending millions
to maintain a national independence," it notes, warning that the nation will
"be nothing but an empty shell without a vigorous and distinctive cultural
life" (59).

Accordingly, the Massey Report sets out a series of recommendations for bolstering the country's cultural defence, including the establishment of the National Library (1953) and the creation of the Canada Council (1957), an extensive funding body that has since funnelled hundreds of millions of tax dollars into the arts. As Kevin Dowler writes, the Massey Report is the primary example of the Canadian government's "use of culture as a disciplinary regime to ensure the development of a distinctive, and therefore defensible, character of the Canadian state" (338). Importantly, the establishment of a national literature was a frontispiece of the Massey Report, identified by its authors as "the greatest of all forces making for national unity" (225). Although there was no shortage of literary work prior to this period, the coming decades would be heralded as having established Canadian literature. In the same way, while there is a substantial amount of literary criticism in Canada that reaches back before Confederation, it was only in the years following the Massey Report's advocacy for the creation of a distinctly Canadian literature that a corresponding criticism came to gain widespread institutional approval, so that Canadian literature emerged in the 1960s both as a cultural institution and as an established area of critical study.[26] Indeed, whether directly the result of the Massey Report or the product of the growing cultural nationalism that accompanied the coming centennial celebrations, the decade and a half following publication of the report saw a flurry of activity in Canadian literature, including the first conference on Canadian literature (1955); the launch of McClelland and Stewart's New Canadian Library series (1957); the first academic journal dedicated to its study, *Canadian Literature* (1959); as well as the massively influential *Literary History of Canada* (1965). What is important for me here, however, is that Canadian literature was institutionalized in the era of the Massey Report less as a description of literary texts in Canada—there was no shortage of these prior to its publication— than as a prescription for national unity.

If the Massey Report called for state intervention into Canadian cultural production in the name of creating a "distinctive cultural life," the following decade began a process that formally problematized the identity to be created. In 1963, the Royal Commission on Bilingualism and Biculturalism was initiated in order to better understand the relationship between the British and the French in Canada, identified in the commission's report as the nation's two "founding races" (xxi). The commission, however, was promptly forced to come to terms with the larger diversity of Canadian culture; as

Bernard Ostry writes, "the fact of multiculturalism in Canada" was "among [its] reluctant discoveries" (107). Significantly, the commission would engage with this diversity through the concept of ethnic identity, a decision that has had long-standing consequences for discussions of Canadian culture.[27] The fourth volume of the commission's report, *The Cultural Contributions of the Other Ethnic Groups* (1969), officially recognized that "the fine arts […] and folk arts of all the people of Canada are part of Canada's heritage" (220), and it recommended widespread governmental promotion of such work. Prime Minister Pierre Trudeau's 1971 White Paper formally accepted the recommendations of the Royal Commission, beginning a process that would see the "preservation and enhancement of multicultural heritage of Canadians" enshrined as section 27 of the Canadian Charter of Rights and Freedoms (1982). In 1988, this process culminated with the passage of Bill C-93, an Act for the Preservation and Enhancement of Multiculturalism in Canada. With these documents, the federal government announced its multicultural ideal for the country, marking a dramatic shift from earlier celebrations of Canada's "bicultural" heritage. The Multiculturalism Act was supported by a series of programs, councils, and further legislation designed to foster the production of distinctly ethnic cultural products in Canada; twenty-five years later it remains official Canadian policy. As Mary K. Kirtz writes, the fact that "the impetus for the production [of ethnic fiction in Canada] has come in the form of monetary grants and other kinds of official support provided by both federal and provincial governments" means that "Canada, at least on the governmental level, has invented its own version of ethnicity" (9).

Within the framing logic of such policies, there is little question that Mennonite identity in Canada constitutes a form of ethnicity. When, in the mid-1980s, political scientist John H. Redekop undertook a wide-ranging survey, he found that ethnicity had so completely overdetermined the meaning of "Mennonite" in Canadian academic and political discourse that, he argued, Canadian Mennonites ought to concede a strictly ethnic understanding of the title "Mennonite" and begin reclaiming the title "Anabaptist" to reassert their religious identity (*People*). In this context, it is hardly surprising to find that Mennonite writing is widely considered part of a larger genealogy of multicultural or ethnic literary studies in Canada.[28]

An understanding of the ways in which the Canadian state interpellated ethnic literature as part of a strategic deployment of culture reveals that the rise of Mennonite Canadian literature, like the critical focus on notions of difference and otherness in Canadian literary studies, was not simply coincident with but also in many ways the consequence of the institutionalization of Canadian literature within the context of an emergent multiculturalism. This is not to suggest, of course, that there was no literature by Mennonites prior to this period or that Canada's policy of multiculturalism created the concept of Mennonite ethnicity on its own—far from it, on both accounts. The point, rather, is that the official recognition and endorsement of the cultural production of minoritized communities in Canada under the aegis of ethnicity encouraged and emphasized the ethnic elements already found in Mennonite writing. What is more, the overwhelming majority of Mennonite authors in Canada have come from Russian Mennonite descent. Given that the ties binding the Swiss, Russian, and other Mennonite communities are primarily theological rather than cultural or ethnic, it is hardly surprising to find that "Mennonite Canadian literature," understood under the banner of ethnicity, quickly became associated nearly exclusively with Russian Mennonites.

The emphasis on ethnicity would quickly overshadow the wider variety of ways in which Mennonite texts were configuring communal identity. Given the importance of religion to Mennonite identity, for example, one might expect theology or issues of faith to be at the forefront of Mennonite literary critical discourse. However, the prominence of ethnicity as a critical concept coupled with the dearth of a significant discourse of religion in Canadian literary studies—where, as Evelyn Hinz writes, "religion or morality are topics rarely [...] overtly addressed" (xiii)—has meant that even those texts clearly engaging with Mennonite religious concerns have been forced to sit uneasily within the genealogy of multicultural or ethnic literary studies. In a footnote to a larger discussion of Mennonite writing in North America, Ann Hostetler underscores this point by contrasting the circulation of Mennonite literature in Canada and the United States. Mennonites "are considered ethnic writers in Canada, where ethnicity seems to be based more on national origin and language than on race," she suggests, while "in the United States, Mennonites are simply one of many hundreds of Christian sects vying for attention" ("Bringing" 149).[29] Canada's multicultural frame for minoritized literature has created a critical context in which religious difference has been consistently misrecognized as representing an ethnic distinctiveness. Religion, one might say, is ethnicized in the discourse of Canadian literature.[30]

It is primarily because the various contexts for the emergence of Mennonite Canadian literature have been forgotten that, as Victor G.

Doerksen has noted, Mennonite writing in Canada is often imagined to have "appear[ed] *ex nihilo*" with the publication of Rudy Wiebe's *Peace Shall Destroy Many* in 1962 ("Recalling" 146). Wiebe's huge presence as the major figure in Mennonite writing in Canada over the past fifty years, along with the controversy that surrounded the publication of *Peace* by a major publishing house, makes the novel an important landmark for any discussion of writing by Mennonites in Canada. However, the coronation of *Peace* as the "first" novel in Mennonite writing is not a simple matter of chronology. In fact, unless we recognize that such a genealogy is not about writing by all Mennonites in Canada but about Mennonite Canadian literature as a distinct body and field of study, it appears to reflect a couple of rather questionable critical assumptions. What about the dozens of German-language Mennonite novels written in Canada prior to 1962? They do not circulate in the English-dominated critical discourse of Canadian literature and can safely be ignored. What about Mabel Dunham's best-selling novel *The Trail of the Conestoga* (1924) or Paul Hiebert's award-winning *Sarah Binks* (1947)? The former represents the Swiss Mennonite tradition, and the latter is not sufficiently attuned to Mennonite contexts; they, too, can be set aside. It is the unspoken presuppositions that commonly guide discussions of Mennonite Canadian literature within the wider discourse of Canadian literary criticism—that it is to refer to works in English, written by "ethnic" Russian Mennonites, which represent Mennonite experiences—that enable critics to so confidently mark Wiebe's 1962 novel as its starting point. As we have seen, these assumptions have their own history, having been formed and affirmed by the socio-political contexts of the field's emergence in Canada.

Although there is a certain appeal to identifying the "first" or "founding" novel in a literary tradition, there are other places where one can turn to date the emergence of bodies of literature, including the anthologies that self-consciously aim to announce their arrival. As Joseph Pivato suggests, the "publication of ethnic anthologies does several things [...]: it creates an identity for the group or generation, it encourages the writers to publish their own work, [and] it begins to create critical and academic interest in the writers" (58). Indeed, the late 1970s and early 1980s saw an explosion of anthologies of ethnic writing in Canada, texts that collectively mark, in Smaro Kamboureli's words, "the first [...] concentrated unfolding of ethnic writing in Canada" ("Canadian Ethnic Anthologies" 47). A partial list of the anthologies published within fifteen years of the White Paper (1971–86) includes the first anthologies of Black, Hungarian, Japanese, Jewish, Chinese, Italian, and Chilean writing in Canada, all published at least partially in English and all published with the financial support of the Canadian government.[31] The first anthologies of Mennonite writing in Canada, *Harvest: Anthology of Mennonite Writing in Canada* (1974) and *Unter dem Nordlicht: Anthology of German-Mennonite Writing in Canada* (1977) emerged alongside these other anthologies, firmly a part of this larger explosion of ethnic writing. If individual anthologies can be taken to signal the existence or arrival of a given body of literature, a burst of such anthologies is clearly less reflective of a critical mass of literary production—is it really possible that all these communities simultaneously reached such a point?—than of a new organizing principle in which such literature is suddenly valued. It is true, of course, that not all of these emergent literatures would go on to enjoy the remarkable critical success of Mennonite writing in the 1980s, but a recognition of the fact that Mennonite Canadian literature emerged as part of a much larger movement of ethnic writing in Canada ought to help dispel the myth that it was a completely singular phenomenon.

The host of first anthologies of "ethnic" Canadian literature during the 1970s demonstrates how minoritized literatures were both enabled by Canadian multiculturalism and, as E.D. Blodgett puts it, "caught in the net of its discourse" (16). Self-published on the occasion of the Mennonites' first 100 years in Canada and with a limited circulation, William De Fehr et al.'s *Harvest* has had no obvious lasting impact on the field of Mennonite literary studies. Nonetheless, the anthology, noted by Pivato in his list of ethnic anthologies of the period (58), remains valuable for its self-conscious attempt to announce (and demonstrate) the arrival of what it calls "Canadian Mennonite literature" (vii). The brief introduction thanks the Secretary of State for funding the anthology and presents the collection as part of the Mennonites' larger attempt "to be accepted as part of this country" (vii). Significantly, it repeatedly opposes the Mennonite community against an imaginary Canadian public to whom it appeals, implicitly excluding Mennonites from the national narrative and thus reinscribing the very alterity that it seeks to address. At the same time, however, *Harvest* also appears to strategically undermine the foundations of that alterity. In an irony that could not have escaped the editors, for example, the anthology's opening two essays offer a stinging caution against understanding Mennonite identity outside the framework of faith—thoroughly undercutting the largely secular account of a Mennonite peoplehood provided by its introduction. What is more, the inclusion of some eighty pages of text in Low or High German (with only the odd translation) shows an editorial refusal to fully accommodate the parameters of the dominant community into which the text is imagined to be emerging. In fact, the editors highlight this gesture by closing the English section of the collection with a short story by Isbrand Hildebrand celebrating the fact that non-Mennonites are unable to understand *Der Bote* or any of the Mennonite church newsletters written in German. "I'm all for German language papers for us," the protagonist says craftily; "in fact, if we could publish in Russian where no one could read what was written, this would be best of all" (98). This desire to publish a text that no one can read is a compelling symbol of the tension of minoritized literatures, encapsulating a desire to express, but not to expose. The structural tensions that mark *Harvest* suggest, on behalf of its editors, a self-conscious attempt to interrogate the framing assumptions under which they are introducing Mennonite Canadian literature.

A decade after the release of *Harvest*, Rudy Wiebe published "The Blindman River Contradictions: An Interview with Rudy Wiebe," a remarkable short essay that shows just how thoroughly the concept of ethnicity had come to define (and restrict) the circulation of writing by Mennonites in Canada. In a faux-interview that satirizes the relationship between ethnicity and writing in Canadian criticism, Wiebe rewrites his own family history to call attention to the absurdities of celebrating ethnicity as a literary attribute. "There's a story around that I was born in Saskatchewan to a Mennonite family but that's not true," he writes, responding to a standard opening question about his formative years (346). He then goes on to parody the exoticism implicit in the discourse of official multiculturalism: "I'm British, I'm English. I never had anything to do with the Mennonites; that's a fiction I made up because of course in Western Canada there's much more point to being ethnic than to being English. Actually, a Canadian writer has an enormous disadvantage in being English, as you perfectly well know, rather than Ukrainian or Greek or Icelandic, or Mennonite" (347). Wiebe's self-interview illustrates and exaggerates the performativity of identity in an age when ethnicity has been endorsed by the government and become a commodity. His claim that "there's much more point to being ethnic than to being English" serves as a reminder of the ways in which the "founding races" logic of official multiculturalism naturalizes a British identity as "non-ethnic" in Canada, and illustrates the shift in Canadian discourse from the silence that surrounded ethnic communities during the "two solitudes" era of Canadian bicultural-ism.[32]

Wiebe's mock interview shows both the cultural cachet of ethnicity in discussions of Canadian literature in this period and the author's deep unease with its larger implications for his work. Wiebe had reason to be uneasy. In 2001, Ervin Beck noted that Wiebe's work remains "so identified [...] with 'ethnic literature'" that other critical perspectives have often "been neglected" ("Rudy Wiebe" 7). At least Wiebe's work itself has not been neglected because of its association with Mennonite ethnicity; the works of others might not have been so fortunate. After all, Enoch Padolsky warns, "when some 'ethnic' writers fill the function within the critical framework, writers from [...] the same group tend to be regarded as further tokens of the same theme and are much less likely to be welcomed. Who needs 17 other Mennonite-Canadian authors when there is Rudy Wiebe?" (377). Although the appetite for Mennonite writing has proven remarkably large—opportunities for Mennonite authors have unquestionably been opened, rather than closed, by Wiebe's successes—significant questions remain. How has the celebration of ethnic identity in Canada facilitated the rise of Mennonite literature? What is the currency in which "Mennonite" becomes a selling feature, and what is the role of the critic in the propagation of such logic?[33] And just what are people buying when they are buying a Mennonite book?

The Mennonite Exotic

When, in the early 1980s, a collection of texts by Mennonite Canadian authors coalesced into something called "Mennonite Canadian literature," it did so in large part in response to the newly ordained and well-funded of-ficial interest in Canada's "other ethnic communities." Just as significant as the financial support that Mennonite authors received for producing "ethnic literature" was the government's sanctioning of such literature's celebration. Consider, in this light, Di Brandt's account of her own emergence as a writer: "It was [...] the time of official multiculturalism in Canada: it was a relief to be able to proclaim our cultural difference in Canada without fear of open reprisal, at last," she writes. "I and my fellow ex-Mennonite writers [...] feel very lucky to have grown up at the time all these things were happening; oth-erwise we wouldn't have found our way into art, and would quite possibly have died or gone crazy instead" (*Dancing* 35–36). Without taking anything away from Brandt's comments, one ought to be able to recognize the interpellation operating in her description of this period: to respond directly to the call of the multicultural ideal is to accept its operative assumptions and to operate, at least initially, within its parameters of possibility. Indeed, in spite of her many other achievements in the larger field of Canadian literature, the success and canonization of her debut book of poetry exploring and exploding her Mennonite heritage, *questions i asked my mother* (1987), means that, as long as Mennonite Canadian literature exists as a concept and as a critical discourse, Brandt will continue to be discussed and understood in relation to its frame. In this sense, at least, she will never fully be an "ex-Mennonite writer," regardless of how she might feel about such a prospect.

The same factors that enabled writers such as Brandt to "proclaim [their] cultural difference in Canada" also made it possible for such proclamations to receive an eager audience. The emergence of a distinctly Mennonite literature was actively facilitated by Winnipeg's Turnstone Press, for example, which published important early work by a host of Mennonite authors during the 1980s, including Patrick Friesen's *The Shunning* (1980), Sandra Birdsell's *Night Travellers* (1982), Armin Wiebe's *The Salvation of Yasch Siemens* (1984), Di Brandt's *questions i asked my mother* (1987), Sarah Klassen's *Journey to Yalta* (1988), along with work by David Waltner-Toews, Ed Dyck, Audrey Poetker, Lois Braun, and Douglas Reimer. In "A History of Turnstone Press," Turnstone editor David Arnason reflects on the close relationship between the press and Mennonite writing by denying that there was any necessary connection between the two. The editors at Turnstone Press "have no interest whatsoever in Mennonite history or anything particularly Mennonite," he insists. "We are interested in good fiction, good poetry, and it just happens that a lot of Mennonites are writing good fiction and good poetry. But again I want to make it absolutely clear that we have very little interest in 'the Mennonite thing'" (213). Arnason's evidence for the disinterest of the press in Mennonites includes his insistence that it has never courted a Mennonite audience. "Our assumptions have been that the things we are interested in would not do particularly well in the Mennonite market anyway," he writes. "They're aimed to be sold to a Canadian mainstream literary market" (213). Such a claim, however, simply reminds us of the economics that underpin the production of literature without doing anything to change the contexts in which Turnstone Press was operating. Intentionally or otherwise, the press was deeply invested in the fascination with (and commodification of) ethnic difference in Canada—that is, in the active production of "the Mennonite thing." The socio-political contexts that encouraged a generation of Mennonite authors to write out of their experiences as "ethnic Canadians" are the same contexts in which it became culturally compelling and economically viable for a small press to begin publishing book after book of and often about a rural, separatist, deeply conservative Christian community, and to be able to reasonably expect a "mainstream literary market" to respond enthusiastically.

Mennonite critics in both the United States and Canada have long been aware—and wary—of the way that the "exoticism" of Mennonite identity can function as a marketing feature for Mennonite writing. Even as he worried that Mennonites were not producing any literature of note, John L. Ruth warned as early as 1978 that "Mennonites don't need [...] evidence that we, too, can be packaged and sold in the marketplace of literary sensation" (68); Peter C. Erb warned in 1985 that Mennonites in Canada were in danger of "preserv[ing] their ethnic peculiarities, as they do canned goods, to sell when the best market conditions arise" (205). Much more recently, Hildi Froese Tiessen reported that a representative from Random House Canada stood in front of a public audience in Waterloo to declare that "Mennonite sells" ("Mennonite/s" 43). Today, with Mennonite authors and playwrights such as Miriam Toews, Sandra Birdsell, David Bergen, Rudy Wiebe, Darcie Friesen Hossack, Carrie Snyder, Dora Dueck, and Di Brandt enjoying widespread popular and critical success for writing that directly engages Mennonite identity, the commodification of literature by Canadian Mennonites *qua* Mennonite Canadian literature is nearly inescapable. In fact, as the German scholar Martin Kuester reports, Mennonite Canadian writing is garnering an increasing readership in Europe, especially, he notes, among the "general readership looking for new and 'exotic' texts" (153). Although, as I noted in regard to Brandt earlier, many writers who happen to be Mennonite have disavowed the position of "Mennonite authors," this disavowal does little to change the fact that their work—especially if it happens to be about Mennonites—gains considerable cultural (and economic) capital from circulating as part of a recognizable literary brand. As crass as the word *brand* might seem in relation to Mennonite identity, I use it as a reminder of the obvious but often ignored fact that Mennonite texts, like all literary texts, are cultural commodities and that their position as "ethnic literature" continues to have currency not only in the Canadian marketplace but also in the larger global market.

The exoticism implicit in the celebration of an aestheticized understanding of ethnic difference has been subject to substantial critique over the past decade. The process of recognizing ethnic difference by promoting cultural production, critics warn, only acknowledges the inescapable fact of difference by attempting to define its political parameters as cultural expression. In *Scandalous Bodies*, Kamboureli argues that the "sedative politics" of multiculturalism work to contain ethnic difference through a celebratory rhetoric that masks, or restrains, the spectre of otherness that it takes to be "scandalous."[34] For Kamboureli and for others, such as Arun Mukherjee, Himani Bannerji, and Rinaldo Walcott, Canadian multiculturalism has allowed for a relatively facile celebration of minoritized cultural production while ignoring the (often racialized) injustices that mark their immediate political contexts. Signifying as "white," Christian, and European, Mennonites occupy a privileged position in the logic of Canadian multiculturalism. As a result, Mennonite literature occupies a difficult position in discussions of multicultural literature for those critics who have attended to the tight relationship between the concepts of ethnicity and race. In "'Race' into the Twenty-First Century," for example, Daniel Coleman and Donald Goellnicht argue "[t]he capacity of the term ethnicity under the aegis of Canadian multicultural ideology to whitewash 'race' into a catalogue of depoliticized differences." They point to the inclusion of Mennonite authors in *Other Solitudes* and *Making a Difference*, the two major multicultural anthologies of Canadian literature during the 1990s, as part of their insistence that the "visible" of "visible minority" cannot be set aside. It is a mistake, they argue, to place "authors of Asian, African, or Aboriginal descent […] alongside authors of Czech, Mennonite, or Italian descent as if the differences of religious or cultural background are equivalent to those of 'race.'"[35] Coleman and Goellnicht trace the rise of racialized fields of literary study to the anti-racism activism of the late 1980s, reading the celebration of ethnic fiction in the 1970s and throughout the 1980s as effecting a displacement of racial anxieties to conclude that, "[i]n certain contexts, some differences are more different than others." In light of their critique, Hostetler's account of the shifting designation of race across the Canadian/American border risks positioning race as a transparently biological concept—as if the inclusion of Mennonites as "ethnic" subjects in Canada means that they are somehow race free—and replicating what Coleman and Goellnicht refer to as "the old Canadian refrain that 'race' is really an American problem, not a Canadian one." Indeed, there is now a real temptation for Mennonite writers (and critics) to capitalize on the status of ethnic otherness rewarded by Canada's enduring multicultural apparatus, on the one hand, while enjoying all the privileges that whiteness, education, and wealth provide in Canada, on the other.[36] This temptation is particularly fraught in the rewriting of a break event, in which, as Julia Spicher Kasdorf notes of Mennonite writing more generally, there is a risk that "[k]eeping the bittersweet memories of past trespasses alive may blind writers to immediate injustice or prevent us from appreciating the privileged positions we now hold" (*Body* 162). Unlike during World Wars I and II, when Mennonites in Canada were understood as "German" (and therefore as potential threats), over the past thirty years they have signified a "safe" form of ethnic difference: distinct enough to benefit from being exotic, but not different enough to suffer from being perceived as a threat.

Although recognizing the exoticizing function of multicultural discourse is an important step in understanding the circulation of minoritized literature in Canada, such a critique in itself is hardly sufficient to undermine the process. In fact, as Graham Huggan discusses in the introduction to *The Postcolonial Exotic*, there are ways in which the academic emphasis on cultural otherness risks reproducing and benefiting from the logic of exoticism, even where it explicitly sets out to critique it. Although critics have long recognized that titles referring to bodies of literature in terms of race or ethnicity—not only "Mennonite Canadian literature" but also "Asian Canadian literature," "Black Canadian literature," and so on—are categories of convenience that do not correspond to any clearly defined communities (or even clearly defined bodies of texts), they nonetheless find themselves returning to them. In doing so, they risk quietly reinscribing their homogenizing politics. Such categories, as Roy Miki points out in reference to "Asian Canadian," are "double-edged site[s]" in that they can offer important opportunities for collective agency, but their deployment also always threatens to remobilize their limiting assumptions (*In Flux* 51). What is more, the "limiting assumptions" that surround such categories often differ greatly between ethnicized and racialized communities. When critics engage with individual texts as examples of "Mennonite Canadian literature"—as I am in this study—they, too, are capitalizing on the commodification of Mennonite identity as exotic. While this need not be understood as irredeemably problematic, neither is it to be taken for granted as ethically or politically neutral. Critics of Mennonite Canadian literature, then, ought to be aware of the ways in which their work—however vital, informed, and self-aware it might be—participates in and benefits from a particular positioning of Mennonite culture within the long-standing nationalist project of Canadian literature.

What does all this tell us about the rewriting of the Russian Mennonite experience across Canadian Mennonite literature? My hope is that, by historicizing Mennonite Canadian literature as a critical concept, I have gently estranged its logic and placed a productive pressure on the ways in which the restrictive politics that once interpellated migrant fiction in Canada as "the cultural contributions of the other ethnic groups" remain implicit in the contemporary moment. This process helps to clear the conceptual ground to enable a more nuanced appreciation of the wider and more varied negotiation of Mennonite identity taking place in the various rewritings of the 1920s migration narrative. If the twinned discourses of Canadian literature and state-sanctioned multiculturalism have worked to shape both the production and the reception of "Mennonite Canadian literature" firmly within the context of ethnicity, the literary texts themselves often work to challenge, reveal, and move beyond the discourses into which they emerge.

Chapter 1

Mennonite History and/as Literature

The history of the Russian Mennonites' 1920s migration experience is outlined in skeletal detail by John Weier's narrator near the beginning of *Steppe*: "This much we know," he writes in his journal: "They lived in Ukraine for about 140 years. They grew a lot of grain while they were there. They had big families and kept horses. Some of them got very rich doing it, growing grain I mean. Some stayed very poor. After the 140 years most of the Mennonites in Russia either left, or died, or stopped being Mennonite. Some became communist. Those last years, that wasn't an easy time for any of them. Eventually they died" (1.26). If it is thin on details, this brief history is not short on power: the narrator's efforts to understand the brief story's impact on his life ends with him on a bus in southern Ukraine, straining his eyes as he looks out onto the steppe in a futile search for evidence of his family's past. In this chapter, I recount a fuller history of the rise and fall of the Mennonite Commonwealth, along with the subsequent mass migration to Canada, in order to provide the contextual details necessary to understanding the remainder of this study. I also begin to trace the process through which this history has become a central narrative in Mennonite Canadian literature. The close but strained relationship among history, narrative, and literature introduced in my opening chapter takes on a particular colouring in Canada's Mennonite imagination, where there exists a substantial "twilight zone" that blurs the boundaries between them.

Mennonites in Russia, Russian Mennonites

The mass emigration out of southern Russia in the 1920s is but one episode in the long and circuitous history of Russian Mennonite migrations. The longer history covers nearly half a millennium, five continents, and at least a dozen countries. In the sixteenth century, a movement of Christian dissenters derisively referred to as Anabaptism grew from varied beginnings in Switzerland and the Netherlands to become loosely organized under the teachings of a Dutch priest named Menno Simons. Stressing adult baptism (hence "anabaptism" or "baptizing again"), the separation of church and state, pacifism, and a commitment to simple living, the Mennonites were considered a threat to the Catholic Church on theological grounds and a threat to the state on political grounds. Since, as De Lamar Jensen writes, the Anabaptists' "radical separation of church and state [...] disrupted the whole structure of politics and society known to the sixteenth century" (89), it is perhaps not surprising that the religious dissenters found themselves among the most persecuted of all religious groups during the Protestant Reformation.[1]

Although recent historical work stresses that the "polygenesis" or multiple and conflicted beginnings of Anabaptism mean that it should not, in its early years, be understood as a single or even cohesive movement, the widespread persecution of this diverse group worked to reorient them inward, beginning what Calvin Redekop calls a "gradual change from being at the centre of the general protest and utopian reform to the periphery through rejection, migration, and isolation" ("Sociology" 181). Many Swiss Mennonites migrated to Pennsylvania in the seventeenth century (of whom a substantial number would ultimately move to southern Ontario following the American Revolutionary War), but the Mennonites in northern Europe found refuge by fleeing to the relatively liberal city-states of the Prussian Vistula delta, in the north of present-day Poland. It was there that they began to organize themselves into the small, tightly structured agricultural villages that would become a defining feature of their communal life, and where they transitioned from Dutch to German as the language of their religious services. Prussian policies, however, became increasingly less permissive toward Mennonites in the late seventeenth century, and Catherine the Great of Russia extended a timely invitation to Germans across Europe to settle on the newly conquered steppes. Having just dismantled the Cossack stronghold in the area, Catherine was eager to promptly settle the territory with farming communities, and she offered the Mennonites not only free fertile land but also cultural autonomy and a set of remarkable privileges, including freedom of religion, control over their own education, and exemption from military service. As a result, many entire Mennonite communities packed up and trekked east to southwestern Russia.

As I noted in the introduction, I adopt the name "Russian Mennonites" because of its wide use, but this is not to say that it is unproblematic. Indeed, as Redekop begins his study *Mennonite Society*, "[t]he term *Mennonite* itself muddies the water when one is attempting to describe the Mennonite society" (3). Although "Mennonite" remains primarily a religious designation—there are roughly 1.5 million adherents to Mennonite churches across the world, with the largest number of members in Africa—my use of the term throughout this study refers to the descendants of this group of "Russian Mennonites," many of whom would prosper in Russia before coming to Canada in two major waves of immigration (1870s and 1920s). Even within the relatively small Russian Mennonite community in Canada, however, the title "Russian Mennonite" is misleading, for it covers over an important distinction between the Kanadier (Canadian) migrants of the 1870s and the Russländer (Russian) migrants of the 1920s. And, in fact, even these titles are somewhat misleading. The Russländer, for example, found themselves targets in Russia at least partially due to their refusal to fully embrace the Russian language, culture, and people during the Commonwealth era. Similarly, the Kanadier were arguably "the least 'Canadian' [of Canada's Mennonites] in their mentality and identification" (Epp, "Problems" 286), often holding tightly to their conservative faith and distinctive Low German language, and refusing to compromise on their ideal of remaining separate from mainstream Canadian society. Moreover, although the Mennonites in Russia spoke German and largely identified as Germans, they officially emphasized their Dutch origins during the Russian war effort against Germany in World War I. So, as Frank H. Epp writes, "they were at the same time Dutch, German, and Russian, yet not really any of those" ("Problems" 283).

Not surprisingly, this complex history has led to some gymnastics of nomenclature in the scholarly literature. A partial list of titles and descriptions for this community gives a sense of the confusion: "Russian Mennonites"; "Dutch Mennonites" (Ens 2); "Soviet-German Mennonites" (Loewen, *Road* 9); "Dutch-North German Mennonites" (Loewen and Nolt x); "Dutch-Ukrainian-Canadian Mennonites" (Kasdorf, "Making" 14); "Dutch-Russian

Mennonites" (Kroeker 5); the "Dutch-Prussian-Russian group" (Reimer, *Mennonite Literary Voices* 2); "Russian-German-Canadian-Mennonite" (Doerksen, "Recalling" 146); "Dutch-North-German-Russian" (A. Anderson 195); and even "North-German/Dutch/'Russian' Mennonites" (Froese Tiessen, "Introduction" 16). Rather than add my own modifiers and claim to focus on "Dutch-North German-'Russian'/Ukrainian Mennonite litera-ture of both the Russländer and Kanadier in Canada," I will simply refer to the community as "Russian Mennonite" and their literature as "Mennonite literature," for these titles reflect what has become accepted through critical convention. It is worth noting, however, that the many modifiers and the multitude of quotation marks, slashes, and hyphens that have accompanied the title "Mennonite" in Canada speak to the self-conscious indeterminacy of this community's geo-political and cultural identity.

Upon their arrival in Russia, the Mennonites established two major colonies (Chortitza and Molotschna) where, over the next 150 years, they overcame initial hardships to enjoy remarkable autonomy and prosper-ity. The roughly 30,000 immigrants would grow to a population of nearly 100,000, owning more than 3 million acres of land by 1917 (Epp, *Mennonites* 141). Aided first by a set of unique and significant privileges granted to the Mennonites as part of their invitation to settle in Imperial Russia, then by Russian reforms that encouraged the creation of a Mennonite bureaucratic structure as part of widespread efforts to further state efficiency, and finally by a shift in government policies that gave that structure the freedom to expand, the colonies developed into an extensive and largely self-governing "state-within-a-state" often referred to as the "Mennonite Commonwealth."[2] Separated from their neighbours by religion, culture, language, and law, Mennonites became—at least in the eyes of their own historians—"the most prosperous and well-developed rural communities in all of Russia" (Epp, *Mennonite Exodus* 27). The magnitude of the Commonwealth was, indeed, re-markable: its infrastructure included social welfare institutions that went well beyond those of the Russian state at the time, including a school for the deaf, an orphanage, and extensive facilities for the elderly. It boasted several hun-dred elementary schools to facilitate its compulsory education programs, in addition to dozens of high schools, as well as teachers' colleges, trade schools, and a business college (Kroeker 25). There were co-operatives, credit unions, a bank, a system of taxation (Urry, "Time" 15), as well as a publishing house that briefly published a Mennonite periodical (Kroeker 26). An elite class of

wealthy Mennonite industrialists emerged, many of whom built elaborate estates and became prominent leaders both within and beyond the community.

Although the Commonwealth period is often recounted nostalgically as a
"Mennonite Golden Age" (Franz 14; Kroeker 28; Toews, *Lost Fatherland* 23),
it was also characterized by deep religious disagreements and class inequalities. The colonialists worked hard to maintain a division between themselves
as a German-speaking religious people and their Ukrainian neighbours,
many of whom they employed (and sometimes treated poorly) as servants,
field hands, and factory workers. Religious disagreements led to the emergence of several distinct denominations in the colonies, divisions exacerbated
by the rise of a vast class of *Anwohner* or landless and often impoverished
Mennonites. When, in the mid-1800s, the Russian state began to with-
draw the special privileges that it had granted the Mennonites—instituting
Russian as the mandatory language of elementary education and requiring
Mennonite men to serve in alternatives to military service—a substantial seg-
ment of the Mennonite population began to worry that wealth and "worldly"
success were diluting the community's faith and distinctive way of life. In
response to class and religious pressures from within, and state pressures from
without, nearly a third of Russia's Mennonites emigrated to North America
in the 1870s, including some 8,000 to the Canadian Prairies, where they lived
as pioneers in present-day Saskatchewan, Manitoba, and Alberta. Just as the
Mennonites had settled on newly conquered land upon their original arrival
in Russia, the Mennonites who arrived in Canada during the 1870s "found
vast tracts of land that had recently been taken from Indigenous people"
(Loewen and Nolt 19). These "Kanadier" Mennonites were generally less
wealthy, less educated, and more conservative than the "Russländer," who,
remaining in Russia, accommodated themselves to the new regulations and
went on to enjoy remarkable levels of commercial and cultural success over the
next fifty years. There is a long tradition of hagiography celebrating this latter
period, nicely summarized by the main title given to Peter Gerhard Rempel's
collection of photographs of the era: *Forever Summer, Forever Sunday* (1981).

Another product of the Mennonite Commonwealth was the con-
solidation of a secular Mennonite identity; in Urry's words, "Mennonites in
Russia would become *Russian* Mennonites" ("Time" 17). The various ethnic,
linguistic, and cultural backgrounds of the Mennonites that had begun to
unite during the Prussian years coalesced in Russia into a secular sense of
peoplehood. According to Urry, the development of a distinct and secular

Mennonite identity was facilitated by two apparently incongruous elements: early positive interaction with the Russian tsars and a tide of rising Russian nationalism at the close of the nineteenth century ("Time"). Upon their arrival in Russia near the end of the eighteenth century, the Mennonites were recognized as a distinct people and singled out by Russian leaders for their "excellent industry and morality," and were held up as "a model to the foreigners" (qtd. in Kroeker 11). As a religious community, the Mennonites were a collection of distinct denominations that continued to divide over time—a practice of particular significance in a context in which faith was so central to identity—but Russian officials ignored such internal disputes and the divisions among the various church groups. In officially recognizing a single, non-religious Mennonite identity, they affirmed—indeed, they effectively created—a distinct people by bureaucracy. "The colonial policy of Czarist Russia," claims E.K. Francis, "was directly responsible for the transformation of this group of German Mennonites into something like a new ethnic unit" (*Interethnic Relations* 172). Urry goes somewhat further, suggesting that the creation of a secular and collective Mennonite identity through the administrative apparatus of the colonies was "precisely the intent of Russian officialdom" ("Russian Mennonites" 34), which had no interest in dealing with the various congregational disputes and divisions.

From the Mennonite perspective, there were clear advantages to be gained with a shift from an oft-splintering religious identity toward a single secular one. As Francis writes, "the most conspicuous factor which held the group together [in Russia] was their common interest in the maintenance of rights granted by the state to all original Mennonite immigrants and their immediate offspring" (*In Search* 105). Indeed, despite the Anabaptists' strong historical stance on maintaining a division between church and state, the Mennonites in Russia began actively collapsing the two in an effort to maintain their state privileges. "Contrary to Anabaptist convictions that admission to the brotherhood depended on spiritual rebirth and personal commitment," Francis notes elsewhere, "anyone born of Mennonite parents now had to be admitted to church membership; for he could otherwise not legally live in a Mennonite colony or partake in the rights granted to the Mennonite group" (*Interethnic Relations* 173). In Russia (and later in Canada[3]), military exemptions given to Mennonites were predicated on a person being both an active church member and a direct descendant of other Mennonites. In a remarkable departure from their core Anabaptist tradition, several colonies simply began baptizing all their young men on their eighteenth birthdays in order to avoid conscription (Francis, "Russian Mennonites" 105). Buoyed by a widespread belief in their superiority over both Ukrainians and other groups of Germans in Russia, affirmed through bureaucratic privileging of the community, Mennonites increasingly thought of themselves in terms of a secular peoplehood.

Being singled out for privilege and praise would return to haunt the Mennonite community, however; when the late-century programs of Russification created a strong anti-foreigner sentiment, the Mennonites found themselves ready examples of the wealthy foreign bourgeoisie. With the onset of the Russian Revolution, these sentiments erupted into a violence that would shatter the Commonwealth. The Germanic language and culture, disproportional wealth, religious beliefs, and (at least theoretical adherence to) pacifism of the Mennonites made them targets for both state and anarchist forces. The Soviets dismissed Mennonite claims to be a strictly pacifist religious community, instead portraying them as ruthless exploiters of the Russian peasants and as eager collaborators with the hated Germans. Even some Mennonite historians have cautiously agreed that it is, as Jacob A. Loewen and Wesley J. Prieb write, "hard to escape the conclusion that the twentieth-century fate of the Mennonites in Russia—to be attacked as a privileged and propertied class and dispersed into the Gulag—is at least partially a consequence of the loss of [their religious] vision" (39). Indeed, Loewen and Prieb report that with the arrival of German troops, some Mennonite estate owners eagerly armed themselves and "organized posse-like groups which attacked the rebels and reclaimed [their seized] estates" (28).

Following the First World War, the Mennonites of Russia would be caught up in one of the bloodiest events in modern history. Over the following decades, millions of Ukrainians and Russians would die from violence and famine. The Mennonite colonies were part of the larger battlefield for the control of Ukraine, with the German Army, the Soviet Red Army, the Russian Imperial White Army, and the Ukrainian anarchists led by Nestor Makhno all occupying the area at various points. As the front swept repeatedly across the colonies, hundreds of Mennonites were killed; in one village alone, Makhno's forces murdered seventy-nine men and three women in a single night. Thousands were lost to labour camps, while famine and disease threatened thousands more. Many Mennonites abandoned the principle of non-violence in order to create the *Selbstschutz,* or armed self-defence units, established to defend their communities, a highly controversial shift away from pacifism that has become a major focus in historical and literary considerations of the period.

Aided by the Mennonites who had immigrated to North America earlier, some 20,000 Mennonites managed to flee to Canada from the Soviet Union during the 1920s, often under the most dramatic of circumstances. Their immigration to Canada was also enabled through a remarkable confluence of political and corporate factors: Mennonites who had settled on the Canadian Prairies during the 1870s successfully lobbied Ottawa to lift the existing order-in-council refusing the entry of additional Mennonites into the country[4] and convinced the Canadian Pacific Railway (CPR) to extend an unprecedented agreement to facilitate much of the mass migration on credit. Those Mennonites who managed to escape Russia took their distinctive agrarian culture, Low German language, and Anabaptist religion to Canada, and, when Canada closed its borders, to Mexico and Paraguay. Although historical studies such as John B. Toews's *Lost Fatherland* (1967) emphasize that "the emigration was a deliberate government-sanctioned movement, not a mass flight" (193), its representation in literature has consistently effaced the ways in which the migration was bound up in governmentality, presenting it simply as a chaotic escape from bloody lawlessness. Indeed, with few notable exceptions, Mennonite Canadian literature has remarkably little to say about the role of the CPR and the Canadian government in enabling the migration, or, for that matter, about the vast number of Mennonites—some 80,000—who remained behind.[5]

Within the critical context of a study such as this, recounting the above history is nearly as problematic as it is indispensable. Marxist scholars familiar with the early-twentieth-century history of the area could protest that I have underestimated the effect of the class divisions between the few wealthy "kulak" farmers and the many landless *Anwohner*, and between the larger Mennonite community and their impoverished Russian and Ukrainian neighbours. A more thorough account would emphasize the ways in which specific Mennonite actions, such as the enthusiastic reception that Mennonites gave the occupying German Army, their role in facilitating reprisals against those who had benefited from the process of collectivization, and the formation of the *Selbstschutz,* undermine those histories that present the violence faced by the Mennonites as unfathomable or entirely unprovoked. Feminist scholars could argue that I have ignored the deep foundation of patriarchy that underpinned Russian Mennonite society, while postcolonial scholars could rightly point out that, over the course of their multiple migrations, these Mennonites were repeatedly "granted" land that had recently belonged to Indigenous peoples, and so have a long history of functioning as "settler invaders"—first on the Russian steppes, then on the Canadian Prairies, and again in South America. Queer theorists might suggest that, by ignoring the homogenizing pressures of ethno-religious life, I have implicitly affirmed the normative models (including sexuality) that it imposes on its members, while conservative theologians might balk at the material focus of the history that I provide or at my quick acquiescence to the claim that these Mennonites are anything other than a religious community. It could be suggested that my account of the early Anabaptists follows too closely the celebratory version of the history that Harold S. Bender constructed in "The Anabaptist Vision" by leaving out the more controversial episodes in the Mennonite past, including the violent and polygamous Anabaptism briefly practised in Münster. Although the history above is offered as a means of providing the geo-political and material contexts for these novels, I must concede that it too is but another retelling of the Mennonite migration narrative, subject to many of the same pitfalls—selection, perspective, and emphasis—that challenge the literary strains of this story.[6] The ordering power of narrative is not limited to fictional narratives, then, and even if the (ever-evolving) historical record remains a privileged anchor for these representations of the past, we must be careful not to reify any single account of that record as an unproblematic ur-narrative, or as the "true" story that the others reflect with greater or lesser degrees of accuracy.

Indeed, early Mennonite historiography is full of examples demonstrating the ways in which ostensibly objective historical studies provide particular perspectives on their subjects. The argument that stands in the foreword to Frank H. Epp's 1962 history *Mennonite Exodus*, for example—that "faithful historical writing […] must be realistic as the biblical story is realistic" (ix)—may no longer inspire academic confidence in its methodology. One way to deal with such histories would be to place them in the tradition of hagiographic literature that James Urry calls the "twilight zone" of Mennonite history, in which, he claims, the Russian colonies are often "seen through child-like eyes and their memories coloured by the tales [that their authors] had heard their parents tell over and over again, of their lost world, their shattered lives, their suffering." Unsurprisingly, Urry reports that such histories usually result in a "strangely sanitized version of Mennonite life in Russia, with a highly simplistic explanation of the sequence of events and their causation" ("Truth" 10). Rather than condescendingly labelling such histories "child-like" and unceremoniously relegating them to the dustbin of the "twilight zone," however, I would suggest that such writings can better be understood as a highly particular form of history—we might call it "sacred history" or "religious history"—that most readers today would recognize as straddling historical fact and theological interpretation. As Harry Loewen has recently noted, Mennonite writings on this period have moved from a "historiography of faith to scholarly history" ("Can" 79), and while there is no question that the more critical analysis of the past several decades has resulted in a much more nuanced account of this period, the earlier work retains an important interpretive function for the community. The novels returning to the Mennonite experience in Russia that I examine in this study occasionally operate in similarly contentious zones of history, sometimes happily simplifying a complex past, sometimes radically self-aware of the limitations of historiography, but always fictionalizing the historical record in an effort to rework and reimagine a Russian Mennonite cultural identity in Canada.

Rewriting the Break Event

Given the historical significance of the Russian experience for many Mennonites in Canada, and given that it is arguably the most dramatic moment in Mennonite history since the martyrdoms of the sixteenth-century Anabaptists, it is hardly surprising that, as E.F. Dyck wrote in 1988, "[t]he Mennonite imagination is [...] fixated on the traumatic Russian experience" (22). The vast collection of works that returns to this period includes innumerable diaries, journals, and self-published memoirs, including Dietrich Neufeld's remarkable diary, translated by Al Reimer as *A Russian Dance of Death* in 1977. It includes collections of historical photos, such as Walter Quiring and Helen Bartel's *In the Fullness of Time* (1974) and Peter Gerhard Rempel's *Forever Summer, Forever Sunday* (1981), as well as an award-winning film, *... And When They Shall Ask* (1984), which combines survivor interviews with historical re-enactments of the period. There are also collections of survivor stories such as John P. Nickel's *Hope beyond the Horizon* (1996) and much of Sarah Dyck's *The Silence Echoes* (1997), and there are a number of polished and published memoirs, including Gerhard Lohrenz's *Storm Tossed* (1976), Harry Loewen's *Between Worlds* (2006), and Arthur Kroeger's *Hard*

Passage (2007). And, when a coalition of Mennonite organizations formally proposed three stories for inclusion in the Canadian Museum for Human Rights, the first story suggested was "A Story of the Mennonite Odyssey from Russia to Canada." This story, they proposed, "should invite people to reflect on how they can maintain courage and commitment in the face of persecution and suffering" (Mennonite Committee on Human Rights 4).

As I discussed at length in the introduction, Rudy Wiebe's 1962 novel *Peace Shall Destroy Many* is commonly identified as the first novel in Mennonite Canadian literature. In essays with titles such as "Canadian-Mennonite Literature: Longing for a Lost Homeland" (1984) and "Leaving Home: Canadian-Mennonite Literature in the 1980s" (1989), however, Harry Loewen has insisted that the "birth" of Mennonite literary culture more generally can be ascribed to the Mennonites' experiences in Russia. "When the Mennonites lived securely in Prussia and Russia for almost three hundred years they wrote almost no creative works," he notes ("Canadian-Mennonite Literature" 73). Then, in the aftermath of the Russian Revolution, when "[t]heir past vanished almost overnight, their present was bleak and dismal, and their future was unknown to them," they abruptly began to write. "Out of this chaotic and hopeless situation," he declares, "Mennonite literature was born" (76). One of the most prolific of the early critics of Mennonite writing in Canada, Loewen expanded this claim in an essay for *Canadian Review of Comparative Literature,* in which he describes the destruction of the Mennonite Commonwealth as spurring the Mennonite literary imagination into action: "Had it not been for the destruction of Mennonite life in Russia, the creative impulses among the Russian Mennonites might not have broken forth to the extent that [they] did. When the Mennonite world in Russia crumbled in the upheavals of World War I and finally vanished in the aftermath of the Revolution of 1917, the Mennonites not only had a story to tell, but they also found a literary voice to tell their story of loss and suffering" ("Leaving Home" 687). As we will see, this is not the only place in Mennonite literary criticism where one can detect a note of appreciation for the Commonwealth's collapse as bequeathing to the Mennonites a subject worthy of literature. Yet, despite the references to "Canadian-Mennonite literature" in the titles of these essays, Loewen's claim in these two essays is not strictly about the beginning, or start, of what we have come to know as "Mennonite Canadian literature" as a body of texts. In fact, while the 1989 essay engages many of the authors that continue to be discussed in the critical literature, Loewen's 1984 essay explores strictly German-language authors, before turning to Rudy Wiebe at the essay's close. And although he is, in this latter essay, cataloguing some of the earliest literary texts in Mennonite history, his claim is not strictly chronological, either. Paul Ricoeur's distinction between "beginnings" and "origins" is applicable here: beginnings, Ricoeur insists, are claims of history, while origins are claims of myth (*Memory* 140). This distinction, he suggests, is often concealed by appeals to the "notion of birth," which collapses the two by way of an anthropomorphizing gesture. To the extent that Loewen's suggestion that Mennonite literature was "born" out of the violence of the Commonwealth's collapse is about the *beginning* of a field, it might well be historically accurate. However, it can also be understood as a mythological claim about the *origin* of a certain form of Mennonite cultural identity, in which the collapse of the Commonwealth is being positioned as the community's break event, or what Vijay Mishra calls its "perceived moment of 'rupture'" that will become a trauma to be worked out "in the artistic domain" (442).

Loewen is the critic who most consistently positions the Russian experience as an origin for the Mennonite Canadian literary imagination, but he is far from alone. Indeed, the first major wave of Mennonite literary criticism was written largely in the 1980s, and if *Peace Shall Destroy Many* was firmly established as the "first" Mennonite novel, the Russian experience was just as quickly established as the origin of Mennonite literature. If, as I argued in the introduction, Mennonite Canadian literature is not a literary construct but a critical one, it is through critical work that the Russian experience is identified as a repeated narrative and, in turn, heralded as a break event. And, as Barbara Herrnstein Smith warns, the "basic-ness" of any repeated narrative is "always arrived at by the exercise of some set of operations, in accord with some set of principles, that reflect some set of interests." Note, in the many examples that follow, the heightened tone that critics use when discussing the Russian experience and the sweeping titles that they give to the essays in which they address it. Setting before himself the task of "tracing the origins of a Mennonite literary tradition, if indeed one exists," for example, Al Reimer spends a dozen pages identifying Anabaptist precedents for Mennonite literature in Canada before arguing that "[t]he tragic upheaval of war and revolution and the destruction of the Mennonite Commonwealth in Russia shocked the Mennonite literary imagination into life as nothing had since the age of martyrdom" (*Mennonite Literary Voices* 1, 15)—

a claim that Julia Spicher Kasdorf cites approvingly in her essay "Writing like a Mennonite" (*Body* 179). When Victor G. Doerksen wrote his essay "In Search of a Mennonite Imagination," he found it in the Commonwealth's collapse as well: "The Russian Revolution," he declared, "was the diabolic engine which drove Mennonite writers" (108). In her essay "Escape from the Bloody Theatre: The Making of Mennonite Stories," Magdalene Redekop sees the tension between the Anabaptist martyrdom stories and the 1920s migration story as working "to account for the fact that the phenomenon of the contemporary literary explosion is happening specifically among *Russian* Mennonites in Canada" (11). In an essay entitled simply "Canadian Mennonite Literature," Jack Thiessen points to "the Russian Revolution with subsequent famine and privation" as having "inspired and even forced" many Mennonites to begin writing (67). Even the original *Mennonite Encyclopedia* (1951), much of which retains its authoritative voice by having been adapted as the *Global Anabaptist Mennonite Encyclopedia Online,* presents this claim as a matter of historical fact. Cornelius Krahn's entry on "Literature, Russo-German Mennonite" posits that Mennonites in Russia had "reached an economic, religious, and educational level by about 1910 in which reflection and literary production could be anticipated." It was, however, "[t]he terrible experiences during the Russian Revolution and under the Communist regime [that] brought about [its] fruition." It would be too much to say that this claim is unanimous in Mennonite criticism, for some critics have attempted to trace the early germs of a Mennonite literary culture prior to the twentieth century, and both the Bible and the *Martyrs Mirror* are commonly raised as precedents. But the claim that the Russian experience marks the beginning of Mennonite literature need not be exclusive: the very fact that its centrality to the emergence of Mennonite literature has been identified so consistently, over such a long period, and in so many different venues, shows its power as an originary event in the Russian Mennonite imagination.

Interestingly, Reimer appears to stage a debate about the role the collapse of the Mennonite Commonwealth played in the emergence of a Mennonite artistic tradition within the plot of *My Harp Is Turned to Mourning,* his fictional rewriting of the Russian Mennonite experience. Wilhelm, the artist figure at the centre of the novel, finds that it is only when he leaves the colony and endures the suffering of working on the front lines of a war that he is finally able to break out of what his art teacher called his "narrow, confining Mennonite *bauernkultur*" (45) and become a true artist. "[A]t last he had done something really first-rate, drawing brilliantly alive and dynamic," he thinks, "even if, paradoxically, their subjects were images of violence and killing" (411). With the death of his first wife, however, Wilhelm wonders "[w]ho would give a damn for [his sketches] in a world where human life was worth no more than a stone kicked underfoot?" (412), and he tosses his portfolio of new work into the Molochnaya River. In Harry Loewen's reading, Wilhelm's destruction of his work "symbolically act[s] out the destruction of his own existence and that of his people" ("Leaving" 690), but I read the passage as reflecting a metafictional anxiety about capitalizing on, or turning into art, the suffering of others. If the shock of war enabled Wilhelm to see the world afresh and unlock his artistic vision, the brutal murder of his wife forced him to reconsider the cost, and value, of this new vision. Read as part of the larger critical debate about the role of this violent history in unleashing a Mennonite artistic vision, it is a remarkable moment of equivocation, a recognition of the deeply difficult politics of rewriting—and thus aestheticizing—a break event.

In the introduction, I worked at some length to mark a distinction between the way that critics have engaged with literature by Mennonites in Canada, and Mennonite Canadian literature. In an important but overlooked essay entitled "The Russian-Mennonite Experience in Fiction" (1980), however, Al Reimer uses the Russian experience to draw a bridge between the two. In surveying early German-language Mennonite writing in Canada, he suggests that those who lived through the trauma of the collapse of the Russian colonies became "obsessed with a need to […] come to terms with that experience by writing about it" (223). He offers a set of brief but valuable readings of rarely discussed early texts focusing on this period, including Gerhard Toews's two novels, *Die Heimat in Flammen* [Homeland in Flames] (1932–33) and *Die Heimat in Trümmern* [Homeland in Ruins] (1936), as well as Arnold Dyck's *Verloren in der Steppe* [Lost in the Steppe] (1944–48), and work by Peter Harder, J.H. Janzen, Gerhard Toews (Georg de Brecht), and Peter J. Klassen. Reimer reports that, in total, some thirty novels were written in German by Mennonite émigrés lamenting the loss of the Russian colonies, collectively constituting what he (rather dramatically) calls a "*Heimatdichtung* style full of nostalgic recollection and yearning for a culture and way of life which had been innocently destroyed by evil forces beyond human comprehension" ("Russian-Mennonite Experience" 223).

When Reimer turns to Rudy Wiebe at the essay's close, however, he pauses to justify Wiebe's inclusion in his essay. One might expect his hesitation to be on the ground that Wiebe wrote in a language different from that of the other authors discussed, but this is not the case. "To include Rudy Wiebe among Russian-Mennonite novelists may seem somewhat arbitrary," Reimer writes. "He is, after all, a native Canadian without any firsthand knowledge of Russian-Mennonite society. Nevertheless, in both *Peace Shall Destroy Many* and *The Blue Mountains of China* Wiebe has found some significant things to say about the Russian-Mennonite experience" (233). That Reimer thinks it necessary to justify including Wiebe in a discussion of Russian Mennonite novelists indicates that, in his discussion of German-language authors, he is consciously working outside the operative assumptions that would come to define "Mennonite Canadian literature." (Not surprisingly, he also names a different text as the "first Mennonite novel": Peter B. Harder's 1913 novel *Schicksale: Oder die Lutherische Cousine* [225].) Nonetheless, after briefly considering Wiebe's work, Reimer argues for a connection between those authors who lived through the Commonwealth's collapse and write in German, and those authors who were born in Canada and write in English, on the basis of their shared investment in what he calls an experience of "special importance" to Mennonites: "But even Wiebe has not said the final word about the meaning of that lost world. That exploration must continue in fiction as in other areas of writing. The writer of fiction can never be done with his examination of the past because he knows that within it lies buried the truth of the present. The Russian-Mennonite experience is of special importance in this respect because it contains the most crucial and tragic confrontation between the Mennonite people and the outside world since Anabaptist times" (235). Anticipating Loewen's argument by several years, Reimer isolates the Russian experience as occupying a key or "special" position in Mennonite writing, using it to bridge the barriers of language, custom, history, and geography that otherwise work to separate Mennonites in Canada. Given the important role that he ascribes to this history in the negotiation of the Mennonites' communal past—that "the truth of the present" remains buried in its retelling—it comes as little surprise when Reimer remarks, somewhat prophetically, that the rewriting of the Russian Mennonite experience "can never be done."

Although one might expect that literary interest in the Russian experience would wane as the émigrés themselves passed on, this was hardly the case. In the mid- to late 1970s, a number of the original German-language texts were translated and republished in English, including Arnold Dyck's *Verloren in der Steppe* (translated in 1974 as *Lost in the Steppe* by Henry D.

Dyck), Hans Harder's 1934 novel *In Wologdas weissen Wäldern* (translated in 1979 as *No Strangers in Exile* by Al Reimer), and Dietrich Neufeld's 1921 diary *Ein Tagebuch aus dem Reiche des Totentanzes* (translated in 1977 as *A Russian Dance of Death* by Al Reimer). More remarkable, perhaps, is the long list of authors who have returned to this narrative in English, writing not as participants in the migration but as members of a community in which the stories and memories of that migration have come to hold a privileged position. Indeed, while Reimer is cautious about connecting the early survivor narratives written in German with more recent narratives written in English by Canadian-born authors, it is only through the retelling of these stories beyond the immediate participants that the experience becomes a part of the larger community, which retains a sense of social cohesion in the present through this investment in a shared past. In 1992, Robert Kroetsch suggested that the loss of the Russian colonies constitutes the "master narrative" of Canadian Mennonite literature (225)—a claim to which I will return.[7] More recently, Jeff Gundy has noted that "[t]he suffering and displacement of Mennonites during the Russian Revolution and its aftermath ha[ve] been a main theme—perhaps *the* main theme—of Mennonite literature in Canada over the last half-century" (review).

I have already mentioned a few of the English-language novels recounting this history, including Weier's *Steppe* (1995) and Reimer's *My Harp Is Turned to Mourning* (1985). Rudy Wiebe wrote two novels returning to this history, first in the episodic novel *The Blue Mountains of China* (1970) and more recently as part of the framing narrative in *Sweeter than All the World* (2001). Barbara Claassen Smucker's award-winning children's novel *Days of Terror* (1979), like Janice L. Dick's *Storm* trilogy—*Calm Before the Storm* (2002), *Eye of the Storm* (2003), and *Out of the Storm* (2004)—shows the community's faith being tested and ultimately refined by trials of the revolution. Other novels, such as Annie Jacobsen's *Watermelon Syrup* (2007), revise these more traditional narratives to reflect roles or experiences that have often been overlooked or ignored.[8] Sandra Birdsell has written the Russian Mennonite story twice: her 2001 novel *The Russländer* and its 2005 sequel *Children of the Day* follow two Mennonite sisters through the violent collapse of the Mennonite Commonwealth, and recount their struggles in Canada to come to terms with the traumas of their Russian past. In other novels, such as Rudy Wiebe's *Peace Shall Destroy Many* (1962), Alayna Munce's *When I Was Young and in My Prime* (2005), and Miriam Toews's *A Complicated Kindness* (2004), memories of the Russian experience serve as the important backdrop for more contemporary narratives.[9] Collectively, these novels have kept the story of dispersal circulating in Canadian literature over the past fifty years, confirming Reimer's prediction that the exploration will be undertaken perpetually, that it will "never be done." Writer Anne Konrad closes her recent article entitled "Why the Soviet Mennonite Story Remains Unfinished" with a pair of staccato sentences that capture something of the stubborn persistence that characterizes Mennonite Canadian literature's compulsive return to this history. "The story is unfinished," she insists. "It matters" (8).

On the Politics of the Narrative Arc

In *Mennonite Literary Voices Past and Present* (1993), Al Reimer offers a telling suggestion regarding why the Russian experience was able to initiate a literary movement among Canadian Mennonites. "Not only was there a sense of faith, peoplehood, and identity in deadly peril," he writes, "but suddenly there were real-life villains (the terrorist leader Makhno and his kind) and heroes (the new Mennonite martyrs) in ready-made dramatic plots" (15–16). Reimer's claim that the past can be understood in terms of predetermined villains and heroes cast in "ready-made" plots is a stark reminder that the ordering power of narrative plays a key role in animating a painful history as a break event. What is more, it reminds us that a narrative's faithfulness to the complexities of the past has little bearing on its power—and that, in fact, just the opposite might be true. In *Recovered Roots*, Yael Zerubavel warns that the use of narrative in the construction of collective memory commonly results in the simplification of "the past into major stages, reducing complex historical events to basic plot structures" (8). According to Zerubavel, however, the simplification of complicated histories is what allows the past to be politicized and deployed in the service of a collective memory. "The power of collective memory does not lie in its accurate, systematic, or sophisticated mapping of the past," Zerubavel argues, "but in establishing basic images that articulate and reinforce a particular ideological stance" (8). Although much of my larger study is given to demonstrating the important differences among the novels that I discuss, Reimer's comments and Zerubavel's critique give me ample reason to pause and consider the politics inherent in many of the novels that rewrite the Mennonites' experience in Russia. Even the quickest glances at these texts reveal a clear narrative arc, one that might not be necessary to establish a single "ideological stance" but that nonetheless provides a basic structure for the function of this history within a collective Mennonite literary memory.

Many of the novels returning to the Russian experience follow a surprisingly uniform three-part structure. They begin with *order,* a stage that establishes the colonies' carefully structured daily life, its simple pleasures, and the natural beauty of its sprawling farms and institutions. This pastoral stage is followed by a dramatic slide into *chaos* as the Commonwealth collapses into a confusion of murder, theft, and rape. These horrors lead almost inevitably to a final stage of emigration or mass *flight.* In many cases, this narrative arc—*order, chaos, flight*—literally structures the story, flagged by section or book titles: the titles of Dick's *Storm* trilogy, for example, are *Calm Before the Storm, Eye of the Storm,* and *Out of the Storm;* the three parts of Smucker's *Days of Terror* are titled "Peace," "Terror," and "Deliverance"; the three parts of Birdsell's *The Russländer* are "In Green Pastures," "In the Presence of Enemies," and "Surely Goodness and Mercy"; and so on. This shared structure underlines the achievements of the prerevolutionary Mennonite world, emphasizes the drama and tragedy of its collapse, and ultimately argues for the necessity of the subsequent mass migration.

One might be tempted to read this larger narrative arc as more reflective of the history that these novels recount than of any shared interpretive strategy, but the parameters of this history reflect both the perspective and the priorities of a particular collective memory. By beginning with *order,* or the Mennonite "Golden Years," rather than, say, the privilegium that welcomed Mennonites into the area by granting them a set of remarkable privileges and advantages, or with Russia's dismantling of the Cossack stronghold that stood on the territory immediately prior to the Mennonites' arrival, this structure effectively effaces the colonial politics that underpin the establishment of a Mennonite Commonwealth in the area. Indeed, much of what the Mennonites refer to as their "Russian" past took place on Ukrainian soil, and the "Little Russians" who populate the literary reconstructions of that world were not Russians at all, but Ukrainians. Although this distinction is largely glossed over in Mennonite fiction, there are a few points at which it is taken up directly, and where its implications briefly become clear. In Dyck's *Lost in the Steppe,* for example, Hans's fourth teacher makes it clear to the students that he is "not a 'Russian' like the others, nor does he want to be one. He doesn't want to be a Little Russian either; he is a Ukrainian, and he wants to be only that" (331–32). The teacher leaves the community after lashing out at the students for the Mennonites' treatment of the Ukrainian people. Dyck leaves the details of the teacher's speech to the reader's imagination, focusing instead on the stunned reaction of the students. Weier's *Steppe* restages the scene, however, and fills in the teacher's voice:

> You think we're worthless don't you, he says. You think we're drunks and thieves. Mechnikov's lips curl. We're just dumb Ukrainians. You look down on us. You like to laugh, and beat us. Whose land is this? Do you know why we're so poor? Speak, Mechnikov says, he hammers at the boy.
>
> By now the classroom is quiet, some of the children are crying. Whose land is this? Do you remember how you got it? Mechnikov's voice turns quieter too. Everything you have you stole from us! You and your God. Once we served the landlords, now we serve you. Remember, you are the foreigners here, you are the guests, this is our land, our country. Someday you'll see the real Ukraine. You won't like it. (1.23)

This passage from *Steppe* is valuable in that by taking up a scene from an earlier novel—a connection that Weier does not overtly signal but that is confirmed by the fact that the teacher's name is the same in each text—Weier makes explicit how the repetition of a key narrative is implicitly a process of rewriting, how the debate about the shape of the Mennonite past extends beyond the pages of any individual text to engage with other texts that return to the same history. More obviously, however, it is important because it is a stark reminder of the imperial politics in which the Mennonites were implicated and from which they benefited. In *Steppe,* passages from Ukrainian history texts and Ukrainian biographies of Makhno are juxtaposed beside nostalgic portraits of the colonies as a Mennonite paradise, and Weier's narrator wrestles with what he calls the "politics of a stolen land" (2.20). Weier's extended engagement with the colonial politics of the Commonwealth's prosperity, however, is nearly unique in Mennonite Canadian novels that return to this period. Dyck's *Lost in the Steppe,* the source of the original passage, is much more typical in this regard: the novel gestures to the larger politics at play but continues to refer to the Ukrainian teachers as Russians, even after drawing our attention to the offensive inaccuracy of the term (102, 332). Without any extended attention to the larger and longer politics in which the Mennonite colonies were swept up, the violence of the Commonwealth's collapse becomes utterly incomprehensible. One need not subscribe to the view that the Mennonites in any way deserved the violence to which they were subjected to recognize that there was a larger political logic at play—including the battle for Ukraine following the collapse of Imperial Russia—that gave meaning, if not structure, to the violence that these novels largely represent as unintelligible *chaos*.

In much the same way, the details of the Mennonites' *flight* to Canada, such as who leaves and who stays behind, where the Mennonites settle, how they get there, or what they do upon arrival, rarely receive more than a page or two in these novels. The emphasis on mass migration as a response to the collapse of the Mennonite world in Russia belies the fact that the vast majority of the Mennonites in Russia—some 80 percent of a population of roughly 100,000—were unable, or unwilling, to participate in the migration. And yet if, from the perspective of Canadian Mennonites, the migration would seem an integral component of this history, the physical movement from one country to another is rarely represented in these novels. Instead, with a few notable exceptions (Wiebe's *Blue Mountains* being the most significant), the migration is almost always simply implied, often through a narrative frame in which the history is recalled by a survivor from the safety of his or her new Canadian home (by interview in *The Russländer*, by diary in *Watermelon Syrup*, by research in *Steppe*) or through a brief conclusion or epilogue showing the protagonist safe in Canada (as in *My Harp Is Turned to Mourning* and *Out of the Storm*). Occasionally, the novels end en route, as in Smucker's *Days of Terror*, or even before the actual migration begins, as in Dyck's *Lost in the Steppe*. In these brief moments in which the destination of the mass migration is presented, Canada is imagined primarily as an empty space of refuge rather than a geo-political landscape with its own complex politics of colonialism or with earlier Mennonite settlements. Not only does the "emptiness" of the Canadian landscape firmly situate the Mennonites' primary location of meaning and belonging elsewhere, but it also echoes, and relies upon, a deeply colonial rendering of the Canadian space. That is, even if the oversimplification of Canada as a geo-political space is an understandable consequence of focus in novels that are, after all, about Mennonite experiences in Russia, it is not innocent in its effects. It participates in a long tradition of constructing the so-called New World as *terra nullius*, at the expense of the many First Nations and Métis peoples with long roots in the areas in which the Mennonites settled. It is a concern that Dora Dueck raises directly, albeit briefly, in *This Hidden Thing* (2010), having her Russländer protagonist wonder, "not for the first time, who'd been here before her, dreaming on this very spot":

> This question was a kind of melancholy that sometimes came over her. It was not generally her way, or the way of her people, to waste worry over what had come before them in the places they lived. It was their own history, with its wanderings and sorrows and triumphs, that they remembered and celebrated, not the land's. The earth they settled upon was assumed to be new and empty. As if prepared, readied and waiting for them. Their memories concerned lines of migration over maps, or lines strung through genealogies of the same names used over and over. Lateral lines, blood lines, not layers of dirt or bone. (224)

Although there are important exceptions—Wiebe's *Peace Shall Destroy Many* and Birdsell's *Children of the Day* primary among them—the larger Mennonite migration narrative, so central to the community's literary and cultural history in Canada, can be said to have relied on an absence of First Nations and Métis in order to position Canada as a safe haven. And little wonder: in recounting the Mennonites' escape from the anarchy of civil war, any mention of the land disputes in Canada might seem to threaten a repetition of the Russian terror.

The narrative arc of *order, chaos, flight,* which structures much of the larger retelling of the Mennonite experience in Russia, should be understood as a clear reflection of the perspective from which this history is being told. One place to turn for an alternative perspective on these novels is in the work of Ukrainian Canadian critics, who, understandably, are often sceptical of the politics at play. In *Leaving Shadows: Literature in English by Canada's Ukrainians* (2005), for example, Lisa Grekul notes that, while many Mennonite Canadian writers "trace their roots back to Ukraine," they are "rarely mentioned in accounts of Ukrainian Canadian history" (xxi), and are never positioned as part of the Ukrainian cultural community in Canada, despite (or perhaps because of) the fact that the Mennonites' experience in Ukraine has "been recorded again and again—rather one-sidedly—in Mennonite literature" (186). In a review of *The Russländer* in the *Globe and Mail,* Janice Kulyk Keefer is even more direct, arguing that Birdsell's focus on the Mennonite experience is "problematic" because it blinds Birdsell to the much larger and more complex political and economic realities in which the Mennonites' experiences were set. "There is another problem with *The Russländer*, not as a novel but as an adequate reconstruction of a tragically complex past," she writes. "For the paradise of what Birdsell calls both Russia and Ukraine was already inhabited—if not productively farmed—when the Mennonite colonizers arrived. The catastrophes of 1917 and afterward engulfed Jews, Ukrainians and Russians as well as Mennonites, whose oasis was as paradisical as it was not only because of the Mennonites' virtues and hard labour, but also, perhaps, because of their exclusionary ethos."

It is Myrna Kostash, however, who most fully engages with what she calls the "Menno Versions of the Revolution." The Ukrainian Canadian author and critic notes her shock at coming across her own people's history in Mennonite Canadian literature, and expresses her dismay at its interpretation of her past. In a rhetorical debate held with an imaginary Mennonite partner, Kostash chastises Mennonites for imagining themselves as being central to Ukrainian history or having any claim to the area in which they once lived. "You would call this empire of Ukrainian pain your fatherland" (140), she writes, retorting that it was the Ukrainians who "were dragged with great violence into the world beyond their here-and-now by the impending drama of revolution and promise of *their own land*. The land had been Mennonite 128 years when the revolution came. A blink of the eye: that's how long it had been Mennonite" (142). After the Mennonites left, Kostash writes bluntly, they were promptly forgotten. "You are utterly gone," she writes. "No one remembers you" (136). Significantly, however, she turns to Mennonite Canadian literature as both her source for the Mennonites' interpretation of their history and as the object of her critique. "I did not know about you from our narratives but from your own, the literature you wrote when you got to Canada and which I read as Canadian texts," Kostash writes. "And there, to my appalled fascination, I learned that you were my raging, guilt-ridden, trespassing boss or his loutish elder son or his bookish younger one. I learned about your secret harbouring rooms and my orphan's homelessness, your plain-speaking God and my avenging revolutionary angel, Nestor" (145). After perusing several of the novels recounting the Mennonites' time in Ukraine (including Dyck's *Lost*, Reimer's *Harp*, and Wiebe's *Blue Mountains*), Kostash parodies their politics in a caustic account that she offers up to her imaginary Mennonite reader:

> First come the Bolsheviks, then comes genocide, the Menno-
> nite people dying of typhoid, cholera, influenza, starvation, and

execution a mere year later. There is no other news between the revolution and the dying, no mention of manifestos or newspapers, programs or decrees, nothing of land reform or workers' councils or women's suffrage, no slogans or songs or eulogies, only death. Or, as the poet writes: "Ruin, ruin, ruin" ... in the place of Menno order. One day you have money, a plump wife, thick crops in the fields and apples tumbling like coins in the orchard, and the next day your wife is dead, your brothers scattered, your children starving, the apple tree limbs broken like sticks. (159)

With section titles such as "Menno Versions of Makhno," "Enter the Ukrainian Servants: The Blockhead and the Slut," and "Shifting Points of View," Kostash's larger chapter carefully identifies, and rejects, many of the stock characters and elements found in Mennonite fiction, offering a deeply (if somewhat ambivalently) critical reading of the way in which Canadian Mennonites have imagined their experience in "Russia." One could certainly argue with some of the terms of Kostash's critique, but in the context of this study her commentary on these novels, along with her own retelling of the Mennonites' break event, serves as a valuable reminder of the political limitations of communal narratives and of thinking of the past in terms of "ready-made plots." Such narratives, Kostash reminds us, are never objective, never complete, and never constructed in isolation.

Conclusion

Although I have taken some time here to emphasize the areas of overlap in the various retellings of the Russian Mennonite narrative (as well as their political limitations), I want to close this chapter by insisting, once again, that the differences among the rewritings are ultimately what is the most important for me here. Even as I opened the section above by citing Yael Zerubavel's caution regarding the way that collective narratives often reduce the past to "basic plot structures," I want to close by noting that she goes on to argue that the apparent singularity of any commemorative practice ultimately breaks down on closer inspection. "The ambiguity may be less apparent within a single performance of commemoration that attempts to emphasize a certain meaning of the past and suppress other possible interpretations," Zerubavel writes. "But the comparative study of various commemorative performances relating to the same event makes it possible to observe these tensions and the amazing capacity of the myth to mediate between highly divergent readings of the past" (10). Although the rewriting of a break event carries with it the threat of repeating the politics of a highly particular and limited perspective on the past, then, there is no reason to assume that these retellings are unable to return and tell the story differently. Robert Kroetsch's use of the term "master narrative" to describe the role that the Russian story has played in Mennonite writing is indebted to François Lyotard's critique of the modernist impulse to create overarching narratives that subsume all experience into an ordering structure, but I want to insist that positioning this history as a "key narrative" is fundamentally different from understanding it as a "master narrative." This is not because the 1920s story is somehow inherently less ambitious or celebratory than the grand narratives of modernity. Although Richard Kearney insists that there is a "crucial difference between the 'little narratives' of the vanquished and the 'Grand Narratives' of the victors" (61), I would suggest that there is no narrative that cannot be rendered grand by its own tellers. Instead, the difference that I want to underline between "grand" or "master narratives" and these "key narratives" is in the latter's multiplicity over and against the monologism of the former. Although a given key narrative might well shape the community's self-perception, its many strains offer few overarching messages apart from underlining its importance. To the contrary, what I find in turning to these novels is that the retelling of a break event functions in precisely the opposite direction of master narratives: they repeat order to multiply, rather than narrow, the possible meanings and forms of the community. In spite of their common historical referent and shared textual structures, the rewritings of this Mennonite break event work within these larger parameters to tell very different stories about the shape of the Mennonites' past and the possibilities of their collective future.

The debate that results from these many retellings is nicely summarized in the opening epigraph to Al Reimer's *My Harp Is Turned to Mourning*, credited to Rudy Wiebe: "Stories must be told and re-told," it reads. "[T]he retelling of stories [...] is so much more important than recounting the original facts because the so-called lies—the accretions and deletions of each new telling—are more humanly significant than literal facts can ever be." The fact that Reimer places this quotation as an epigraph to his own retelling of this key story shows how widely acknowledged, and how self-conscious, the repetition of this narrative has become. And it is to the various strains of these retellings, and to their so-called lies, that I now turn.

Chapter 2

Gelassenheit *or Exodus:* My Harp Is Turned to Mourning *and the Theo-Pedagogical Narrative*

It might come as a surprise to some that a study of Mennonite Canadian literature would devote just a single chapter to novels with a theological focus. After all, in studies such as John L. Ruth's *Mennonite Identity and Literary Art* (1978), *all* authentically Mennonite writing is theological by definition. Ruth, who earned his PhD in English from Harvard, does not make a naive call for Mennonite authors to offer simplistically evangelistic literature or to sanitize the difficulties and shortcomings of the community. Nonetheless, he insists that the proper aim of Mennonite authors is ultimately to present the community's story in such a way that "the over-arching Salvation-story in which it participates may be grasped" (70). In turning to the Russian experience specifically, Ruth can barely contain himself at its theological potential. "How monitory, how paradigmatic of difficult issues in the Mennonite soul, with its lessons of apocalyptic extremism, territorial religion, class conflict, schism, patience, persecution, faith!" he exclaims. "What a saga, how replete with incident!" (69). Writing two years earlier than Ruth, Paul Erb is even more explicit in his expectations for Mennonite literature. The "Mennonite dynamic has spiritual roots, and can only be understood and interpreted spiritually," he writes. As a result, true Mennonite art is therefore to be "evangelism in the best sense of the Word" (5). Much more recently, American critic and poet Jeff Gundy—a central figure in an emerging "theo-poetics" movement among American Mennonite poetics—literally defines "Mennonite literature" in North America as "work that seeks self-consciously and more or less directly to promote Anabaptist faith and practice" (*Walker* 32).

Where some might be surprised to find just one chapter focusing on the theological implications of Mennonite writing, I suspect that for many more, even among Mennonite critics, the surprise would be that I would give it even this much space. In *Mennonites in Canada, 1939–1970,* for instance, T.D. Regehr declares that "[a]n essentially redemptive or didactic model of story telling was inadequate for conveying the pathos of the disintegration of the Russian Mennonites' world" (287), while Victor G. Doerksen worries that the tradition of "religious fiction" in Mennonite art has resulted in "the subversion of the imagination by referring to a frame of reference that is falsely artificial" ("Search" 107). Rudy Wiebe complains about what he calls the "propagandizing sort" of Christian literature, which aims at the salvation of its reader, calling such literature "cherry-flavoured medicine" and dismissing it with a literal "[b]ah!" ("Artist" 41). Even Gundy, after defining Mennonite literature as religious in scope and intent, places it aside as being interesting only from a "sociological point of view," opting to focus on all other literary work by Mennonites, which he calls "Mennonites writing" (*Walker* 32).[1]

Even if we dismiss the idea that all "authentically" Mennonite literature ought to be religious in an evangelical sense, it might seem reasonable, given the deeply and thoroughly religious nature of the Mennonite world in Russia, to expect that any novel recounting the collapse of that world would need to engage deeply with its religiosity. That this is not the case—that there are Mennonite novels set in the Russian colonies that manage to avoid nearly any mention of faith or religion—says much about the secularization of the Mennonite Commonwealth in its latter stages and the competing interests of other strains of the Mennonite migration narrative. Of course, the majority of novels retelling this history *do* engage with theological concerns, yet most are not "theo-pedagogical" in the sense that I intend by this term. Although theo-pedagogical novels need not be nakedly didactic or embarrassingly evangelical in their educational intent, they must tell their stories in such a way that they both undertake the education of readers regarding a particular religious faith and actively advocate its promotion. Both John Weier's *Steppe* and Annie Jacobsen's *Watermelon Syrup* wrestle extensively with theological issues, yet neither novel is properly theo-pedagogical in that they do not envision a fully religious perspective on events, nor do they ultimately articulate a pedagogical intent that seeks to advocate for the Mennonites' Anabaptist faith, religion, or theological tradition.[2] Similarly, several chapters of Wiebe's *The Blue Mountains of China* are complex and powerful theological renderings of Canada's Mennonite community, and the concluding chapter has been read as didactically theological (Ferris). Nonetheless, in my reading of the novel, the cumulative effect of its fragmented narrative works away from the coherence and totalizing claims of its conclusion. Perhaps more to the point, the religious vision suggested in its closing chapter is not explicitly Mennonite. As such, though Wiebe's novel is clearly theologically engaged, I do not consider it a theo-pedagogical rendering of the Commonwealth experience in the sense that I am articulating in this chapter. What I am interested in here is Mennonite literature as articulated by Gundy—that which "seeks self-consciously and more or less directly to promote Anabaptist faith and practice" (*Walker* 32)—even as I want to question the suggestion that such literature cannot be complex or sophisticated enough to be interesting from a critical standpoint.

In this chapter, I begin my literary analysis of the Mennonites' 1920s migration narrative by considering two very different examples of this theo-pedagogical strain: Al Reimer's *My Harp Is Turned to Mourning* (1985) and Janice L. Dick's *Out of the Storm* (2004). Both novels are saturated in religious imagery, assume a thoroughly theological perspective on the history that they represent, and, I will argue, take as their primary focus the spiritual significance that the Russian experience holds for the Mennonite community. Wrestling with, but ultimately affirming, the Anabaptist principle of non-violence, both novels present the trauma of the Russian experience as a painful but necessary process of spiritual purification and renewal. Although *My Harp* will be my primary focus here, I juxtapose it to *Out of the Storm* because their striking thematic similarities illustrate how extensively the biblical paradigm structures a theological rendering of the Russian experience, and because the differences between the novels help to demonstrate what is at stake in critical discussions of faith in fiction more generally. Critics have consistently argued that, as a genre traditionally invested in realism, the novel is particularly ill suited to convey religious concerns—indeed, this is a key element in Benedict Anderson's argument regarding the construction and maintenance of imagined communities. A careful reading of *My Harp*, however, suggests that narratives can be firmly anchored in the realist tradition and historical record while insisting on a larger transhistorical religious significance. In *My Harp*, the collapse of the Commonwealth is revisited not only as a means to document a key moment in Mennonite history, to confirm a contemporary community through a shared history of suffering, or simply to subject that community to a theological critique. Instead, I want to suggest it rewrites the collapse with a startling pedagogical thrust: to enable the contemporary community to return vicariously to this violent history and experience something of the theological value of suffering for itself.

Faith in Fiction

In spite of Northrop Frye's declaration in 1965 that "[r]eligion has been a major—perhaps the major—cultural force in Canada" (229), religious literature has remained nearly absent from the larger purview of Canadian criticism. To be sure, there have been rare occasions in which religion has been the focus of consideration, including the uneven half-dozen essays in a *Literature and Theology* special issue on Canadian literature (2002) and in William Closson James's *Locations of the Sacred: Essays on Religion, Literature, and Canadian Culture* (1998). However, in each of these venues, the discussion focuses almost exclusively on the religious or spiritual subtexts of canonical texts rather than on "religious fiction" per se. Barbara Pell's *Faith and Fiction* (1998) does take on overtly Christian elements of fiction, claiming to be "the first of its kind in Canadian literary criticism" (4). However, her focus is canonical works, and Pell, like many others, dismisses the "religious novel" as "that minor genre written for the encouragement of the faithful" (4). There are other exceptions (including some to be found at the long-standing Christianity and Literature Study Group that meets each year as a subsection of the annual Association of Canadian College and University Teachers of English conference), but the overwhelming critical assumption in Canada seems to be that religious novels, by definition, are not worthy of serious academic attention. Although it has been possible to consider the Bible as a "great code" for literature, the prevailing wisdom is that the "religious factors in Canada [are] doctrinal and evangelical," as Frye puts it, "stress[ing] the arguments of religion at the expense of its imagery" (229).

The larger relationship between religious faith and literature is clearly too complex a topic to explore in detail here, but one of the implicit arguments of this chapter is that the Mennonite literary tradition suggests that it is a relationship worth reconsidering. The arguments to be made more directly will concern a different set of questions. What is at stake in novels rendering the collapse of the Russian Mennonite world in theo-pedagogical terms? What are the various biblical paradigms available to authors working in this strain? What assumptions—about time, history, and the nature of repetition—underpin novels in the theo-pedagogical narrative strain, and what generic or formal strategies do these authors use to support their representations of the Mennonite experience? In short, how does the theo-pedagogical strain reimagine the Mennonites' 1920s migration narrative?

Although *My Harp Is Turned to Mourning* and *Out of the Storm* are, in many ways, a study in contrasts, they are remarkably similar at the level of both plot and biblical framing. Both are large, sweeping novels told in the third person using multiple linear plotlines and showcasing a wealth of historical research in the service of their theological renderings of the Russian experience. Reimer's 439-page novel tells the story of Wilhelm Fast, an aspiring artist who becomes a village teacher in the Molochnaya colony. The central character in Dick's 430-page novel is Johann Sudermann, also a young Mennonite teacher, also living in Molotschna.[3] The central love interests of both men are the beautiful daughters of wealthy Mennonite business owners, whose parents meet traumatic ends during the chaos of the post-revolutionary years due to their status as "kulaks": in *My Harp,* Clara Bock is raped, and her parents are murdered, at Selenaya, their large country estate, and Wilhelm's first wife, Katya, is raped and killed while pregnant; in *Out,* Katya's sister is raped, and her parents are murdered, at Succoth, their large country estate. Both Wilhelm and Johann wrestle with the morality of placing aside the Mennonites' historic peace position and taking up arms, and while both men ultimately do fight—Wilhelm volunteers for the *Selbstschutz* (Mennonite self-defence units), and Johann is conscripted by the Red Army—their participation is shown to be theologically and strategically regrettable. Both novels include a rebellious brother figure nicknamed Kolya: in *My Harp,* Wilhelm's brother, Nikolai, rejects the Mennonites as hypocritical bourgeoisie and joins the anarchists; in *Out,* Katya's brother, Nicholai, voluntarily leaves his Mennonite community to fight with the White Army. Both novels make much of the potential for the brothers to unknowingly fight each other—in *My Harp,* Wilhelm unknowingly shoots and wounds his brother—and, in both, the rebellious brothers ultimately see the errors of their ways. Finally, each novel concludes with a short chapter telling of the primary characters' arrival in Canada: both sets of couples settle in Saskatchewan with their children, where both teachers will try their hand at farming.

Without setting aside the possibility of intentional intertextuality, many of these novels' textual overlaps can be traced to the fact that the texts share not only a historical referent but also an ultimately theological focus. The "rebellious brother" in their storylines, for example, has its clear precedent in the biblical parable of the prodigal son (Luke 15), a connection made explicit in *Out* (70). Similarly, their shared critiques of the militarization and material decadence of the Mennonite communities in Russia—the former stronger in *Out,* the latter more prominent in *My Harp*—are derived from the Anabaptist principles of non-resistance and simple living. What is more, both novels draw on the same biblical paradigm for their retelling of the migration story, each taking its title and epigraph from the book of Job.[4] Given the centrality of scripture to Mennonite identity historically—Robyn Sneath goes so far as to suggest that appeals to the Bible in Mennonite writing function as an appeal to a "part of their homeland, [the] place where they all belong" and "a way of referring to their collective memory" (216)—these biblical titles make the novels' theological assumptions clear while appealing to a communal identity via a common source of authority that helps to explain their similar structures.

If *Out* and *My Harp* have similarities in focus and detail, however, they offer dramatically different theo-pedagogical arguments. *Out,* the final novel in Dick's trilogy retelling the Mennonite migration narrative, is a straightforward example of evangelistic literature. Although the novel raises theological questions about Mennonite spiritual decadence and the use of force in self-defence, the answers that it provides are so strictly in keeping with Mennonite convention that they come across as predetermined and programmatic. *Out* is peppered with scriptural references, and several of the novel's subplots are straightforward object lessons, including Anna's recovery from rape (which demonstrates the redemptive power of her faith), and the wanderings of the Russian Paul Gregorovich Tekanin and the Mennonite Grisha (which are transparent occasions to stage debates in support of Anabaptist theology). In Dick's novel, Mennonites are largely innocent victims of forces beyond their control, and the perpetrators of the violence, such as Makhno's men, are "assorted bands of embodied demons" (127). The primary protagonists are so unwaveringly righteous that the impact of the novel's critique of individual Mennonites as selfish, arrogant, or hypocritical is limited. Indeed, the fate of *Out*'s main protagonists is never seriously in doubt; by the novel's close, the major characters have their faith justified and their hope renewed, with only one significant character presumed to have died. The novel is admirably researched and ably written, and is particularly valuable as one of the few novels retelling this history that represents the political and material processes of the migration. From a theological perspective, however, *Out,* as Wiebe suggested of such works, is pedagogical in the propagandistic mode: the faith that it works hard to promote is never interrogated rigorously enough to rise to the occasion of the history that it engages.

Although *My Harp,* like *Out,* ultimately argues for a theological interpretation of the Russian experience, Reimer's novel eschews straightforward or dogmatic answers to the theological questions that it raises. In fact, the novel levels a stinging critique of the Mennonites' long-cherished principle of separation from the world and the vapid religious rhetoric that did little to address the serious material inequalities that marred the colonies. The major characters of Reimer's novel endure devastating tragedies that do not lend themselves to glib responses—Wilhelm, for example, loses his father, both of his brothers, his in-laws, and his pregnant first wife during the chaos—and few in the novel are able to hold unquestioningly to their faith. What is more, Reimer refuses to succumb to the caricature of Makhno that, as Sarah Klassen writes in her review of the novel, otherwise dominates "Mennonite mythology," where "he is the Evil One, the Anti-Christ" ("Everyman's Story" 59). If Makhno is cold blooded and (nearly) merciless in *My Harp,* he is also given a historical perspective that helps to explain, if not to justify, his actions: he was a victim of crushing poverty, he was beaten when he worked on a Mennonite farm as a young man, and he was introduced to radical politics during his time in prison. *My Harp* is not free of didacticism (as the novel's rather awkwardly staged debates about Mennonite identity make clear), but its two explicitly religious subplots, that of the charismatic evangelist Erdmann Lepp and that of the failed church reformer "Old" Daniel Fast, are compelling accounts of how the power and promise of religious faith are deeply intertwined with, but need not be overcome by, the attendant dangers of corruption and fanaticism.

Both Dick and Reimer have commented on their understandings of the relationship between faith and fiction, and while there is always a danger in relying too heavily on an author's critical commentary to understand her or his literary work, their contrasting opinions nicely illustrate the very different directions of their theo-pedagogical texts. Dick's view of the role of art, as she explains it in a brief interview with Darlene Polachic, offers an explicitly evangelical mandate for Mennonite literature: "One of the things I want to portray in my stories is the truth that God is faithful no matter what, and His faithfulness goes beyond the Mennonite story to whatever situation a person is in." Arguing elsewhere that "fiction is one of the finest and most effective means of communicating the message of faith and hope" (qtd. in Lindquist), Dick suggests that the pedagogical focus of her work demands a sanitized version of the history it represents in order that its spiritual message remains clear. "I don't want anything I write to make Him sorry He gave me the gift," she explains to Polachic. The demand for Christian fiction is growing, she argues, precisely "because it's clean and it's safe." Even as Reimer warns against "the old Mennonite habit of reading fiction as though it were a form of discursive writing like history or theology" (*Mennonite Literary Voices* 67), he, too, has advocated for what can be understood as a thoroughly religious framework for understanding Mennonite art. His study *Mennonite Literary Voices Past and Present*, published eight years after *My Harp*, refers to Mennonite authors as "prophets" (56), affirms the long tradition of understanding the artist as "divinely inspired, a bearer of highest truths" (56), and insists that the "early spiritual bias in Mennonite literature has never been entirely lost" (3). Distancing his own work from precisely the readers whom Dick is courting— rather caustically referring to them as "lower tier" readers "who still want only a safe, didactic Christian literature devoid of challenge or any view of the world as it actually exists" (64–65)—Reimer nonetheless insists on a thoroughly theological role for Mennonite literature. Suggesting that Mennonites have only recently begun to "question our triumphalist view of our own history and achievements and tak[e] a more critical view [of] ourselves" (57), he argues that the community "desperately need[s] artists who have wrestled long and hard with evil—both outside and inside of themselves—and who are committed to exposing our spiritual hypocrisies, our shallow moralism, our incessant but often aimless church activities" (57). Although his understanding of the role of the Mennonite author is every bit as faith based as the one expressed by Dick, Reimer's expectation is that Mennonite literature will best serve the faith community by interrogating it, rather than by celebrating it.

Although *Out* and *My Harp* return to the same historical moment, the authors' divergent expectations for religious literature make for two very different novels. There are, of course, differences of style and quality, but the theological differences are illustrated nicely by the fact that each novelist pays careful attention to a historical character that the other largely ignores. As I noted earlier, *Out* is the only retelling of the migration to recount the minutiae of B.B. Janz's administrative efforts to secure permission for the Mennonites' migration to Canada, and *My Harp* is the only novel that attempts to detail the formative experiences and rise of the anarchist leader Makhno. These very different historical foci—the former focused on a Mennonite leader and seeking to understand the effort that made their mass migration possible, the latter focused on a Ukrainian leader and seeking to understand the events that made the migration necessary—reflect the conflicting directions of these texts' theo-pedagogical gazes. Dick's novel is theo-pedagogical in the evangelistic mode, presenting the Mennonite migration as a biblical parable of God's goodness, whereas Reimer's novel allows the Anabaptist faith to critique the Russian experience (and vice versa) in an effort to understand God's willingness to allow the colonies to collapse.

Exodus versus *Gelassenheit*

Both *Out of the Storm* and *My Harp Is Turned to Mourning* signal, in their titles and epigraphs, their use of the book of Job to offer theological interpretations of the Mennonites' Russian experience. The biblical story lends itself as a parallel to the Mennonite experience in Russia because of the dramatic turn of fortune Job experiences while being celebrated as "blameless and upright, a man who fears God and shuns evil" (Job 1:8). When Satan suggests that Job loves and fears God only because of the protection and wealth that God has provided, God decides to allow Satan to test Job's faith by inflicting a litany of horrors on the faithful servant: a neighbouring people sweep in, kill his servants, and steal his livestock, and a wind collapses his house, killing all of his children (1:14–20). Although Job questions God's decision to allow his suffering, he remains faithful, and he seems to accept God's rebuke for daring to question his omnipotence. Importantly, Job's faith is ultimately rewarded: he is granted a second family, even more riches than he had before, and an extra century and a half of life to enjoy it all.

In *Out*, the Job paradigm is used to position the Mennonites as a holy and upright people who are afflicted in their innocence. If Dick's characters occasionally question their suffering, they steadfastly refuse to turn away from God, with declarations such as "[f]aith is often nurtured in the school of adversity" (23) and, "[i]f your faith is no good in trials, then it is no good at all" (127). *Out*'s three primary couples migrate to Canada and get married at the conclusion of the series, a reward for their steadfastness that is in keeping with the Job paradigm and is underlined by the biblical passage that stands at the end of the novel. The epilogue reads, in part, "[f]or you, O God, tested us; you refined us like silver ... you brought us to a place of abundance" (Psalm 66:8–12). Yet *Out*'s use of Job raises a number of concerns as well. The most obvious is the fact that, in the biblical narrative, Job resolutely refuses to flee from the violence that has come upon him. In fact, it is precisely his willingness to endure his suffering as the will of God that leads to the re-establishment of his successful farm and family. Even if the Mennonites were historically as blameless and upright as Job—which is surely too much to ask of any people— the mass migration seems to stand in direct opposition to the lesson of *Out*'s chosen biblical parallel.

Dick addresses this apparent contradiction by supplementing the Job paradigm of suffering with the Israelites' deliverance from slavery in Egypt. In this context, the Mennonite emigration becomes a repetition of the biblical Exodus, with the historical B.B. Janz serving as a Mennonite Moses.[5] As an ethno-religious community with a history of migration and suffering, Mennonites have a long tradition of comparing themselves with Jews, and the Exodus frame appeals to their sense of themselves as a distinct or even chosen people.[6] The Exodus provides a coherent theological model for understanding the Mennonites' Russian experience, but it also proves a tenuous parallel if pushed too far. The Mennonites as a people, of course, were anything but slaves in Ukraine, and Ukrainians and Mennonites alike were caught in the violence of the period. More importantly, the Mennonites fled *out* of the land that they believed had been set aside for them by providence. The significant incongruities between the Exodus narrative and the Russian Mennonite experience produce a number of contradictory uses of biblical tropes in *Out*.[7] What is more, the parallel not only deeply misrepresents the material and political history behind the migration—which the novel itself otherwise works admirably to catalogue—but also holds unfair implications for the vast majority of the Mennonites in Russia. That is, comparison of the Mennonites' flight from Russia with the Israelites' flight from Egypt would only work if the Bible suggested that Moses demanded that Pharaoh let one-fifth of his people go. As I noted in the first chapter, of the more than 100,000 Mennonites in Russia, only a small minority—roughly 20,000—actually escaped the country. A novel need not follow its intertextual gestures in their entirety, of course, but appealing to the Exodus model of migration to sidestep the uncomfortable implications of the Mennonites' response to their suffering afforded by the Job paradigm *Out* only compromises the clarity of its theological message. Ultimately, the novel offers a generalized but largely unsubstantiated sense of biblical support for the Mennonite community in Russia.

Like *Out, My Harp* takes Job as its primary biblical paradigm, but rather than supplementing it with additional scriptural references to address the complications that arise Reimer emphasizes Job's willingness to suffer, allowing the biblical narrative to critique the historical Mennonite community. I will return to how Reimer attempts to address the incompatibility between the Job narrative and the migration narrative shortly. In order to understand its logic, however, it is important to first note that the clearest connection that *My Harp* draws between Job and the Russian Mennonites—and the clearest summary of the novel's overarching theological interpretation of the history that it represents—is not with those caught in the collapse of their Commonwealth but with an earlier collapse of the religious ideals meant to animate that community. Apart from the title and epigraph, the novel's most explicit reference to Job comes some seventy years *before* the Russian Revolution, in the four chapters presenting the arrival of failed church reformer "Old" Daniel Fast to Russia in the early 1800s. Daniel, who immigrates to Russia in search of a religious purity he believes impossible in Prussia, takes a strong stand against the Mennonite hypocrisy he encounters in the Russian colonies. In one of the novel's most explicitly pedagogical passages, Daniel insists that the Mennonites' physical isolation is no guarantee against the lures of the world, and he predicts the coming collapse of the Commonwealth. "Perhaps our big mistake right from the start was to think we could live in our little world like ducks on a pond," he begins (140), before comparing his spiritual suffering with that of Job: "The fox is calling oh so sweetly from the bank, and we are listening. We think we'll always be able to come back to the safety of our pond. But it won't work. We separated ourselves from the world so we could live for Him, not so we could build bigger *wirtschaften* and richer estates. [...] [L]ike Job's, my harp is turned to mourning. Give me release. From memory. From earthly life. [...] 'It is a terrible thing to fall into the hands of the living God.' Ach, Heavenly Father, Thy terrible, loving will be done ..." (141). As part of the novel's larger criticism of the Mennonite ideal of separation from the world, the passage marks a significant departure from conventional Mennonite theology, and clearly echoes Reimer's own argument in *Mennonite Literary Voices*, in which he warns that the Mennonite practice of separation has "bred its own strains of sin—from false humility to a subtle sense of pride in our own superiority" (57). Moreover, in suggesting that the idea of separateness, ostensibly meant to allow Mennonites to focus on their faith, has only led them to build larger estates, the passage points to the material inequalities that characterized the Mennonite colonies in Russia as a primary cause of its collapse.

The apparent paradox of Daniel's final words in the passage above— concluding with his resignation to the Lord's "terrible, loving will" (141)—crystallizes the novel's overarching promotion of *Gelassenheit,* a difficult Anabaptist theology of suffering characterized by a radical submission to the will of God. In order to establish the spiritual value of suffering central to the novel's conclusion, Reimer has Daniel define the church as a "family of suffering believers" and insist that it is "only through persecution [that] we could discipline ourselves into a true group of suffering disciples" (79–80). Daniel goes on to explain that he "reminded our group in a sermon of the Anabaptist aim of achieving *gelassenheit,* serene self-surrender and resignation to God's will," and turns to a common Mennonite metaphor with obvious application to the violence that occurs later in the novel. "[B]read is made of kernels ground and mixed, and wine of grapes crushed and blended," he declares. "And what has not been ground or crushed is a husk only fit for swine" (80). The novel also warns, however, against the masochism that such a stance seems to invite. The members of Fast's new church compete among themselves to prove themselves the most sinful and prideful, and they undertake extreme, even ridiculous, acts of penance. Several church members sleep overnight in a ditch in winter, for example, and when one of their children dies of pneumonia they take it as evidence that they have not gone far enough. Yet the larger novel affirms Daniel's theology of *Gelassenheit,* even to the point of calling into question the theological legitimacy of the migration effort itself. As we will see, however, the invocation of Job as part of a material critique has its own limitations.

It is worth pausing briefly over the concept of *Gelassenheit,* which, though once a well-established Anabaptist principle, is likely new to many readers. As possible translations for the German word, Donald Kraybill offers "yieldedness; surrender; submission; resignation; [and] abandonment" ("Gelassenheit"). "Those who embody the virtues of *Gelassenheit* surrender themselves to God, yield to the authority of the church, and defer to those in authority over them," he continues. "They exhibit a meek and mild personality that is willing to suffer rather than defend itself." Although resignation or "yieldedness" to God's will and pacifism as a way of responding to violence are not synonymous, they overlap on the question of the suffering believer, which has been a central tenet of Anabaptist theology since the 1527 confession of faith known as the Schleitheim Confession. The confession lays out the Anabaptist principles of adult baptism, church discipline, and separation from the world, and, though it does not use the term *Gelassenheit,* it makes clear that the early Anabaptists understood Jesus's teachings as rejecting all use of force, even in self-defence. "Thereby shall also fall away from us the diabolical weapons of violence," it reads, "such as sword, armor, and the like, and all of their use to protect friends or against enemies—by virtue of the word of Christ: 'you shall not resist evil'" ("Schleitheim Confession"). Other early Anabaptist leaders would echo this principle: Conrad Grebel, for example, described Christians as "sheep for the slaughter ... [who] must be baptized in anguish and affliction, tribulation, persecution, suffering and death" (qtd. in Klaassen 26), while Menno Simons noted that "gold is tried in the fire, and acceptable men in the furnace of adversity" (qtd. in Klaassen 27). This difficult theology of *Gelassenheit,* concisely described in *My Harp* as the "serene self-surrender and resignation to God's will" (80), was at the centre of the widespread martyrdom of Anabaptists during the sixteenth century (Friedmann). Although its lived application—at least in such dramatic form—has rarely been necessary in subsequent centuries, the theology of a suffering church has remained a constant throughout Mennonite history.

My Harp participates in the tradition of Anabaptist thought that accepts the spiritual value of suffering. Although the novel works hard to represent the self-defence units organized by Mennonites in Russia as understandable responses to extraordinary circumstances, it ultimately renders them both a tactical error and a betrayal of Anabaptist principles. Speaking at the funeral of a young Mennonite man who died fighting in the units, for example, the evangelist Erdmann Lepp reiterates the Mennonites' historical peace position. Even as he suggests that the Mennonites ought to "honour their memory with love, respect and compassion," he nonetheless insists that "[w]e all know that as Anabaptist Christians we Mennonites believe it wrong to live by the sword" (361). The larger novel is more resolute in its critique. Although Wilhelm ultimately joins the self-defence units, he is unable to prevent the rape and murder of his pregnant wife, and he unwittingly shoots his own brother. The novel suggests that the units were ineffective at best, and self-destructive at worst, illustrating how the decision to pick up arms worked against the Mennonite pacifist claims and ultimately lent credence to those who saw them as legitimate targets in a larger military-political fight.

More surprising than its critique of the self-defence units, perhaps, is *My Harp*'s relatively sympathetic portrayal of Nestor Makhno. Makhno is introduced as a young man working on the wealthy Loewens' estate, first shown when he is being whipped for having taken a small tool. Reimer uses the passage not only to provide a historical context for Makhno's hatred of the Mennonites—"[T]he big Loewen was nothing but an accursed land-owner who had gotten rich by bleeding the peasants" (39), Makhno thinks—but also to show Makhno accepting and even appreciating the violence as necessary discipline. "Unexpectedly the black hatred within him gave way to a sudden rush of tenderness that almost choked him," the reader is told. "He wanted to say, 'Papasha, you were right to beat me, I deserved it. You are my Papasha, my Little Father, and I must feel your power when I do wrong'" (38–39). Reimer likely overreaches in presenting the charismatic anarchist leader and terror of the Mennonites as secretly appreciating his employer's beatings (to say nothing of his portrayal of Makhno's remarkably wholesome crush on his employer's young daughter), but the passage affirms the novel's larger portrait of the pedagogical value of violence by presenting it as a form of necessary discipline. Echoing "Old" Daniel Fast's resignation to the "terrible, loving will" of the "Heavenly Father" (141), Reimer has Makhno recognize a form of love behind his "Little Father"'s violence. "For the first time in his life [Makhno] had felt what it was like to have a father," Reimer writes, "a father who cared enough to hurt you" (39).[8]

It is in the conflicted figure of Lepp, however, that *My Harp* most fully explores the relationship between suffering and faith. Early in the novel, Lepp is a deeply unsympathetic character; he is an arrogant and aggressively didactic travelling evangelist who terrifies Wilhelm and attempts to bully Wilhem's brother at the dinner table. By the novel's close, however, he emerges, as Herbert Giesbrecht writes, "as a towering figure of indomitable faith, awesome courage, and deepened compassion" (258). Importantly, Lepp's dramatic transformation is shown to be the direct result of his response to the violence of the period. In a passage that many reviewers noted as the novel's finest, Reimer stages a dramatic ideological confrontation between Lepp and Makhno, with Lepp preaching the peace teachings of Jesus to the notoriously ruthless anarchist leader. Lepp echoes Daniel's material critique of the Mennonites by recognizing the legitimacy of Makhno's complaints regarding the disproportionate wealth accumulated by the Mennonites. Indeed, when Makhno asks Lepp "[w]here is that part about the rich getting what's coming to them, their flesh eaten by fire[?]" Lepp's answer—"Epistle of James, Chapter Five"—implicitly affirms its applicability to the Commonwealth. Although Reimer does not actually quote from James 5, the biblical passage is remarkable in its implications for the novel's representation of the Mennonites.[9] Lepp, however, refuses to condone the anarchist's use of violence. Instead, he challenges Makhno's legitimacy as a revolutionary figure and counters with a scriptural reference in support of non-violence. "There has only been one true revolutionary on this earth, and that is Jesus Christ, the life-giving Redeemer," Lepp tells the anarchist leader. "And he said just the opposite of what you're saying. He said: 'When a man hits you on the cheek, offer him the other cheek too'" (396). Although Makhno mocks and strikes him, Lepp manages to live out the scripture that he has just quoted, literally turning his face for Makhno to strike a second time. In this central moment in the text, Lepp's willingness to submit to Makhno's fist wins Lepp the leader's grudging respect. He is whipped, rather than killed, and released. Importantly, his submission does not noticeably change Makhno's actions, nor does it ultimately earn him his freedom. It is true, as Edna Froese writes, that "Lepp is the only one who successfully turns the other cheek and who, for that reason only, remains alive and still preaching" (*Write* 108), but his "reward" is little more than the opportunity to continue his evangelism under even more trying conditions. In the novel's final passage, Lepp has been exiled to the worst of the Soviet punishment camps, where, along with Soviet and Ukrainian prisoners, he bears unimaginable sufferings. Even as several other major characters are beginning to climb the social ladder elsewhere—Wilhelm and Clara have fled to Canada, for example, where they have succeeded as farmers and are moving to Winnipeg to restart their careers in the arts (435)—Lepp remains a portrait of suffering faith, continuing to preach "the love of Christ and the peace that passes all understanding" and serving as a "living symbol of hope" for his fellow inmates (438).

In *My Harp,* the reward for patient suffering as a response to violence lies neither in earthly wealth nor in a miraculous migration but in a transformation into a genuine witness of faith. Having survived his confrontation with Makhno, Lepp comes to a new understanding of the Mennonites' difficulties in Russia, one that runs directly counter to that offered by the more celebratory history that seems to proliferate in the theo-pedagogical strain. "Bad as he was, Makhno was not the Antichrist," Lepp tells Wilhelm. "He was sent by God as a scourge to us, a vicious dog to snap at our heels so we would change direction, a catalyst to stir us to a new spiritual awareness. I'm convinced that God intended something creative in this prolonged ordeal of violence against us" (421). Like Daniel, Lepp emphasizes the spiritual value of suffering, and, like Daniel, he presents this image of a suffering faith as a counter to the Mennonite history of isolation from the world. "The greatest sin of temptation for Christians is to avoid exposure to hostility and oppression," Lepp insists, "to seal themselves safely off from the world, as we Mennonites have done here in Russia" (421). From Daniel's suggestion that "[i]t was only through persecution that we could discipline ourselves into a true group of suffering disciples" to Lepp's insistence that "God intended something creative" in the violence, *My Harp* shows suffering to be a powerful force for spiritual growth.

My Harp's valorization of Lepp's refusal to flee the violence in Russia for a new beginning in Canada is consistent with the Job paradigm and marks Lepp as the novel's closest parallel to the Anabaptists of the sixteenth century. What is more, in its affirmation of his suffering faith, the novel follows the Job paradigm to a controversial conclusion, questioning the theological justification for the migration itself—implying that, far from being an answer from God, the mass flight was not in keeping with what Daniel Fast names "the Anabaptist aim of achieving *gelassenheit*" (80). Indeed, while John L. Ruth suggests that both the martyrdom stories and the Russian experience are parts of the "over-arching Salvation-story" in which the Mennonites participate (70), they differ in significant ways. "The Anabaptist story and the Russian story are not, after all, the same story of a cycle of martyrdom," insists Magdalene Redekop: "The making of the story of the Russian Mennonites is painfully split between those who made their escape and those who did not. That split cannot be interpreted so easily in the context of the theology of martyrdom. From the perspective of Canada, the place of escape, it is a refugee story. To tell it as a story of exodus helps but it cannot hide the tension between the survival story and that other one, the one that pulls towards the spectacle of torture and death" (19). Redekop's insights anticipate the difficulties that I located in Dick's attempt to impose the Exodus model onto the Russian migration narrative. Although a representation of the migration as divine intervention might seem an appealing theological interpretation, within the Anabaptist tradition that understands yieldedness and suffering as expected parts of Christian discipleship, the decision to emigrate can also be understood as a refusal to fully participate in the sacrifices expected of faithful believers.

Just as the theo-pedagogical narrative in *Out* is complicated by its movement away from its primary biblical paradigm, however, *My Harp*'s representation of the material inequalities within the Mennonite Commonwealth complicates its theology of suffering. After all, the biblical narrative is clear that Job's suffering is not a consequence of material wealth or spiritual shortcoming, just as the suffering of the Anabaptist martyrs is most commonly understood as a fulfillment of their deep faith rather than as a corrective to their departures from that faith. In dramatizing Makhno's beating at the hands of a Mennonite employer, in emphasizing Mennonite decadence and hypocrisy, in criticizing the Mennonite practice of separation from the world, and in gesturing to biblical passages such as James 5, Reimer's novel implicitly positions the violence of the collapse as the necessary discipline or purification of the Mennonite world in Russia, and this marks an important departure from both the Job paradigm and the standard Anabaptist understanding of *Gelassenheit* that the novel attempts to invoke.

To this point, I have focused on the representations of Mennonite history through the prism of religion in Dick's and Reimer's novels, suggesting that the similarities between the two texts demonstrate how thoroughly they have been structured by a shared theo-pedagogical vision, even as their many differences indicate the wide range of texts swept from critical view when "religious fiction" is too quickly dismissed. Both *Out* and *My Harp* adopt a biblical paradigm to render a theological portrait of the suffering of the Russian Mennonite experience, and in both novels violence functions to purify the Mennonites' faith by testing it. In *Out,* the largely blameless Mennonite Commonwealth becomes a land of suffering from which mass migration comes as a divinely ordained exodus. In *My Harp,* the violence exposes the inequalities that lay at the root of the Mennonite Commonwealth, and, on the rare occasions when it is received with a spirit of *Gelassenheit,* it offers a means to re-establish a right relationship with God. Although the theology offered by Reimer's novel is difficult, to be sure, one of its most valuable contributions is that it demonstrates that a theo-pedagogical narrative is able to challenge the inherited, complacent, and celebratory spirituality common to some of the more traditional Mennonite renditions of these events. However, many of the most conventional arguments regarding the limitations of religious fiction are based less on content than on form. For the remainder of this chapter, I want to focus on how texts in the theo-pedagogical strain are problematized by the formal qualities that, it has been commonly suggested, make the novel an ill fit for religious concerns, and how they negotiate these challenges as part of their complex theological portraits of the Mennonite experience.

Fiction, Time, History

In the opening chapter of *Faith and Fiction,* Barbara Pell suggests that many literary critics have seen a "paradoxical tension inherent within the concept of the 'religious novel'" (5), in that "the novel has been constructed as a 'realistic' genre, a mimesis of secular life" (6). She cites a litany of critics who have understood this tension to be fatal, including Charles Glicksberg, who insists that "[t]here are no religious novels *per se,*" and Georg Lukács, who defined the novel as a genre to be "the epic of a world that has been abandoned by God" (qtd. in Pell 5). As I traced briefly in the introduction, the inability of the novel to convey a spiritual reality is a foundational assumption in several influential arguments regarding the structural effects of narratives on communal identity, including Benedict Anderson's suggestion that the novel form facilitates the imagining of national communities through a shift from religious to secular understandings of time. Before I concede that the theo-pedagogical strain is marred by the inappropriateness of the novel form to convey religious concerns, however, I want to look more closely at *My Harp Is Turned to Mourning* and its relationship to historical detail, realism, and time, in order to consider what happens to all three when they are corralled in the service of the sacred.

Although Reimer's novel has garnered little critical response, the reviewers' consensus on its historicizing function speaks volumes into this relative silence. Helmut-Harry Loewen, for example, praises Reimer's combination of "the minutiae of historical scholarship with the skillful shaping of character and setting" (56), while Sarah Klassen reports that, "[w]hen the reader emerges from the reading, he will have completed a mini-course in Mennonite history" ("Everyman's Story" 60). Ervin Beck writes that the novel "will probably shape our knowledge of Russian Mennonite history for many years to come, since more Mennonites will read (and believe) this novel than they will scholarly books or [*Mennonite Quarterly Review*] articles on the subject" (review 91). Similarly, historian John B. Toews, whose *Lost Fatherland* is a best-selling historical study of the period covered by Reimer's novel, calls *My Harp* a "painless history lesson," and, somewhat anxiously, he also recognizes the increasingly primary importance of literature to Mennonite identity. "Somewhere in the future I can envisage the following scenario," he writes. "Students in a Russian

Mennonite history class are using this novel as a text and [...] as an assignment [are] asked to separate fact from fiction. Unanimously they decide it is all true. Where will that leave us historians?" ("Compelled" 7). The historicizing drive of Reimer's novel appears to place it squarely in what J. Hillis Miller would define as the Platonic tradition of repetition, in that, as Miller writes, "the validity of the mimetic copy is established by its truth of correspondence to what it copies" (6).

If Ian Watt was correct in his oft-cited 1962 proclamation that realism is "the lowest common denominator of the novel genre" (478), the historical focus of Reimer's novel, evident in its insistence on the specificity of the Russian experience, might seem to stand in tension with the theological paradigm within which that experience is presented. A closer look at the nature of the history so prevalent in the novel, however, suggests otherwise. First, for all its supposed investment in the historical record, the larger geo-political context for the collapse of the Mennonite Commonwealth is rather conspicuous in its absence. There is little, if any, discussion of the details of World War I; Lenin and Stalin are rarely mentioned, and the only references to Russian or Soviet policies are those that directly impact the Mennonites themselves. Similarly, while the novel is relatively sympathetic to Makhno, there is no discussion of the wider anarchist or Ukrainian independence movements. In place of a larger military or political history, the novel offers a mass of historical detail, peppering its pages with the minutiae of daily existence in the colonies, lengthy passages on the particularities of Mennonite food, careful accounts of village layouts and church organization, extensive depictions of agricultural implements and factories, and so on. In an ironic reversal of the novel's critique of Mennonite separatism, the realism in which *My Harp* is invested is constrained by a close focus on the community itself. What is more, while it is true that the novel is theological in scope, the supernatural never intervenes directly into this history. There are no angels, no heavenly voices, no miraculous healings. Instead, Reimer offers a theological interpretation of historical events that is nonetheless deeply invested in a realistic portrayal of the past—albeit one tightly constrained by the contours and concerns of a very specific community.

However, there is reason to believe that the novel's traditional investment in realism—such as it is—need not be understood as necessarily fatal to its representation of religious belief. Although Klassen suggests in her review of *My Harp* that the novel's plethora of historical details might distract from the plot to the point that "the reader will suspect that Reimer the novelist is in competition with Reimer the historian" ("Everyman's Story" 59), an argument can be made that it is precisely the *excess* of details that enables it, as a religious novel, to achieve what Beck calls its "absorbing ring of truth" (review 90). According to a well-known essay by Roland Barthes, the "reality effect" of realism is best achieved through a "great mythic opposition of the true-to-life (the lifelike) and the intelligible." Those details not "intelligible" within the plot of a novel, Barthes suggests, are assumed, by their very unintelligibility, to be evidence of how "true-to-life" the novel is ("Reality Effect" 231). This is, I think, a compelling way to understand Helmut-Harry Loewen's approval of the "minutiae of historical scholarship" in *My Harp* (56) or Herbert Giesbrecht's claim that "the cumulative impact of the narrative as a whole [...] is one of compelling reality, even of verisimilitude" (255). The effect of such details is to assure the reader that the novel's portrait of the past is *how it really was,* and this effect is achieved precisely through their very superfluity to the narrative itself. If, as Barthes suggests, there is a "mythic opposition" between the "true-to-life" and the "intelligible" that opens up to a space in the representation of reality that is beyond comprehension, then perhaps it is here, where realism reaches its theoretical limit, that the theo-pedagogical strain locates a theological reality that supplements, rather than supplants, the secular realism in a novel's representation of the world.

In order to better understand what is at stake in the theo-pedagogical narrative's representation of the past as simultaneously religious and historical, I want to return to Benedict Anderson's well-known argument regarding the contrast between secular and sacred renderings of time, and their relationship to the novel. For Anderson, as I noted earlier, the beginning of modern nationalism in the eighteenth century was marked, or made possible, by a fundamental shift in the human experience of time. Building on the work of Walter Benjamin, Anderson tracks a shift from "messianic time, a simultaneity of past and future in an instantaneous present," to "an idea of 'homogeneous, empty time,' in which simultaneity is [...] transverse, cross-time, marked not by prefiguring and fulfillment, but by temporal coincidence, and measured by clock and calendar" (24). According to Anderson, the former is exemplary of a medieval Christian temporality, in which there was "no conception of history as an endless chain of cause and effect or of a radical separation between past and present" (23). Rather, Christendom "assumed its universal form through a myriad of specificities and particularities," each of which is equally representative of the divine rather than of human progress (23). In a passage worth recounting at some length, Anderson quotes Auerbach's description of how the messianic conception of time enabled a theological link between the Old Testament sacrifice of Isaac and the New Testament sacrifice of Christ: "[A] connection is established between two events which are linked neither temporally nor causally—a connection which it is impossible to establish by reason in the horizontal dimension. ... It can be established only if both occurrences are vertically linked to Divine Providence, which alone is able to devise such a plan of history and supply the key to its understanding. ... [T]he here and now is no longer a mere link in an earthly chain of events, it is *simultaneously* something which has always been, and will be fulfilled in the future" (qtd. in Anderson 24). According to Anderson, the formal qualities of the novel as a genre—in particular its presentation of multiple, simultaneous plotlines—enabled readers to break this link to the divine and conceive of a simultaneity encompassed only by a horizontal, linear, causally related understanding of temporal progression. Although a novel's seemingly disparate characters rush from one place to another unaware of each other's actions, the omniscient reader is able to comprehend their relations and imagine them as meaningfully connected as part of a distinct community (25–26). For Anderson, this is the shared "homogeneous, empty time," characteristic of the "structure of the old-fashioned novel," which enables people to imagine themselves as part of a national community, and it is, by definition, secular.

Although James Urry's examination of the shift from sacred to secular time in the Russian Mennonite colonies works from a different critical genealogy, his argument runs largely parallel to Anderson's account. According to Urry, the Mennonites' physical and social isolation—particularly in the mid-nineteenth century, before the Russification of the community—buttressed by their theology of separation from the world, "produced a continuity of existence for members of the congregational communities, out of time, away from the 'world' until the time that the living and the dead would face the Day of Judgment" ("Time" 7). The effect of this separation was to create for the Mennonites a sense that, "[j]ust as congregational communities were situated *in* the 'world' but were not *of* it, so they were also in time but not of it. In a sense, the communities lived a kind of timeless time" (7). According to Urry, the Russification (which included the secularization) of the Mennonite community during the later years of the nineteenth century and the early twentieth century would effect a profound shift in their understanding of time, moving the community away from a strictly religious temporality and toward a secular temporality. This shift both mirrored and enabled their shift in self-understanding away from themselves as a strictly religious community and toward a "distinct people with an origin in time and space expressed in nationalist sentiments" (18).[10]

In some senses, *My Harp* seems perfectly suited to illustrate how Anderson's argument regarding the form of temporality enabled and reflected in the novel as a genre maps onto Urry's account of the Mennonite experience in Russia, for Reimer tells his story in multiple, simultaneous plotlines framed and united by a careful adherence to chronological calendar time. To take a single example: the varied and largely unrelated events of 10 March 1919 are described in no fewer than six separated sections across a dozen pages.[11] The chapters themselves trace a host of only loosely connected plots and characters, and each is similarly marked by calendar time, many beginning with the date and location listed above the text. The result is that the novel's mass of historical details is carefully catalogued through a portrait of simultaneity-along-time that appears both to assume a secular notion of "homogeneous, empty time" (what Anderson calls the complex "meanwhile" at the heart of a secular imagined community [24]) and to affirm a distinct Mennonite identity as its unifying principle.

Yet, as we have seen, the correlation between Auerbach's portrait of divine or sacred time and the function of mimesis in the theo-pedagogical strain is equally obvious: the connection that Reimer seeks to establish between the biblical narrative of Job and the Mennonites' traumatic experience in Russia is clearly "vertically linked to Divine Providence," to adopt Auerbach's turn of phrase. Many novels rewriting this history adopt biblical narratives as parallels for their stories, but they do not necessarily adopt them as their interpretive paradigm.[12] For those novels in the theo-pedagogical strain, the biblical narrative so thoroughly structures both the content and the form of this history that it can fairly be considered a paradigm rather than a simple parallel. In their formal qualities and in their adherence to historical details, these novels are deeply invested in the linear and horizontal concept of time. However, I want to suggest that they are also, at the same time and to an approximately equal extent, invested in a non-linear, messianic, and vertical concept of time. They are retelling the story of the Mennonites in Russia, of course, but they are also retelling the biblical story. To pick up on Ruth's terms, they render the highly specific history of Mennonites in Russia as part of a larger salvation story, marking the temporality of the theo-pedagogical strain as both secular and sacred.

In fact, speaking at a roundtable discussion on Mennonite literature and history alongside Rudy Wiebe and Hildi Froese Tiessen, historian Royden Loewen suggested that the experience of multiple, seemingly contradictory temporalities is a central characteristic of contemporary Mennonite identity. Like many other communities, Loewen notes, Mennonites "are always living with a couple of different basic ideas of time at the same time," so that the experience of daily, immediate concerns are overlaid with, or given meaning through, an intimate and enduring connection to both historical events and the promise of eternity. "[T]hese layers of time are always there simultaneously," he continues, suggesting that the layer to be emphasized will depend both on the topic at hand and on the medium being used. Elsewhere, writing in the context of the mid-twentieth century migrations from North to South America by rail, Loewen argues that Mennonite migrants "viewed time in multi-linear ways, with a strong sense of the present as located in a continuum of the past and future—even the afterlife—and as related to abstract ideas of tradition or progress" ("Trains" 124). Contrasting the representation of time in diaries, letters, memoirs, and oral accounts of these inter-hemispheric migrations, he goes on to show how "different media of communication solicited perspectives that produced a multi-linearity of the present" (136). While Loewen's paper emphasizes the impact of media on the representation of time, his larger argument about the experience and expression of a "multi-linearity of time" in relation to Mennonite migrations suggests we ought not to be surprised to see narratives focusing on the Mennonites as a faith community working to reunite sacred and secular time into something like a dual or doubled temporality, and to find that this doubled temporality contains ample room for both a theological and a thoroughly historical engagement with the past.

Importantly, it is only through such a doubled temporality that the repetition of violence in Reimer's novel takes on its full theological significance. If Urry's description of the Mennonites' earlier conception of time as sacred helps to explain the way in which history and theology buttress each other in the theo-pedagogical strain—that is, that they are "in time but not of it" ("Time" 7)—*My Harp* offers a challenge both to Urry's description of the Mennonites' temporal shift as being complete and to Anderson's largely binary use of Benjamin's description of time in the novel's construction of communal identity. Even if, as Urry seems to suggest, the Mennonite community in Russia retained just the shell of a sacred temporality as it came to be dominated by a secular temporality in the early twentieth century, what we see in the theo-pedagogical strain is an attempt to reintegrate the two conceptions of time by rewriting a deeply historical narrative through the lens of Mennonite faith. In the final section of this chapter, I hope to show how the temporality operative in *My Harp* means that the theo-pedagogical narrative does not so much seek to *remember* the catastrophe of the Russian Mennonite experience as it looks to *repeat* its effect for a contemporary audience.

Violence and Repetition

Earlier I suggested that the theo-pedagogical investment in history places Dick's *Out of the Storm* and Reimer's *My Harp Is Turned to Mourning* squarely in the Platonic tradition of repetition, in which the validity of their narratives would be measured by the accuracy of their representations of the past. Understanding the secular-sacred temporality at the base of the theo-pedagogical strain, however, enables us to see that there is a slightly different mode of repetition operating in these texts. The doubled temporality of the theo-pedagogical narrative rejects the chronology implicit in an exclusively linear understanding of repetition—that is, what happened once in the past is happening again in the present—and replaces it with a shared simultaneity in which, as Auerbach writes, an event becomes "something which has always been, and will be fulfilled in the future" (qtd. in Anderson 24). In the same way, *My Harp* represents the Russian Mennonite experience in its historical minutiae while simultaneously aiming to re-present, or repeat, the biblical narrative of Job. On one level, as I noted earlier, the biblical narrative functions as a simple parallel to historical retellings of the past, whereby the story of Job becomes a loose model or guide for understanding the theological significance of the Russian experience. But there are hints that Reimer's novel invites a more substantive equation of the two stories. *My Harp*'s representation of the Russländer experience, I will argue, works to decontextualize the violence of the Commonwealth's collapse by overlaying it with the martyrdoms of the sixteenth century and the eschatological violence of a coming apocalypse. Coupled with an insistence on messianic time, the pedagogical effect of this layering of past and future violence is to invite contemporary readers to understand the historical violence and suffering as immediately applicable in the present moment.

Consider, in this light, Reimer's invocation of the original Anabaptist martyrs in his novel. The wonderfully descriptive full title of the *Martyrs Mirror* makes clear the important relationship between faith and suffering that I have been discussing throughout this chapter: *The Bloody Theater or Martyrs Mirror of the Defenseless Christians Who Baptized Only upon Confession of Faith, and Who Suffered and Died for the Testimony of Jesus, Their Savior, from the Time of Christ to the Year A.D. 1600.* As the full title makes clear, the theological significance of this sixteenth-century text is grounded in its historical claims. That is, the *Martyrs Mirror* is theologically important precisely because it presents the detailed history of early Anabaptists who died for their faith. As Urry notes, it also enables a "sense of a connection between the Christian past and the present" for the Mennonites ("Memory" 34). This connection, importantly, is not limited but supported by its status as a historical document; indeed, many entries in this massive collection of martyr tales are preceded by the date and location of the execution. In this marking of religious testimony with "clock time," *Martyrs Mirror* reflects the unification of secular-sacred temporality that the theo-pedagogical strain invokes in its efforts to make the particular events of the past witness to an eternal reality. And it is hardly a surprise to find that *Martyrs Mirror* is the favourite childhood reading for both of the prominent spiritual leaders of Reimer's novel, "Old" Daniel Fast (28) and Erdmann Lepp (171). Lepp, we are told, "read and reread the ghastly accounts of early Anabaptist martyrs who in their thousands were whipped, gouged, torn apart, smothered, buried alive, crucified, stoned, beheaded, drowned from boats, and burned to cinders for their faith, with horror and outrage that such terrible things could be done to true believers" (170–71). It is a lesson that he is to learn again in the collapse of the colonies, and his refusal to join the Mennonites' mass migration out of Russia positions him as an heir to the Anabaptist martyrs' willingness to suffer for their faith. Importantly, this is not to say that the novel equates the violence suffered by the twentieth-century Mennonites and the sixteenth-century Anabaptists (though there is certainly no shortage of Russländer narratives that do position the 1920s victims as martyrs[13]). Rather, Reimer's material critique of the colonies makes it clear that his retelling of the Russian Mennonite story is not about martyrs in the mould of the *Martyrs Mirror.* Instead, the Anabaptist martyrdoms are invoked in *My Harp* to provide a model of willing suffering that is seemingly absent from the larger migration narrative, and to suggest that the proper response to violence transcends its historical particularity.

If *My Harp*'s references to the sixteenth-century martyrs invoke an important history of religious violence, the eschatological prophecies of the novel's many evangelists look forward to a different wave of religious violence. Indeed, the novel is dominated by prophet figures—even Rasputin makes a brief appearance (248)—many of whom espouse a millennialism that keeps present the looming possibility of the apocalypse and the end of time itself. Not only is Lepp an ardent believer in the imminence of the apocalypse, but the Bocks also hold a religious conference on their estate on the topic of millennialism, gathering like-minded preachers from all over Europe to preach to the Mennonite colonies. Moreover, Reimer makes much of the Mennonite tradition of reading eschatological fiction, including Jung-Stilling's allegorical novel *Heimweh,* which, we are told, "had become almost a second Bible for many Mennonites" (178). Indeed, at least one critic thinks that Reimer focuses too much on the end-times movements: Waldemar Janzen worries that Reimer "has given a prominence to the religious fringe phenomena (such as fanatical millennialism) that, in my opinion, they do not deserve." Janzen's concerns might well be appropriate from a historical standpoint, but the novel's claims about the Mennonites' eschatological focus are not strictly historical in nature. Like the novel's invocation of the sixteenth-century martyrs, the portrayal of millennialism fever as part of his historical narrative expands the sacred temporality in which the novel operates; the apocalypse pushes the narrative as far forward into the future as the Job paradigm has pulled it back into the past.

It is in this multi-temporal structure of violence that repetition takes on its full significance in the novel. *My Harp* dovetails the violence of Job's testing, the martyrdoms of the sixteenth-century experience, and the coming apocalypse into the violence experienced by the Mennonites in the aftermath of the Russian Revolution. Because the continuum of history necessary for conventional, Platonic repetition is unable to fully supplant the community's investment in sacred time, these moments of violence are not so much echoes or parallels of each other as they are manifestations of a single, overarching experience of violence, which erupts repeatedly in the historical narrative (albeit for very different reasons). Stripping the violence of the Russian experience of its firm location in the historical record, the novel itself aims not simply to represent this experience of violence, then, but to "re-present" it to the reader in the present. In this limited sense, at least, the suffering of the Russian experience is not being rewritten here simply to bind the contemporary

Mennonite community closer together in its shared history of sacrifice and survival but also to allow the religious impact of this violence—what Urry calls the "sacredness of suffering" ("Time" 39)—to be experienced anew by the (reading) community. Consider, in this context, Reimer's closing comments in his foreword to *Storm Tossed*, the remarkable memoir of the Russländer experience by Gerhard Lohrenz: "Anybody who has listened to the fascinating stories of these aging survivors of South Russia [...] has had an insight into the love and devotion these people had for their lost fatherland," Reimer writes. "Their heritage is also our heritage, and we can live it—even if only vicariously—through such books" (9). Here Reimer makes explicit the implicit claim of his novel, arguing, once again, that what he has called the "tragic curve of the Russian-Mennonite experience" ("Coming" 263) can be understood as part of the "heritage" of all Mennonites. In the theo-pedagogical strain, the object of mimesis, or repetition, is not simply the history of the Mennonites' suffering but also the vicarious experience of the suffering itself.

Conclusion

Both Dick's *Out of the Storm* and Reimer's *My Harp Is Turned to Mourning* offer a biblical paradigm for the collapse of the Mennonite Commonwealth in Russia, each taking the story of Job as a precedent for both the scale and the suddenness of that collapse. Each novel relies on a mimetic concept of repetition, buttressed by a linear, coherent narrative structure that works to ensure that the fictionalized accounts are received as the more-or-less accurate history of a distinct community. Although Raylene Hinz Penner is correct to note that *My Harp* is nowhere near as overtly religious or deferential to the Mennonite faith as the Job references seem to suggest (29), nowhere does Reimer's novel counteract the basic theology that gains its biblical justification from Job: suffering is allowed by God, and the proper response is submission, not flight or separation from the world. What is more, by overlaying its historical focus with a sacred conception of time, *My Harp*'s representation of historical violence becomes a means of enabling a type of vicarious experience of that violence for its contemporary readers.

In the larger historical record, of course, the collapse of the Mennonite world in Russia is a relatively small footnote within the drama of the Russian Revolution, the violent rise of the USSR, the battle for Ukrainian independence, and so on. Whether novels in the theo-pedagogical strain use their biblical parallels to offer straightforward endorsements of Mennonite history or to critique the community, they share not only their religious concerns but also a willingness to circumscribe those concerns within the particular framework of Mennonite identity and history (rather than adopt larger geopolitical or broader religious perspectives). Even as Reimer's novel interrogates and critiques the theology of separateness that worked to establish the distinctiveness of the historical Mennonite community, *My Harp* is every bit as insistent as *Out* that the Mennonite experience in Ukraine is the story of a distinct people. In the next chapter, I will show just how quickly this insistence on the Mennonites' distinctiveness as a spiritual community can collapse into ethnocentricism, in which Mennonite history in Ukraine is imagined as the experiences of a *Völklein,* or ethnic community, with the Commonwealth itself serving as its timeless, originary landscape.

Chapter 3

Dreaming das Völklein:
Lost in the Steppe *and the Ethnic Narrative*

Harry Loewen is likely overreaching when, in the introduction to his edited collection *Why I Am a Mennonite* (1988), he claims that "the question of Mennonite identity has become a burning issue among Mennonites and non-Mennonites everywhere" (11). Nonetheless, there is no question that the nature of Mennonite identity has long been of central concern within the community itself, especially in regard to the problem of Mennonite ethnicity—and even a passing glance over the long debate about whether such a thing exists shows that it is, indeed, a problem. Given that the formation of an Anabaptist identity in the sixteenth century coalesced around a set of religious principles that specifically defined community inclusion by adult baptism rather than by accident of birth, the enduring focus on kinship, genealogy, and ancestry among Russian Mennonites is a remarkable development (even if, as we have seen in Chapter 1, it is historically understandable). Answering the question of whether or not Russian Mennonites constitute a distinct ethnicity is well beyond the scope of this study, but this chapter engages with the debate on the grounds that, as Mennonite literature entered into Canadian literature as an example of what the Royal Commission on Bilingualism and Biculturalism named "the cultural contributions of the other ethnic groups" (volume 4), the rewriting of the Russian Mennonite experience is inextricably bound up in its politics.

Of the various authors who have sought to foster an ethnic Mennonite identity in Canada, none has been more persistent or successful than writer, editor, and playwright Arnold Dyck (1889–1970). Born in the Russian Mennonite colony of Hochfeld (now Yazykovo, Ukraine), Dyck studied art in both Germany and St. Petersburg until the outbreak of World War I forced him to return to southern Russia and, ultimately, to move to Canada. In Canada, Dyck attempted to re-establish the emerging Mennonite cultural life that was cut short in the Russian colonies. Although he was largely disappointed by the reception that his efforts received, he quickly became the dominant figure in German Mennonite writing in Canada. As a long-suffering editor, Dyck ran a number of increasingly short-lived German newspapers and journals,[1] as well as the Echo Verlag series of historical texts, which focused nearly exclusively on the Mennonite experience in Russia. He was also a prolific author: the four volumes of his recently published collected works run well over 2,000 pages, but the editors were left apologizing for its omissions (4: 4). Dyck's only novel, a High German *Bildungsroman* first published in serial form as five short books collectively entitled *Verloren in der Steppe* (1944–48), was collated and translated by Henry D. Dyck as *Lost in the Steppe* in 1974.

Like many of his émigré contemporaries, Dyck's work often focused on the colonies that the Mennonites left behind in Russia, and critics have often identified his writing as having recorded, and exemplified, the nostalgia that many of his generation held for their lost homeland. Dyck's oeuvre, however, stands out from his contemporaries' work in both quality and style, as well as in his consistent relegation of religion to the periphery of Mennonite identity. Indeed, Dyck's writings reflect a deep belief that Mennonites were a distinct Germanic people, or *Völklein,* bound together more by their shared language, culture, history, and genealogical ties than by their faith. As Al Reimer writes, Dyck "remythologized his Mennonite world as a vital ethnic reality where human relationships exist for their own sake in a social setting, without much regard given to the church as controlling force or inhibitor" ("Role" 33). In this chapter, I read Dyck's *Lost in the Steppe* as an attempt to "remythologize" the Russian Mennonite migration as an ethnic narrative. Although the novel was written over half a century ago, it continues to be, as critics suggest, "of major importance to Mennonite history" (Hadley 199) and a "basic text" for the "self-understanding of the Mennonite tradition" (Doerksen and Loewen 78). By rendering the Mennonite colonies of Russia as a timeless, comprehensive, and fully integrated agricultural Germanic world, Dyck positions the Mennonite Commonwealth as an originary landscape for a distinct Mennonite ethnicity. His portrait of the maturation of Hans, the novel's bright young protagonist, suggests that the community was on the verge of fulfilling its potential as a culturally sophisticated *Völklein* before being tragically lost to the political revolution that lurks just beyond the novel's conclusion.

The Mennonite Identity Crisis

In a 2008 essay entitled "The Poetics of Peoplehood: Ethnicity and Religion among Canada's Mennonites," Royden Loewen identifies, and briefly discusses, six distinct approaches to ethnicity common among Mennonite Canadians, ranging from its complete rejection (by those who find it an affront to a faith-based identity) to its embrace over and against a religious identity (by those who want to retain selected qualities from the Mennonite community while rejecting its religious beliefs). Some of the most conservative Mennonites, he notes, understand markers of community distinctiveness as integral to and inextricable from a separatist religious identity, while some of the newest groups who call themselves Mennonite manage to "resonate with neither a Mennonite ethnicity nor with Anabaptist pacifist and communitarian religious ideals" (356). Although Loewen focuses on the question of Mennonite ethnicity in its present form, the question itself is anything but new. In 1984, sociologist Calvin Redekop christened the community's debate over ethnicity "The Mennonite Identity Crisis," reporting that "the simultaneous pride in the Anabaptist-Mennonite belief system and the embarrassment at the 'ethnic' and cultural trappings of that heritage ha[ve] created a tension which is reaching the breaking point for many Mennonites" (98). More recently, Hildi Froese Tiessen has acknowledged that the "identity crisis" and its attendant tensions are ongoing. After briefly raising the debate, she promptly sets it aside in exasperation. "Ah, there's a quagmire I have no desire to wade into," she writes ("Critical Thought" 244).

As Loewen's article makes clear, concerns over the prospect of a Mennonite ethnicity have been especially prevalent among those evangelically minded Mennonites who "believe that any link of religious faith to Mennonite ethnicity will make that faith unattractive to mainstream Canadians or members of other ethnic groups" ("Poetics" 349). Loewen singles out the Mennonite Brethren as being particularly concerned about this point, noting that many of the denomination's churches have begun dropping "Mennonite" from their names. Indeed, the Mennonite Brethren have been concerned about the impact of Mennonite ethnicity for some time. The release of John H. Redekop's study *A People Apart: Ethnicity and the Mennonite Brethren* (1987) resulted in an international symposium on the issue. Tellingly, even in a context explicitly framed by religion—it was, after all, entitled A Symposium on Faith and Ethnicity among the Mennonite Brethren—agreement on this issue proved impossible: the Symposium Planning and Findings Committee reported a debate over the appropriateness of ethnicity in the Mennonite context that was lively, but ultimately inconclusive. For a broader and clearer warning about the dangers of understanding Mennonite identity in ethnic terms, it is worth revisiting historian Frank Epp's opening essays in *Harvest* (1974). In the first essay, Epp points out that the larger Mennonite faith community has "become an international, interracial, multicultural, and multilingual brotherhood," and he worries that Canada's Mennonites have resorted to using scripture to "defend our favourite customs, cultures, and kingdoms" (2). Epp's second essay is even more direct: "One form of group egoism among Mennonites is ethnocentrism," he writes. "By this definition Mennonites are a Volk, a race, with strong ethnic, linguistic, and cultural traits" (5). Epp's essays are strong critiques of the overemphasis on Mennonite ethnicity and a clear call for the community to return to an inclusive Christian faith as the sole marker of their identity. The editors of *Harvest* made a significant decision to begin the first anthology of Mennonite Canadian writing, published to mark the Mennonite centennial in Canada, with a stark warning to the community that it was ostensibly celebrating.

Those arguing for the importance, or at least the existence, of a Russian Mennonite ethnic identity often point to the linguistic, cultural, historical, and kinship ties that sharply distinguished Russian Mennonites from their neighbours for centuries. Historical and sociological studies, for example, have largely accepted that the Russian Mennonites historically developed into an ethnic identity (though many stress that this distinctiveness has largely disappeared in Canada). As early as 1948, E.K. Francis declared that in Russia the "group which was ethnically heterogeneous but united by a specific religious ideology was transformed into a new ethnic group" ("Russian Mennonites" 101). Forty years later, Donald B. Kraybill echoed Francis's conclusion: "The abundant sociological evidence makes it virtually impossible to argue that the Mennonite phenomenon is merely a religious one devoid of ethnic expressions" ("Modernity" 158). In 1989, Calvin Redekop suggested that, while "it is perfectly obvious to thoughtful Mennonites as well as to outside observers that Mennonites are more than a religious fraternity or even a denomination," Mennonites are likely to resist identifying themselves in ethnic terms. "Mennonites are conditioned by their self-conscious heritage to think of their identity as entirely religious," he points out (*Mennonite Society* 137). Writing two decades after Redekop, however, Loewen speculates that, for a "large, quiet majority" of the community today, Mennonite ethnicity is strictly "symbolic" and "seems to exist almost naturally alongside Mennonite religious faith" ("Poetics" 354). Although he diplomatically covers a range of perspectives on Mennonite ethnicity, then, Loewen can conclude his article with the rather unambiguous declaration that ethnicity "is an integral component in the narrative of Canadian Mennonites" (358).

Whatever its risks might be from a religious perspective, it seems clear that a Russian Mennonite ethnicity exists, or has existed, in Canada. Equally clear, however, is that any simple equation between Russian Mennonite ethnicity and the larger term "Mennonite" remains a gross oversimplification. Given that Canada's Mennonite authors have come overwhelmingly from a Russian Mennonite community with a distinct ethnic identity, and given that Canadian literary discourse is strongly predisposed to (mis)recognize religious difference in ethnic terms, it might not be surprising to find that the "Mennonite" in "Mennonite Canadian literature" often functions as a synonym for "ethnic Russian Mennonites." Nonetheless, we ought to be mindful of the implications of this critical convention. First, it implicitly presents "Mennonite" as a primarily ethnic term rather than a religious one. To the extent that Mennonite writing in Canada has become a primary force shaping the "new cultural memory of the Mennonites" in Canada (Tiessen, "Mennonite/s" 48), this might well have implications beyond the realm of literary criticism. In this sense, at least, the so-called Mennonite miracle—the explosion of Mennonite Canadian writing whose most consistent relationship to Mennonite faith has been a rigorous and often caustic critique—can be understood as participating in, and actively contributing to, a larger effacement of religious concerns among the negotiation of Mennonite identity in Canada. Second, it effectively obscures Mennonite writing that comes from outside the Russian tradition. In fact, even within the Russian Mennonite tradition, a consideration of ethnicity is complicated by the fact that the 1920s migrants, along with those Mennonites who migrated to Canada immediately following World War II, understood themselves as much more deeply connected to High German culture than those Mennonites who migrated from Russia to Canada in the 1870s (Loewen, "Poetics" 337). As a result, the particular "ethnic narrative" that surrounds the 1920s migration is much more explicitly Germanic than one might find in other (Russian) Mennonite Canadian novels expressing a clear ethnic vision, such as Armin Wiebe's *The Salvation of Yasch Siemens*.

In this chapter I am interested in novels that present the Russian Mennonite experience as the story of a distinct community that exists beyond, or outside, its religious heritage. In Chapter 1, I followed anthropologist James Urry in tracing the historical emergence of a distinct, secular conception of Mennonite identity back to the late nineteenth century in Russia as part of my effort to historicize the concept of Mennonite ethnicity. Although Urry intentionally avoids the terminology of ethnicity—elsewhere he explains that he prefers "peoplehood" on the ground that it better reflects what he sees as the Mennonite sense of "being and belonging [...] informed by a culture of faith rather than a faith in culture" (*Mennonites* 6)—I have retained it here because, as I argue in the introduction, it is the concept through which Mennonite literature emerged in Canada. More importantly, the form of Mennonite identity constructed in the work of Arnold Dyck demonstrates precisely the "faith in culture" that Urry suggests is characteristic of an ethnic understanding of identity.

Although the question of Mennonite ethnic identity remains both open and contentious, there is no debate regarding where Dyck stood on the matter. Al Reimer, the critic who has engaged most thoroughly and consistently with Dyck's work, declares matter-of-factly that it was Dyck's "cherished conviction that the Russian Mennonites, and by extension Canadian Mennonites, were a genuine *Volk* (or *Völklein*), a people that had developed a distinct ethnic identity along with its unique religious heritage" ("Role" 32–33). Gerhard K. Friesen argues that "the concept of a distinct Mennonite identity, which for [Dyck] is based on pride in collective achievements as well as the German ethnic and cultural heritage," is "[c]rucial to the pedagogical function underlying all of Dyck's works" (137). Indeed, Dyck's writing consistently aims, implicitly or explicitly, to construct and affirm a distinctly Germanic identity for his Russian Mennonite people that he (rightly) saw as being threatened in Canada. In fact, several of his works liken the loss of the German language among Mennonites to the murder of their ancestors,[2] while the short story

"Die Neue Weltmacht" [The New World Power] imagines the Mennonites leaving Canada and constructing an independent Mennonite nation-state. Although the latter story is, like much of his writing, humorous and self-dep-recating, his private letters show that it also reflects his dream of organizing a mass migration of Mennonites to South Africa, where they were to set up a *Mennostaat* and fulfill their destiny as a people. "I would have liked to go [to South Africa] with our Mennonites and to establish our own state in proximity to our ethnic cousins, the Boers," Dyck writes, "in order to make it manifest—especially to ourselves—that we are truly capable of the utmost accomplishments" ("Life" 128). As I noted in the introduction, Dyck was not entirely alone in such dreams. Although he expressed reservations about J.J. Hildebrand's dreams of "an independent white settlement" of Mennonites on Australian territory, Dyck nonetheless gave Hildebrand ample space to promote the project in the newspaper that he edited (Urry, "*Mennostaat*" 73). The politicization of ethnicity into nationalism is rarely this explicit in Dyck's work, but the emphasis on both land and peoplehood as expressed in *Lost in the Steppe* is not far removed from its logic.

At times, Dyck's emphasis on the Mennonites' Germanic identity slipped into a problematic politics. George K. Epp and Elisabeth Peters note in Dyck's work evidence of "racial biases in favour of German culture" (221), for example, and Al Reimer concedes that the concept of ethnic identity held by Dyck was "tinged with the notion of racial purity and 'Germanness' that prevailed in the Nazi Germany of the 1930s" (*Mennonite Literary Voices* 16–17). Although it is easy, in retrospect, to overstate the significance of prewar German sympathies in light of Nazi atrocities during the war, Dyck's editorial and literary work in the lead-up to World War II did show sympathy for National Socialism: as noted above, Dyck allowed his newspaper, *Die Post*, to print articles arguing for the establishment of a Mennonite state with an "unmixed white population" (Urry, "*Mennostaat*" 75, 66) as well as a poem by Fritz Senn entitled "Der Führer" (Doerksen, "Recalling" 149). Moreover, his own *Koop enn Bua* series briefly featured a schoolteacher, Teacher Wall, who directly expressed sympathy for National Socialism. In one skit, Bua briefly plays apologist for prewar German anti-Semitism: "To kill the Jews is not their intention," he says. "All they want to do is slap their hands a little, so that they won't always poke into things that don't concern them" (qtd. in Reimer, "Creation" 261). Although clearly problematic, there is little doubt that such views would have received a favourable hearing among some in

Dyck's audience. Several critics have suggested that prewar Mennonite society in Canada was "fertile and fruitful soil for Nazi propaganda" (Redekop, "Roots" 81), and Urry recently suggested that implicitly pro-Nazi sentiments can still be found among Mennonite Canadian scholars "of a certain age"—a claim that resulted in a minor uproar in the pages of the *Mennonite Quarterly Review* ("Fate" 126).[3]

In an irony that cuts to the heart of the paradox of the Canadian national policy that claims no official culture but two official languages, Dyck remains nearly absent from the larger discourse of Canadian literature. Despite being a significant talent with a clear vision of Canada's Russian Mennonites as an ethnic community, Dyck wrote in the years before Canada's official interest in the cultural work of "the other ethnic groups" and, importantly, understood writing in Low and High German to be foundational to his expression of Mennonite ethnicity. Critics of Canadian multiculturalism, as I discussed at some length in the introduction, have often argued that the policy is homogenizing and tokenizing, encouraging a problematically essentialist and static notion of ethnic identity. Dyck's work, however, indicates that exaltations of origins and dreams of cultural purity are not always unwelcome in minoritized communities. To the contrary, *Lost in the Steppe* is a reminder that, for Mennonites concerned with the retention of their Germanic heritage and distinct cultural identity, the essentialist notion of ethnic identity implicit in multicultural discourse, along with its conceit of a homogenized community whose present and future are fully determined by its linguistic and cultural past, might be something to be embraced.

Evidence of Ethnicity

Lost in the Steppe tells the story of Hans Toews, a young boy growing up in a small Mennonite village at the height of the Mennonite Commonwealth's golden years. In five parts originally published separately, the novel carefully catalogues the agricultural world of the Russian Mennonite colonies while tracing the personal, artistic, and educational development of Hans within that world. His unfailingly kind and honest parents alternate between being proud of his artistic and educational achievements and being worried that those very achievements might take him away from the farm. It is his older brother Berend, however, less academic than Hans but much better with his hands, who is destined to take over the family farm. At the novel's close, the young Hans is shown to be leaving his small village for

Chortitza, the Mennonite urban centre, where he will continue his education. Although the novel is often considered a *Bildungsroman*,[4] or coming-of-age story, his development is almost completely overwhelmed by the novel's loving portrait of Mennonite life in Russia. In fact, one could argue that the primary protagonist of *Lost* is the Commonwealth itself, the novel serving as a biography of a distinct people on the verge of coming into their own as a cultural community. With Hans as the attractive embodiment of the community's artistic and intellectual potential, the tragedy of the collapse that stands just beyond the novel's conclusion is the tragedy of a promise unfulfilled.

Through its exhaustively detailed representation of Hochfeld, the Mennonite village on the northern edge of the Chortitza colony where Hans spends his formative years, *Lost* provides one of the most fully developed portraits of Mennonite identity in all of Canadian literature. Dyck revels in the intricacies of the former Mennonite world in Ukraine, overloading the plot of *Lost* with historical details as part of his effort to reconstruct "the old Russian Mennonite world in all its minutiae" (Doerksen, "Recalling" 150). The novel's early sections are peppered with meticulous descriptions of the Toews family house, the household items, the farmyard, and the surrounding landscapes, all illustrated by dozens of Dyck's own sketches, as well as blueprints of important buildings and a map of the larger colony. No aspect of the Mennonite world in Russia is too mundane to be featured prominently; there is, for example, a lengthy description of a milk bench and milk rod in Hans's house (11–12), for which Dyck provides two illustrations. In fact, large sections of the novel are little more than lengthy descriptions of typical Mennonite houses at the time, including the three chapters that Dyck takes to describe Hans's house (entitled "The Small Room," "The Corner Room," and "The Great Room"). Each of these chapters includes a hand-drawn blueprint of its respective room, and is illustrated by sketches of everything from a Kroeger clock to a lamp. After the first five chapters cover the house in exhaustive detail, the next five describe Hans's yard and barn in similar fashion, with chapters such as "The Chicks" and "The Kittens" accompanied by further sketches. It is a testament to Dyck's abilities as a writer that this episodic structure does not unravel the novel. Instead, his use of Hans's naive perspective keeps the text fresh and engaging throughout.

The use of a historical detailing to construct a past reality is not unique to *Lost* or to narratives of ethnicity. As we saw in the previous chapter on the theo-pedagogical strain, both *Out of the Storm* and *My Harp Is Turned to Mourning* are marked by a plethora of historical details. There I argued that the cumulative effect of such details is to assure the reader that the novel's portrait of the past is *how it really was,* and that it does so precisely through the details' superfluity, which I identified as exemplifying what Roland Barthes calls the "reality effect." Before I describe the key differences I see between the two strains on this point, it is worth stressing that the theo-pedagogical narrative and the ethnic narrative do have several striking overlaps. Both strains assume the Russian Mennonites to be a clearly definable historical community, which they take as their central focus, and neither of these strains ultimately threatens the community itself, even where it subjects that community to critique. Moreover, the novels that I consider in each strain are supported by linear narrative structures and a mimetic conception of repetition that work together to ensure that the fictionalized accounts of the Russian Mennonite experience are understood as the accurate, "true" history of a distinct community. As we will see in the coming chapters on trauma narratives and meta-narratives, none of these points is to be assumed in the retelling of this history.

Despite these similarities, the theo-pedagogical strain attempts to weave its mass of details into a larger narrative progression in order to draw out (or insert) a theological message, while in *Lost* the details are, at least initially, themselves the focus of the text. This difference can be traced in the reviews of the novels: although reviewers of *My Harp* have occasionally worried that its extensive historical detailing becomes a distraction from the progression of the novel, Dyck's critics willingly embrace those details as the raison d'être of the work. Edna Froese, for example, calls *Lost* "a disarmingly detailed description of the integrated agricultural community" ("*Lost*" 149), pointing to the early, descriptive sections and suggesting that, to "the exiled Mennonite who with Dyck would relive his/her own childhood in just such a village, these chapters are a pastoral delight" (148). Similarly, Gerhard Wiens has suggested that "no other work about our Russian past [...] gives us so complete, so vivid a picture of our everyday life"; he calls the novel "a panorama, vast in scope and rich in loving detail, of Mennonite life during a whole period" ("Arnold Dyck at Seventy" 84). If Dyck was, as Al Reimer suggests, "convinced that his *Völklein,* the Russian Mennonites, [...] had a rich history that deserved to be recorded and preserved in a more formal and permanent form than [a] transitory newspaper could offer" ("Arnold Dyck"

73), *Lost* can be understood as the repository for all of these details. When we recall that the novel was originally published in serial form, it becomes clear that his readers were hardly purchasing a novel at all. By the time Dyck was publishing, say, the fourth book in the series, what they had on their shelves was an eighty-page encyclopedia, detailing and illustrating Mennonite life in the Commonwealth, offered as evidence of the distinctiveness of the Mennonite people.

Faith and the Ethnic Ghost

Perhaps the most remarkable thing about Dyck's portrait of the Mennonite Commonwealth is what it lacks: for all its careful accounting of the world of the Mennonites in Russia, *Lost* somehow manages to forget their faith. In the earliest chapters, much of the novel's descriptions are of the farmhouse and surrounding yard, but the absence of religion in *Lost*'s reconstruction of the Mennonite world in Russia cannot be attributed to an entirely material focus. After all, Dyck records the socio-cultural aspects of Mennonite Russia nearly as exhaustively as he does its physical attributes, with entire chapters dedicated to annual community events such as "Spring Riding," "Pig-Killing," "The Days of the Calves," and so on. However, the characters of *Lost* are never shown reading the Bible, praying, or entering a church. There is no mention of the early Anabaptists, or of the denominational schisms so prominent during the period in which the novel is set. Religious concerns are, as Michael L. Hadley notes, "conspicuous by their absence" (201).

In Edna Froese's reading, the novel's "completely secular stance" ("*Lost*" 154) is part of Dyck's larger attempt at "defusing potential conflict between the artistic individual and the community" (153). The "all-important religious dimension of Mennonite life is taken for granted in *Lost in the Steppe* as merely part of the background," Froese suggests (154). It is worth noting, however, that even the few hints at the Mennonites' religious beliefs in the novel are stripped of their theological significance. For example, there is a brief discussion on the possibility that the school's Christmas pageant might be blasphemous, but Jesus' birth is dismissively presented in three quick sentences. "Now comes the Christmas story, presented by Hans Toews," it reads. "He speaks loudly, monotonously, and much too fast. But then everybody knows the story" (168). Similarly, Hans's knowledge of his catechism is presented as a feat of memory rather than as laying a theological foundation for his faith. What is more, as Froese points out, the novel's insistence on defining the Mennonites in non-religious terms extends to the word *Mennonite,* which is never actually mentioned; instead, the community is depicted simply as "German" ("*Lost*"154). In my reading, the novel's effacement of religion reflects something more than an attempt to defuse Mennonite concerns about education or art. To ignore religion in an otherwise careful account of the Mennonite world in Russia is to leave all of its cohesiveness to be attributed to the cultural and secular—that is, the ethnic—elements of a distinctly German *Völklein.*

The community that Dyck presents in *Lost* is clearly marked by what Urry calls "the agrarian roots of Mennonite identity" ("Russian Mennonites" 22)—or, better, by the idealization of those roots, in what Calvin Redekop has called "the Mennonite romance with the land" ("Mennonite Romance" 83). "[T]o think Mennonite," Redekop insists, "has been tantamount to thinking land, agriculture, and rural life" (83), noting that the "zenith of their love relations with the land occurred in Russia during the Commonwealth period" (88). While *Lost* is, at times, quite critical of the Mennonites' agrarian world—indeed, Hans yearns to avoid the mundane life of a farmer and study art in the city—it nonetheless firmly establishes the farm as the starting point, or origin, for whatever the community might become in the future. Redekop's argument that "the encroachment of modern civilization and modern technology served to drive the final wedge between Mennonite love and infatuation for the land" (90) also helps to explain *Lost*'s dearth of references to the technological revolution that was well under way in the colonies by the time in which the novel is set. Hans's brother Berend is interested in the technological advances taking place elsewhere, but the novel consistently defers their arrival in the Mennonite colonies, so that airplanes, cars, and other technologies remain in Berend's mind, always yet to come, always in the near future.[5] In Froese's reading, this absence is not an oversight but, again, the direct result of the novel's focus. "[Dyck] does not describe the enormous technological advances that have taken place in the Mennonite Commonwealth," Froese reasons, because he is more interested in tracking Hans's development ("*Lost*" 152). Without disputing such a reading, it is also clear that Dyck's idealized version of the larger Mennonite past is agricultural and pastoral, rather than industrial and urban. Given the Mennonite "romance with the land," one can see how a context that presents the Mennonites as a *Völklein* benefits from returning to a "simpler," more natural, or "pure" state, in which there would be little room for the dramatic changes and challenges sparked by modern technology. If it is true, as Redekop suggests, that "[t]he 'ethnic ghost' of Mennonitism is largely attributable to the retreat to the land," we can say that *Lost*, with its thoroughly secular and pastoral vision of the Commonwealth, is a text haunted by the Mennonites' "ethnic ghost" ("Mennonite Romance" 93).

Before moving on to further consider how the novel works to construct and define a distinct ethnicity for the Mennonites, it is worth noting that, while *Lost* is steadfast in its refusal to engage with the religious aspects of Mennonite identity, this refusal is not fully explained by the novel's ethnic claims. After all, the exclusionary politics implicit in many expressions of the ethnic narrative are often at their most powerful when cloaked in the language of religion. In Barbara Claassen Smucker's *Days of Terror*, for example, the Germanic and religious aspects of the Mennonite identity are so interwoven that each implicitly supports the other. Taken to an extreme, this ethnicized religious logic can become deeply problematic, as is most clear in the work of American Russian Mennonite Ingrid Rimland. Rimland, who was born in Ukraine and lived for a decade in Canada before she emigrated to the United States and began her literary career, writes unapologetically anti-Semitic work that has been classified as hate literature by the Canadian government (see "Canada"). The relatively tame ethnocentrism of her award-winning first novel about the Mennonites of Ukraine, *The Wanderers: The Saga of Three Women Who Survived* (1977), exploded into explicit racism in her *Lebensraum!* trilogy (1998), released by Toronto-based Samisdat Publishers (owned and operated by Rimland's well-known husband, Ernst Zündel). Like *Lost* and *Days*, Rimland's novels stress the Russian Mennonites' Germanic heritage, but unlike Dyck or Smucker, Rimland explicitly embraces the racial politics of National Socialism and props it up through the rhetoric of Christianity.[6] By avoiding religion in his portrait of the Mennonites in Russia, Dyck emphasizes the Mennonites as a distinct ethnic community—but he also manages to avoid deploying religion in the service of race, nation, or ethnicity.

A People Apart

Lost in the Steppe argues for a Mennonite ethnicity by downplaying the religious aspects of Mennonite identity while offering an elaborately detailed portrait of a Germanic and agrarian Mennonite world in Russia. Given, as Werner Sollors has suggested, that ethnicity "refers not to a thing-in-itself but to a relationship," one that is "typically based on a contrast" (288), it is perhaps not surprising to find that the distinctiveness of the Mennonite world in *Lost* is buttressed by its juxtaposition against the Ukrainian context in which it is set.[7] Language, class, and biological markers are raised consistently in Dyck's novel as a means of contrasting the Mennonites with their neighbouring communities. Although the Mennonites' interactions with their neighbouring Jews, Ukrainians, and Russians reveal the heterogeneity of the larger context of the colonies, *Lost* carefully polices the borders between these communities, using these others as foils for the unambiguously Germanic Mennonite identity. The Mennonite Commonwealth might be located *in* a larger, more multi-ethnic world, but in Dyck's novel, it is certainly not *of* it. Stripped of its theological underpinnings, here the Mennonite ideal of remaining separate from the world—so strongly critiqued by Reimer in *My Harp*—functions simply to affirm the distinctiveness of the Mennonite people.

In the chapter entitled "Hershke, the Jewish Peddler," for example, Dyck draws several lines of connection between Mennonites and the Jewish merchant before insisting on their fundamental difference through a number of backhanded compliments. "In appearance he is a typical representative of his race, but only in appearance; in his character and in his whole being he doesn't seem to be one," we are told. "He is modest, unassuming and not nearly as verbose as many of his clan and profession" (68). When Hershke brings greetings from other Mennonites, the narrator casually notes that he does so "*as if* he doesn't do this from shrewd business reasons but from sheer courteousness and human kindness" (69; emphasis added). Earlier in the novel, readers are told that Spitz, the family dog, guards the house against the visit of any undesirable others, such as "a Russian, or a gypsy, or a beggar of any nationality" (50); accordingly, it is no surprise to find Hershke's chapter ends with Spitz "accompany[ing] the Jew up to the street" (71). The lesson of Hershke's visit is echoed in a parallel scene at the novel's close, when the Jewish tailor Abraham Yankel visits the Toews household for several days. Hans's father and the tailor enter into a debate that, while ostensibly about their differing faiths, functions primarily to affirm their ethnic differences. Abraham, we are told, "races up and down the corner room, gesticulates with his arms in the air, and gets pale and red in turn. He is that seriously concerned with his faith [...] His voice cracks repeatedly, his lips are covered with foam," while "the Low German Christian Berend Toews [...] remains composed, unaffected, and unconvinced" (344–45). Dyck includes almost nothing of the content of this debate, and there is certainly no danger of anyone converting. Instead, the focus is on the contrast between the frenzied Jewish man and the serene "Low German Christian," and it is clearly meant to reveal much more about their temperaments than about their respective religious beliefs. "In the end," Dyck assures his readers, "they remain what they were, one a Christian, the other a Jew" (345).

The larger distinction of the novel, however, is not between Mennonites and Jews, but rather between Mennonites and their Ukrainian / Russian neighbours, and it is drawn primarily through the novel's portrayal of the non-Mennonite teachers who cycle through the colonies. Education plays a central role in *Lost*, as indicated by the small body of reviews of and criticism on the novel: Michael L. Hadley reads *Lost* as a novel of "Education and Alienation"; Andre Oberle classifies *Lost* as "a novel of education" (252); while Edna Froese notes that the novel wrestles with, but ultimately affirms, education as a force that will "strengthen the community" (*"Lost"* 153). Without taking anything away from these readings, I want to draw attention to the ways in which the process of education is mediated through a cultural, ethnic, or even racialized structure that reaffirms the distinctiveness of the Mennonite people.

Dyck, using a series of "Russian" teachers who are increasingly bold in voicing their frustrations with the "German colonists" (316), reveals the class and ethnic tensions that structure the Mennonite colonies. Hans describes the first teacher hired to work in the village school as being as "pretty as a picture" (105), for example, but his friends make it clear that they "will not be ordered around by a Russian wench" (106). Although Dyck works hard to show the Russian teacher in a positive light, he also makes the differences between her and her German students categorical. "People of two different worlds were confronting each other here," he writes, underscoring the "alien outlook" of the teacher: "Marya Ivanovna embodied the Russian being, while the village community represented a far deeper consciousness of the German nature than she realized, or deeper than one would have thought possible after a hundred years of lostness in the Russian steppe. Isaac's submission to the 'Russian wench' was an acceptance of the attractive person of Marya Ivanovna, not of the Russian people. The children's attitude toward the latter didn't change; it remained negative. It couldn't be otherwise" (106–07). With Hans's first teacher, Dyck establishes a pattern for the remainder of the text in which the Russian teachers are treated unjustly by the Mennonite children and quickly leave the community. Although Dyck uses this trope to criticize the parochialism of the Mennonites and to argue for the enlightening value of education, it also serves to affirm what the novel presents as the fundamental differences between the Mennonites and their neighbours. Like Ivanovna before her, the Russian teacher who arrives in Hans's seventh year at the school is an effective teacher, but "an ever-increasing rift develop[s] between teacher and pupils, until [she] began to hate the German children" (314). Taking Hans into her confidence, Varvara Pavlovna confesses her frustration over teaching in a Mennonite school and of the injustice of having to work for "the foreigners." "Because I am Russian I was rejected and treated as an inferior," she begins. "That's how you German colonists are. You look down on the Russians with disdain. — And yet, all the time you are the foreigners here, you are our guests, because this country belongs to us, the Russians, after all! — Yet look around, observe the German villages and then look at the Russian ones, a few steps away from your door. What a contrast! It seems our landlords had to perish in order to make room for you Germans" (316). Dyck uses Pavlovna's speech to indicate that, to the Russians, the Mennonites are not only non-Russian but also temporary guests—even as Pavlovna later expresses her hope that "we Germans and Russians some day will live beside each other and with each other peacefully and in friendship, complementing each other" (317). Although the text recognizes the legitimate grievances of the impoverished Russians against the "German colonists," here, as elsewhere in the novel, the full extent of its redemptive vision is that the Mennonites are Germans who might one day "complement" the Russians. Whether or not such a vision is achievable, however, is far from clear. Like the first Russian teacher, Pavlovna is pushed out of the community, "never to return" (315).

The tensions that the novel establishes through Hans's earlier teachers come to a head with his fourth and final "Russian" teacher. In a passage that I discussed briefly in the introduction, readers are told that Sergei Ilarionovich Protsenko is, in fact, "not a 'Russian' like the others, nor does he want to be one. He doesn't want to be a Little Russian either; he is a Ukrainian, and he wants to be only that" (331–32). That "Hans finds out only now that 'Little Russians' are really Ukrainians" (332) is indicative of the Mennonites' larger ignorance of the geo-politics of their colonies. Just as telling, however, is the fact that the narrator continues to refer to the new teacher as Russian, even after drawing our attention to the inaccuracy of the term (332). Protsenko manages to earn the respect of the Mennonite students and their parents, but one day, in what is described as "a moment of spontaneous arousal of national feeling" (333–34), he loses control and lashes out at the students for the Mennonites' treatment of the Ukrainian people (334). The narrator leaves the details to the reader's imagination, choosing instead to show the effects of Protsenko's words on the class. "None of the children says a word in their defense, in explanation; they hardly dare to breathe," Dyck writes. "Dear God! They haven't deserved this and everything is really a misunderstanding! — But what their teacher said just now, couldn't be misunderstood; all of them had understood it…" (334). Like Ivanovna and Pavlovna before him, Protsenko lasts only one year in the colony. After that, we are told, he "returned to his own people" (335). One of the primary lessons of Hans's Russian and Ukrainian teachers, it is clear, is that the inequalities between the Mennonites and their neighbours are regrettable. Another lesson, however, is that they are also inevitable, the unfortunate consequences of inalienable differences between them.

The most consequential division within the novel, however, is the one between the German Mennonite landowners and their Ukrainian and Russian workers, a distinction that effectively racializes the class divide. The only Russian mentioned in the novel's first book is Olga, the family's kindly maid (11, 28). As the novel progresses, however, the interactions between the Mennonites and their Russian workers become increasingly common and threatening. The field workers are presented as drunks and thieves, and Hans becomes frustrated with how the Russian workers "plunder the Germans' gardens year after year; how they lead the horses from the stable at night, steal the sheaves from the field, take along anything from the yard that isn't bolted down and safe" (328). As the tensions between the Mennonites and their neighbours rise, Hans and his friend Isaac begin to hear the jeers of Russian men who, readers are told, are "disposed to let the German devils' children know what they think of the accursed Germans and what they will do to them some day when their time has come" (282). Near the novel's close, Hans hears reports of arson and murder by Russian workers on the German estates (328), and he begins to have a recurring nightmare of "a Russian advancing towards father, with a pitchfork" (328).

The growing tensions lead Hans to consider the divisions between the Germans and the Russians and to make explicit the dream of *das Völklein* that has implicitly structured the novel as a whole. Wondering if "the Germans must live forever among the Russians, who hated them" (283), Hans takes a more reasoned position than Isaac—the young hothead argues that "[t] he Russians just need more thrashings […] then they will become tame"

(283)—but he is not convinced by his father's efforts to help the Russians. Instead, he wishes that all the villages in the area were strictly German, with all the workers German as well. In a passage that clearly echoes Dyck's own dreams of establishing a *Mennostaat,* Hans dreams of the Mennonite Commonwealth becoming entirely German—a fantasy that he expresses in unambiguously biological terms. Considering the various Ukrainian villages surrounding his own town, he asks Isaac, "what if all these villages were German like Hochfeld? And what if the police sergeant and his men were German," he continues, and if the inspector of schools was "a blond one with blue eyes ... speaking German?" (284). Isaac's objection—"You mean everybody German? And where would we get workers?" (284)—only further underscores how class and biology work together to construct a distinct Mennonite identity throughout the text. The narrator suggests that Hans has never had such thoughts before and that they "came over him suddenly just now, perhaps because he can not see how relations between the Russian neighbours will ever change or improve" (284), but this is not the first time that Hans dreams of racial purity. Midway through the novel, for example, the narrator notes in passing that the people "in [Hans's] dreamworld are always German. All the sailors, fishermen and fishermen's children have always spoken German [...] blond, blue eyes, and fair skin, that is the way they may look" (147).

    In Edna Froese's reading, Dyck stresses the biological elements of the Mennonite community in order to "anchor Hans rather firmly within his ethnic community, despite his desires to experience the wider world" (*"Lost"* 155). Without the threat of Hans losing his Mennonite identity, Froese suggests, Dyck is free to explore the potential of education and the arts. Although this is certainly true, the (bio)logic that underpins the novel's representation of ethnicity is, at times, striking and significant. It runs along sharp class and linguistic lines, and it seems to reflect a troubling set of assumptions about the relationship between race and cultural identity. As I have already made clear, the novel expresses an informed empathy for the difficulties faced by the Russians and Ukrainians with whom the Mennonites interact, and it critiques many of the Mennonites who consider themselves superior to their neighbours. In fact, some of the Mennonite characters are shown to be greedy, most are ignorant, and nearly all, it seems, are arrogant. Nonetheless, the sympathies expressed for the Mennonites' neighbours, along with the critiques of the Mennonites themselves, are couched firmly within the fact of their separateness. Even where the implications of these divisions are to be lamented, as in the children's overtly anti-Russian sentiments, the narrator assures the reader that "[i]t couldn't be otherwise" (107). Whether the Mennonites' neighbours are Jewish, Russian, or Ukrainian, travelling salesmen, teachers, or workers, their function in the novel is effectively the same: to affirm a coherent and separate German identity as normative for the Mennonites in Russia.

Time and Ethnicity

Early in *Mennonite Literary Voices Past and Present,* Al Reimer claims that the collapse of the Russian colonies "swept away [...] the complacent old tradition of devotional and didactic writing, the sentimental accounts in the papers and journals of Mennonite bucolic bliss, of dreamy, self-absorbed village life" (16). One page later, however, he suggests that Dyck's *Lost in the Steppe* "captured the Mennonite experience in Russia in a definitive mythic form" (17). It is to the temporal structure of this "mythic form" that I would like to turn now, for it shows not only a clear attempt to return to precisely the tradition that Reimer suggests was swept away by the Commonwealth's collapse, but also an attempt to remain within it indefinitely. In fact, I want to suggest that *Lost* not only covers a different historical span than the other novels in this study, it also attempts to position the Mennonite colonies as being outside time altogether.

In the introduction, I noted that many of the novels that engage with the Russian Mennonite experience follow a three-part narrative arc that moves from *order* to *chaos* to *flight.* By establishing the colonies' carefully ordered daily life, simple pleasures, and natural beauty, I suggested, this structure emphasizes both the drama and the tragedy of the Commonwealth's collapse, and implicitly argues for the necessity of the mass migration. In contrast to the other novels considered in this study, however, *Lost* remains almost exclusively within the opening stage of *order.* Despite (or perhaps because of) the fact that Dyck is the only writer in this study who actually lived through the collapse of the Mennonite colonies—at one point he came face to face with Makhno (Reimer, "Arnold" 71), and he worked in an administrative role to facilitate the migration before emigrating himself in 1924 (Wiens, "Arnold Dyck at Seventy" 80)—the characters in *Lost* never experience the chaos of the collapse or the hardship of mass flight. Dyck has written work that wrestles with the violence of this period elsewhere, including a devastating Low German short story about the loss of the colonies translated as "Two Letters." In *Lost,* however, he merely gestures to the coming trials, concluding the novel well before the outbreak of any significant violence. Rather than using the paradisiacal period before the revolution as a foil for the terror of the collapse, or as part of an argument for the migration, Dyck's novel remains firmly within the "Golden Age" that preceded them both. Read within the context of the Canadian rewritings of this migration history, *Lost* is best understood as an exile narrative, as Edna Froese's reading implies:[8] it emphasizes the Russian colonies as the rightful and natural homeland for the Mennonites, with Canada well outside its purview.

While Reimer's *My Harp Is Turned to Mourning* and Dick's *Out of the Storm* use datelines to carefully historicize their detailed portraits of the Mennonite Commonwealth, Dyck's *Lost* is, remarkably, a historical novel with nearly no reference to calendar time. Only the passing of the seasons, the occasional reference to the month of the action, and Hans's progression through the grades of elementary school mark the passage of time in the text. The historical period in which it is set can only be determined by references that assume a working knowledge of Mennonite history, as in the descriptions of an item in the house that "has come all the way from Prussia to Russia, more than a hundred years ago" (25). There are a number of references to calendars and clocks, but these are most notable for their inability to historicize the narrative. Readers are told that Hans's father likes to look at the family calendar "around Christmas," for example, but only because the calendar makes for "very welcome reading material" (159)—a reminder that the calendars used by Mennonites during this time functioned as almanacs, and that they retained a clear connection to sacred time.[9] The house also includes no fewer than three Kroeger clocks, those distinctive symbols of Russian Mennonite identity—of which Dyck provides an illustration, of course (13)—and Hans's brother Berend receives a pocket watch midway through the novel, the same Christmas that the family receives an additional Kroeger clock (176). Notably, however, none of these clocks is ever shown to indicate the time of day. Some of the novel's clocks, such as Hans's toy "blind" clock with no hands (175), or Berend's failed attempt at building a clock from scratch (13), do not tell time at all, while Hans seems unable to read those that do. He describes the "big Kroeger clock" in the Great Room as "deliberately ticking off the time," for example, but he immediately suggests that it is impossible to participate in its count. "When one joins the pendulum in its count, from boredom or without really wanting to," he notes, "one gets probably as far as thirty, when suddenly all is gone—pendulum, clock and also the last number" (23–24). Here, then, is the timeless temporality that characterizes the originary moment of *Lost*'s ethnic narrative: a Mennonite clock carefully ticking off time that never actually progresses.

Lost's refusal to engage with historical or chronological time as part of its construction of an ethnic communal identity directly challenges Benedict Anderson's suggestion that the move from sacred to secular identity is facilitated by a move toward the "homogeneous, empty time" of the clock and calendar. Indeed, according to Anderson's work on temporality examined earlier in this study, one would expect narratives of ethnicity to reject sacred time as a vestige of a theological understanding of community and to explicitly embrace secular clock time as a means of insisting on the Mennonites as a national or ethnic community. Yet, if it is true, as Caren Kaplan argues, that the process of "historicizing displacement leads us *away* from nostalgic dreams of 'going home' to a mythic, metaphysical location" (7; emphasis added), then the novel's refusal to historicize its narrative should not come as a surprise, for it is precisely the construction of the Mennonite colonies as a "mythic, metaphysical" home that is accomplished by the novel. What is more, Dyck complements the novel's absence of historical dating by using the present tense throughout—*Lost* is the only novel in this study to do so with any consistency—effectively placing the reader in the ambiguous present of the novel's setting. In the same way, the encyclopedic structure of the early chapters can be understood as a deferral of narrative itself, which, as a representation of a series of events over time, would seem to insist on a temporal progression of some kind. With no reference to a Mennonite past beyond the first arrival in Russia and an imminent collapse that never arrives, with a collection of calendars and clocks that never manage to convey the date or time, and through a present-tense, episodic structure that minimizes the narrative drive for progression, Dyck's detailed construction of a distinct, Germanic people is preserved in an originary moment outside the bounds of time itself, reflecting what Michel Foucault calls the "timeless and essential secret" of an originary moment. For Foucault, the search for origins can be understood as an "attempt to capture the exact essence of things, their purest possibilities, and their carefully protected identities" (142). Consider, in this light, Victor Peters's claim that the books that make up *Lost* "pulsate with life of a world, a Mennonite world, which has forever receded beyond the horizon of time. ... [O]ne forgets that there were but a few Mennonite villages scattered in the vastness of Russia; one is only aware that here life was good, life was full, life had meaning" (88). It is precisely this structure of ethnicity preserved within a timeless temporality—of "a Mennonite world" in which "life was good, life was full," and which has now receded not to the past but "beyond the horizon of time"—that characterizes Dyck's efforts to retell the narrative as the origin story of an ethnic community.

In its construction of the Russian experience as an originary moment outside time, *Lost* reflects what Urry describes as the sense of despair that characterized Russländer historical writings following World War II. Urry reports that, as any hope of a German-Mennonite return to Russia disappeared, the writings of the Russländer in Canada focused solely on the past. "Time seemed to have either stopped or stood still for an entire generation of Russian Mennonites," he writes. "[T]ime present had turned into time past without any real links to the future" ("Time" 26). Unlike the "timeless time" that Urry says characterized the Mennonites' earlier, religious understanding of themselves as being at once *in* time but not *of* it, or the secular clock time that he suggests the Mennonites of Russia had embraced by the turn of the century, the rewriting of the Commonwealth experience as an originary event is neither messianic nor secular. Outside both the forward march of "homogeneous, empty time" and the transcendental grounding of "messianic time," the temporality of the Mennonite world in Russia as presented in Dyck's nostalgic novel is sacred without religion. In *Lost*, we could say, it is the community itself that is sacred.

"Remembering What Will Happen"

I have argued above that the suspension of conventional clock and calendar time in Dyck's novel, along with the novel's lack of engagement with a past or future outside the so-called Golden Years of the Commonwealth, works to position the prerevolutionary Russian Mennonite colonies as the mythological origin of an ethnic Mennonite community. But it is not entirely accurate to suggest that there is no sense of the forward progression of time in the novel, or that the collapse of the colonies is fully absent. In fact, while *Lost in the Steppe* presents an overwhelmingly positive portrait of Mennonite Russia, the novel's nostalgic portrait is marked—or, to pick up on Robin Cohen's terminology about the break event, "colour[ed]" (28)—by the horrors that stand just beyond its pages. While Dyck's decision to write in the present tense creates the illusion of an organic, natural present unfolding in front of the reader, that present is repeatedly troubled by images of a future-to-come that calls into question the very naturalness of the novel's dominant vision. In fact, as I will try to show, the very structure of the novel begins to shift in the fourth and fifth books to reflect the Mennonites' threatened future in Russia.

Although *Lost* begins and ends in the peaceful and most prosperous decades of the Mennonite Commonwealth, Dyck foreshadows its collapse in a number of ways. Most obviously, as I discussed above, the narrator draws a sharp distinction between the Mennonites and their neighbours, a line that bears a growing tension as the novel progresses. There are reports of arson and even murder by Russian workers, and the threat of revolution is given voice through the Russian and Ukrainian teachers. But the novel gestures toward the collapse of the colonies in less overt ways, as well. Its recurrent interest in the violent death of farm animals, for example, demonstrates not only the ruthless extermination of heterogeneity in the colonies, as Edna Froese rightly suggests, but also the transitory nature of its pastoral vision. In the same way, Hans's recurring dreams of owning a gun (24, 70, 175), along with his habit of playing war (23, 98, 232), are not only surprising in a portrait of an ostensibly pacifist community, but also function to anticipate the coming violence. Similarly, though it might be surprising that Dyck begins "[t] his happy book" (Wiens, "Seventy" 84) with the death of the protagonist's sickly sister, this, too, serves to establish a tenor of tragedy for the novel that is never fully erased by the narrator's faux naïveté. The young Hans's complete inability to comprehend what is happening with his sister's death, along with the opening image of the Russian Mennonites constructing coffins for their loved ones, can hardly fail to conjure up—at least in the mind of the informed reader—images of the chaos, confusion, and mass funerals that would end the world of the novel only a short while after its close.

Dyck does more than simply insert the possibility of violence into the mythic temporality of the Mennonite origin, however. The novel's use of prolepsis, or flash forwards, to draw the reader's attention to the coming collapse seems to work against its larger temporality, which is otherwise structured by the limitations of a present-tense (albeit omniscient) narrator. Although the novel's third-person narration largely adopts Hans's young perspective on the world, it occasionally shifts focus and leaps ahead into a violent future. At times, these shifts are obvious, with the narrator's suddenly earnest voice interrupting the story to inform the reader of the horrors to come. In Chapter 1 of the second book, for example, readers are told that the house and belongings of

Hans's grandfather will one day be destroyed. In one of the few passages in the novel in which readers get a glimpse of Hans's feeling about the collapse of the colonies, the narrator abruptly leaps forward in time to report on what the grandfather (and the reader) will never see. "What about the books and papers" that his grandfather kept?

> They too were dead. They were burnt when all Russia burned, when the hundred-year-old house with the blue-edged white shutters, with grandmother's chest and grandfather's corner cabinet went up in flames, when all of Neuhorst was reduced to ashes.
>
> It is good that the old man did not see all that. If, like his grandson, he had been forced to stand before the burning Neuhorst, before the smoking ruins of all the other colony villages, and before the countless graves of those overtaken by this cruel destruction, he would have joined his grandson in a bitter accusation of those who, a hundred years ago in Danzig, caused the emigrant wagons to roll. (114)

This short section exaggerates the complex temporality at work throughout *Lost*. In announcing that Hans's grandfather's house will soon be destroyed, the novel offers a sudden glimpse of the future that lies just outside the novel's frame. Or, to be more precise, the narrator comments on what might happen in the future, should the grandfather survive long enough to see it—which he does not. In the emptiness of the novel's mythic time, the "reader cannot help *remembering what will happen*," as Froese nicely puts it in her own analysis of this passage ("*Lost*" 155; emphasis added). Echoing Harry Loewen's argument about the collapse of the Commonwealth as the Mennonites' break event, Froese writes that these "brief glimpses into the future acquire particular relevance, [for] if anything else was yet lacking to cement the Mennonite sense of a peculiar identity, the experiences of the Revolution fulfilled that lack" (155). This picture of the young Hans's future, in which Hans stands before the smoking ruins and graves of the Commonwealth, cannot but shape the reader's impression of the novel's larger, much more peaceful portrait of that landscape. Dyck, however, seems eager to resist, or at least ease, what Mark Currie calls the "teleological retrospect" implicit in prolepsis (33). Although the spectre of the end of the colonies serves to "cement the Mennonite sense of a peculiar identity," as Froese puts it, the narrator immediately insists that these horrors should *not* be allowed to colour the innocence, or purity, of the timeless originary period. The first sentence following the above description of the colonies' collapse, for example, attempts to immediately return the reader to the bucolic empty time of the mythic past, insisting, paradoxically, that the horrors just discussed are not yet relevant: "That all happened many years later," the narrator explains. "Today the small Hans still avoids getting near the strange old man" (114).

A remarkably similar scene is staged in Chapter 8, in which the ingenuity and prosperity of the Mennonite farmers are illustrated by the amount of violence that it will take to overcome them. "This farmhouse and the adjoining barn and feed shed truly contain an almost inexhaustible store of supplies of all kinds," the narrator boasts. "It took a world war, a revolution, a drawn-out civil war with billetings of pillaging and murdering bands of anarchists, and a subsequent total crop failure to bring the Hochfeld farmers, who thanks to their ingenious self-sufficient economic system had never experienced a lack of the bare necessities, not to speak of famine, to a state of starvation. Finally, after everything broke down, when in the surrounding Russian villages bodies of the victims of famine lay along the roads, the Hochfeld farmers also didn't have enough to eat" (155). This litany of horrors in store for the Mennonites, casually invoked as evidence of the community's present glory, draws attention to the violent future ostensibly only in order to focus the novel more fully on the glorious past. Once again, the narrator quickly ushers the reader back into the prerevolutionary moment. "This disaster overtook the village only some twenty years later," begins the next paragraph. "Today [...] nobody in Hochfeld thinks of war, pestilence, and famine" (155).

In *Lost*, then, Dyck does not simply present a nostalgic portrayal of the Mennonites' Russian colonies that is entirely outside of time. Instead, he presents a portrait of the Commonwealth that, though it is never grounded in clock and calendar time, is nonetheless framed as occurring immediately before its destruction. That the terror or trauma, which lies just outside the narrative's purview, haunts the novel can be seen in the way that critics have echoed the structure of Dyck's novel by describing its positive portrayal of the past by referencing the violence that it ostensibly omits. Gerhard Wiens, for example, celebrates the novel as a portrait of Mennonite life in "those peaceful, contented decades when everything seemed right with the world and actually pretty much was right with our little Mennonite world which never dreamed that it was soon to be drowned in blood and horror" ("Arnold Dyck at Seventy" 84). Similarly, Edna Froese describes *Lost* as "a celebration of an earthly paradise now lost to his immigrant readers" ("*Lost*" 147–48), and Harry Loewen says that in *Lost* Dyck "recreates the lost world of the Russian Mennonites" ("Canadian-Mennonite Literature" 79). Indeed, it is difficult to read the novel, at least for a reader with any understanding of Mennonite history, as anything other than what Doerksen and Loewen call it: a "portrait of what it is that was lost in the catastrophes to follow" (12).

Importantly, it is precisely the *loss* of the Russian Mennonite world that makes its preservation a pressing concern for Dyck. Earlier I suggested that the extensive detail and illustrations that *Lost* offers of the Mennonite world is encyclopedic, but an understanding of the complex temporality of the novel, in which the future structures the details of a past that is ever present, suggests that a better word might be *archival*. In its mass of details, descriptions, and illustrations, *Lost* might seem to be simply cataloguing the Mennonite past, but, on closer inspection, it becomes clear that this past functions in the service of a particular vision of the future. In this sense, the present of the novel is structured not as a present at all, but rather, paradoxically, as the past of a future that is being actively deferred. As Jacques Derrida writes in *Archive Fever*, the "structure of the *archiving* archive also determines the structure of the *archivable* content even in its very coming into existence and in its relationship to the future. The archivization produces as much as it records the event" (17). An understanding of the archival function of *Lost* helps to make sense of the extent of the detailing that Dyck undertakes in its early books. The multiple drawings of the milk pail, for example, are of value and interest only when we realize that they are meant to help construct, for readers in the future, a particular interpretation of the past. As we have seen, the novel's archival opening books not only produce the (ethnic) object that they claim to record, they also actively regulate its parameters.

Recognizing *Lost*'s representation of the Mennonites as a distinct ethnic community and the Commonwealth as its originary agrarian landscape also helps to explain a shift that occurs between the third and fourth books of the novel. In the first three books, the narrative of Hans's development offers but a loose ordering principle, as the novel establishes the Commonwealth period as a timeless, bucolic origin, and fills it with an exhaustive account of the Mennonite world. With the fourth book, however, a noticeable shift in focus and structure occurs. The episodic descriptive passages begin to fade, and the narrativity of the novel—that is, its representation of a series of events over time—comes to the fore. Similarly, the illustrations disappear: the first book of *Lost* has forty-two drawings, and the second and third books each have fifteen; the final two books have no illustrations at all. Having established the setting into which Hans is born, Dyck begins to focus more on his protagonist's educational and cultural development. If, as Doerksen and Loewen suggest, "the young man represents not only the young intellectuals and artists who ha[d] begun to emerge from among the Mennonites, but also the first literary and artistic achievements of Russian-Canadian Mennonitism" (11–12), we can see in Hans's development both his growing cultural and educational ambitions and the potential of the larger community. Just as Benedict Anderson suggests that novels conventionally represent an idealized national subject operating in a carefully constructed and clearly defined national landscape—"we see the 'national imagination' at work in the movement of a solitary hero through a sociological landscape," he writes (30)—Hans's growth, frustrations, and dreams offer a portrait of a distinct community on the verge of an important transformation from its rural, agricultural roots into an urban, culturally mature community, even as it is increasingly threatened by the context in which it has grown.

In this reading, the novel's closing gesture, in which Hans is set to leave the village of Hochfeld for the city of Chortitza, seems to clearly suggest the imminent transformation of the agrarian Mennonite world prior to the outbreak of the war. Surprisingly, however, the final words of *Lost*—"Hans Toews stands before the threshold of a new life" (354)—have been repeatedly read as signalling his taking leave of the Mennonites altogether. Michael L. Hadley, for example, suggests that "Hans does eventually leave his village, taking his Mennonite legacy into an alien culture" (206). In the English translation of the novel, even the preface states confidently that the "theme [of the novel] is the growth of the small Hänschen Toews into the fourteen-year-Hans, who at the end of the novel leaves his native village for the beckoning outside world" (Mrs. Henry D. Dyck iv). Although Froese is right to note that "the discourse of tradition rather than of belief" makes "Hans' eventual defection from the community less controversial" ("*Lost*" 154), it seems important to note that Hans never truly attempts to "defect" from the community. Not only is it true, as Hadley concedes, that his leaving Hochfeld at the novel's close "neither rends him from his past, nor makes him betray his origin" (206), but Hans is also not taking leave of the Mennonite world at all. He is simply moving from Hochfeld, a village on the border of the larger Mennonite colony, to attend a Mennonite school in Chortitza, the Mennonite urban centre, described earlier in the novel as "the cultural and ecclesiastical center of the whole so-called Old Colony" (307). If anything, Hans is moving away from the place where the Mennonite people are understood as having stagnated, and where the constant presence of Russian neighbours has turned them inward, and toward a location where he will be more thoroughly enmeshed in an emerging Mennonite world. "[A]fter all, he is leaving the Russians," as Dyck's narrator points out in the closing pages, "because Chortitza is surrounded by German villages far and wide" (350–51). Although Hans does believe that he is leaving Hochfeld "completely" behind him at the novel's close (351), this should not be understood, as Hadley suggests, as some type of "emancipation" from the Mennonite world into "an alien culture" (206), but rather as indicating the possibility of the transformation of the agrarian Mennonite villages into a more vibrant Mennonite cultural community.

It is in this spirit of transformation, rather than rejection, that the novel's focus on education heralds the potential transformation of the agricultural Mennonite world in Russia. It is, as Hadley writes, a portrait of "a culture in transition" and "social metamorphosis," in which Hans embodies a "liberalizing spirit" (200). If Hans represents the potential that we know will be cut short, it is not merely that of an individual Mennonite artist in Russia, but the Russian Mennonite community in general that, like the young protagonist, is in the process of transforming itself into something much less parochial, and much more culturally sophisticated, at the novel's close.[10] Indeed, just as Dyck would later dream of a *Mennostaat* "in order to make it manifest— especially to ourselves—that we are truly capable of the utmost accomplishments" ("Life" 128), so too *Lost* expresses an ardent desire for the Mennonites to live up to their potential as a *Völklein*. The tragedy of the coming collapse, in this context, is that it will cut short the community's educational, technological, and cultural transformation and prevent the Mennonites from realizing their vast potential. In fact, the novel spatializes this transformation in a brief but fascinating manner, describing Hans's first steps toward advanced education as a move to "the New World" (336). This replacement of the "New World" of North America with a "New World" of a culturally sophisticated Mennonite Commonwealth in Russia stands as a crystallization of the novel's attempt to rewrite the lived migration narrative with the dream of an ethnic transformation narrative.

Before closing, I want to turn to one final example of the novel's insistence on what I have identified as the timelessness of an ethnic origin. Near the end of the novel, Berend and Hans briefly discuss the possibility of emigrating to America, with Hans expressing his fear of the Russian workers' mounting anger. "Berend, they will kill us all one day," he says. "I want to leave here, and I want you and father and mother and everybody to go away, else they will kill us all" (329). Berend, however, dismisses the fears of his "foolish brother" (329). In the same passage, the narrator reveals that the Toews family had once considered migrating to America to join a distant relative but decided against it on the ground that, as Hans explains, "they don't speak our language." Given the prominence that Dyck ascribes to the Mennonites' language—in his introduction to the third volume of Dyck's *Collected Works*, Al Reimer suggests that Dyck understood Low German as "the very epitome of Mennonite peoplehood" (2)—Hans's passing comment is a strong critique of what is in store for Mennonite identity and culture in North America. After the brothers again reject the possibility of emigration, the narrative abruptly turns, once again, to the subject of time, and offers one of the novel's few references to a specific hour of the day. "Berend rises. He turns toward the sun and, stretching out his arms, lays his palms, edge over edge, holding them against the eastern sky. 'It's ten o'clock,' he says, 'we must go home.' Hans checks the correctness of Berend's time report the same way. It's right, ten o'clock and dinner is at eleven on Sunday" (329). Placed at the end of the novel's single discussion of emigration, the boys' use of their hands, rather than Berend's pocket watch, to accurately judge the time reflects the Mennonites' "romance with the land" (Redekop, "Mennonite Romance" 83) and quietly affirms the novel's larger portrait of the community as agrarian, organic, and natural. In a gesture that is equally quaint and tragic, Hans accurately sees both the time of day and the violence that awaits the Mennonites in the near future.

Conclusion

Lost in the Steppe's success in rewriting the Russian Mennonite experience as an origin narrative for a Russian Mennonite ethnicity is well attested to in the reception that the novel received on its translation and publication in English. A 1975 review by Mary Saveson, for example, assured readers of the *Mennonite Mirror* that "[t]he translation captures the essence of both the German Mennonite community life and the sensitive feelings of the boy Hans growing up there" (17). Gerhard Wiens was somewhat more philosophical in his review but affirmed the thrust of Saveson's account. "The world of *Lost in the Steppe*, the Mennonite settlements in the southern Ukraine at the turn of the century, is gone now," he wrote, before continuing with a passage worth quoting at length:

> [T]he history of a people is quite incomplete if there is not an artist in its midst who can see beyond events and conditions and look into the souls of the people who experienced them—the world of their day. For no world has meaningful existence except as human experience. And when the artist reports this human experience, then we no longer have a mere objective record of that world, we have its magic re-creation in which the life of long ago again pulsates with vigor and eagerness, a world sparkling with the brilliance of never-fading color. Arnold Dyck was such an artist. *Verloren in der Steppe* is such a magically re-created world. ("Translation" 7)

Lost returns to the prerevolutionary Mennonite Commonwealth to create an archival portrait of a distinctive, agricultural community defined in contrast to its neighbours by its linguistic, cultural, and ethnic markers. Buttressed by a present-tense narrative presented in an episodic structure, the timeless temporality of *Lost* renders the "Golden Years" of the Mennonite Commonwealth a mythic origin for a Germanic *Völklein*. Indeed, in announcing but deferring the collapse of that world, Dyck offers his readers a "magically re-created" past for a distinct Mennonite people, with the promise of their vast potential equalled only by the tragedy of their demise.

Chapter 4

The Individual in the Communal Story:
The Russländer *and the Trauma Narrative*

Sandra Birdsell's 2001 novel *The Russländer* begins with what is likely the biggest plot spoiler and almost certainly the most ghastly character list in all of Canadian literature: a brief newspaper article that reveals, in stark list form, that eleven of the novel's main characters will die in a mass murder on 11 November 1917.[1] Among the dead are seven who share the last name Vogt, including three children under ten. A short paragraph beneath the list provides the grisly details in blunt, staccato prose. The dead, readers are informed, will be found strewn about the yard of Abram Sudermann's large Mennonite estate, shot or with their throats slit; the estate owner himself will be decapitated. The larger narrative of the novel sets out to retell the story of this massacre from the perspective of Katherine (Katya) Vogt, one of its few survivors. From the comfort of a Canadian retirement home some eighty years later, Katherine recounts, for the first time, the story of her youth in Russia to Ernest Unger, a young Mennonite man travelling the country and recording Russländer stories for the Mennonite Heritage Centre in Saskatchewan. In its two-part structure, the novel repeats its single story with a critical difference: the detached tone of the very public and detailed account of the massacre offered by the opening newspaper article is not only supplemented but also, as I will argue, interrogated by the deeply personal and subjective account of a survivor struggling to work through its impact on her life.

The story told in *The Rußländer* is dramatic, but by this time it should also be familiar. The Vogt family lives and works on the Sudermanns' beautiful estate in southern Russia at the turn of the twentieth century. Katherine's father, Peter, is employed as the estate's overseer; though the Vogts' social standing is well below that of the unscrupulous owners, it is also well above that of the many disgruntled Ukrainians employed on the estate. One November morning in 1917, a group of "bandits," led by the historical figure Simeon Pravda, rides onto the estate and forces the Mennonites to line up in the yard. After some initial banter provides a glimmer of hope for the Vogt family, the estate owner provokes the men, and the massacre ensues. Katherine's parents, along with five of her siblings, are killed. Together with her younger sister, Katherine escapes to a hole in the estate's greenhouse, dug by their father as a hiding place for just such a moment. In marked contrast to the brief account of the massacre offered in the opening newspaper article, the narrative goes on to trace the impacts of these events on Katherine over the months and years that follow, and it closes with her marriage to an older Mennonite man and their immigration to Manitoba.

Birdsell's decision to present the Russian Mennonite experience through the memory of a single character shifts the larger narrative of the break event's mimetic aim away from the conventional historical claim (i.e., "this is how it was") and toward a psychological one (i.e., "this is how I remember it"). As both Maurice Mierau and Janice Kulyk Keefer have pointed out in reviewing Birdsell's work, there are political risks to representing complex histories through such a subjective, individual focus.[2] Problems of perspective are not restrained to texts adopting an intentionally subjective focus, however, and Birdsell shows herself well attuned to such dangers throughout the novel.[3] Moreover, when placed within the context of the various strains of the Mennonites' 1920s migration narrative, it is precisely the novel's self-conscious focus on the individual as an individual within the community—rather than the individual as a *representative* of that community—that makes *The Rußländer* significant. The novels that I considered as part of the theo-pedagogical narrative focus on the violence of the Russian experience and its impact on the Mennonites as a community of faith, and the novel that I read as an ethnic narrative displaces that violence into an immanent but ever-deferred future as part of its efforts to present the Mennonite community as a distinct ethnic group. In *The Rußländer,* the destruction of the Commonwealth is once again foregrounded, but here it is presented through the memory of a single character, routed through the prism of trauma that both occasions and, as we will see, structures her account. By having its elderly narrator recount her tragic story into the microphone of an eager young archivist, *The Russländer* calls into question the role that this key history continues to play in the larger Mennonite Canadian community, and offers what I read as an extended critique of the adoption of individual trauma narratives in the construction of communal identity.

The Individual Story in/versus the Communal Narrative

The brief newspaper article with which Birdsell opens her novel establishes the larger collective experience of the massacre as the context—or, more accurately, as the foil—for Katherine's personal narrative, and it offers a set of clues to the shape of the (imagined) community into which Katherine is born. In fact, Benedict Anderson identifies the newspaper as a primary medium for the construction of a communal identity, calling it "an 'extreme form' of the book, a book sold on a colossal scale" (34). Indeed, the newspaper's ostensibly objective voice, its deep investment in "homogeneous, empty time" evinced by the date in its byline that serves as its primary ordering principle, and its gathering together of a dispersed audience, all work to simultaneously reflect and construct a larger imagined community. The source of the newspaper article that opens *The Russländer* is the *Odessaer Zeitung*, a German-language Ukrainian newspaper that James Urry calls a "rich and varied source" regarding Russian Mennonite life in the Commonwealth period ("Listing")—and which, incidentally, Hans's father is shown enjoying in Arnold Dyck's *Lost in the Steppe* (159). Just as the untranslated German header running across the top of the article quietly establishes the Mennonites as unassimilated foreigners in Ukraine, so too the article's brevity and adjectives—such as a description of the Mennonites as having been "piteously slain by bandits"— suggest an author and audience who share a set of political and religious sympathies. Its dearth of background details indicates less a lack of historical contextualization than a set of assumptions about that context that operates powerfully in reserve. In fact, the very structure of the death list, which separates the names of the estate owner and his wife and sets them above those of the other nine victims, quietly bears witness to (and implicitly affirms) the social and class stratification in the Mennonite Commonwealth that proves an animating force behind the violence that the article records. Moreover, while both the perpetrators and the survivors are left unnamed, the article manages to identify both the *Ältester* (church elder) and the church that first broke the news of the massacre, reminding its readers of the theological frame through which the violence is to be understood. This is indicative, in fact, of the function of religion and class throughout the novel, where, along with gender, they are emphasized as the primary cultural contexts through which Katya must negotiate her traumatic experience.

But the story told in the newspaper, the communal and theological one, is not the story told in *The Russländer*. According to Birdsell, her decision to begin the novel by announcing the deaths of many of its primary characters was meant to encourage readers to attend more closely to the particularities of the lives represented—lives, she suggests, that often blur into the background in the many retellings of the Russian Mennonite experience. "I had read so many accounts of sufferings that I began to feel numbed by them," she explains. "Soon they all began to sound the same. I didn't want the reader to forget for a moment that these people would be gone and therefore to pay attention to their lives, to the smallest details that make them unique" (Birdsell, Loewen, and Thomas). In using graphic violence as a means of emphasizing the specificity of history, Birdsell invites readers to set aside generalized claims of the role of the Commonwealth's collapse in the larger Mennonite "world" or "cultural identity," and to consider instead its impact on the individuals who survived the collapse.

In stark contrast to the newspaper's official, communal account of the massacre, the opening of Katherine's narrative presents a much narrower focus for the larger novel. "She would always remember the awe, the swelling in her breastbone when she'd first seen her name written," the first chapter begins, establishing the personal, subjective, and reflective nature of the narrative to follow. "When she had learned to make her name she began to put herself forward, traced K.V. in lemon polish on a chair back, through frost on a window, icing on a cookie. K.V. Which meant: Me, I. Which was, Her" (5). Although her name is conspicuously absent from the opening newspaper account, Katherine begins her story by inscribing it repeatedly—even if her initials, traced with a finger in polish, frost, and icing, seem hopelessly ephemeral after the print of the newspaper. The passage also establishes the doubled perspective that will characterize the larger novel; although *The Russländer* ostensibly entails Katherine recounting her memories to Ernest Unger for the Mennonite Heritage Centre, it is presented to the reader almost entirely in the third person. Here this disjuncture is underlined as the shift from "Me,

I" to "Her," which has the effect of splitting the speaker into both subject and object, a double consciousness not inappropriate to a narrative of subject formation marked by a traumatic event. As Paul Tiessen suggests, the novel's opening lines "invite readers to enter the subjective realm of the protagonist Katherine Vogt," and in doing so they promise a radically different perspective on the Mennonite break event than those that I have discussed thus far in this study.

In Tiessen's reading, the novel's focus on Katherine's subject formation, emphasized through its trope of naming, can be understood as paradoxically demonstrating its larger concern with the community in which Katherine lives. "In laying stress on Katya's name, Birdsell's interest actually moves beyond questions of naming and personal identity," Tiessen writes, moving on to unpack the ways in which the novel critiques the economic and social structures of the community into which Katya is born, and against which she struggles to define herself. "What Birdsell seems to be exploring," Tiessen suggests, "is the functional usefulness of one's name in a society bent on commodifying its participants." Without precluding such a reading, the novel's framing device, which routes this material history through the memory of its central character, suggests that a slightly different emphasis might be more appropriate. That is, the novel's critique should be taken less as an exposé of the decadence and class stratification that characterized the Mennonite colonies of this period, and more as an exploration of the individual's experience of trauma within that deeply stratified community. I will return to the implications of this suggestion below. For now, I simply want to underscore that, in the contrast between these two opening scenes, the reader is invited to look beyond generalized claims regarding the shape of the Commonwealth or the role that this traumatic history has played in the larger Mennonite community, and to consider instead its impact on the individuals who suffered its full force.

As should be clear from *My Harp*'s portrait of Wilhelm in Blumenau and *Lost*'s portrait of Hans in Hochfeld, the tension between the community and the individual is not, in itself, a new subject for Mennonite literature. In fact, Hildi Froese Tiessen has rightly noted it to be a well-worn binary in both Mennonite literature and Mennonite criticism ("Artist"), while Jeff Gundy suggests that it constitutes "the Ur-myth of the modern Mennonite writer" (*Walker* 25). Yet Birdsell's novel is not a part of the well-established Mennonite literary tradition of juxtaposing an enlightened artist figure against an overly conservative religious community. In *The Russländer,* published simply as *Katya* in the United States, the tension lies between the communal and the individual memories of trauma, and in an examination of what is at stake in the effacement of their difference.

"Na Ja. And So They Killed Them All": *The Russländer* as Trauma Narrative

The rise of trauma studies is often linked to the American Psychiatric Association's first recognition of Post Traumatic Stress Disorder (PTSD) as a diagnostic category in 1980. Following the lead of Cathy Caruth's influential collection of essays, *Trauma: Explorations in Memory* (1995) and her seminal study *Unclaimed Experience: Trauma, Narrative, and History* (1996), however, critics interested in the representation of trauma have drawn less on the current clinical tradition than on the work of Sigmund Freud. In "Beyond the Pleasure Principle" (1920), Freud defines the traumatic as "any excitations from outside which are powerful enough to break through the protective shield" (607). According to Freud, victims are unable to comprehend or fully experience the traumatic event in the moment of its occurrence, and are forced to unconsciously return to it through sudden flashbacks, nightmares, or sublimated repetitions in an attempt to master the traumatic event. Victims are not in control of these returns, however, and, since they are unable to fully return to the original act through repetition, they are doomed to repeat the process over and over, a cycle defined by Freud as the "repetition compulsion." For Freud, the victim is "obliged to *repeat* the repressed material as a contemporary experience instead of, as the physician would prefer to see, *remembering* it as something belonging to the past" (602). Accordingly, a primary goal of Freudian psychoanalysis is to move the trauma victim away from this painful *remembering by repeating* and toward a reflective *remembering by working-through.*[4] As such, the experience of trauma is structured by a belatedness, wherein the victim only truly experiences the traumatic event at some later date, if and when she manages to work that event back into the narrative of her past.

Given Freud's focus on language and the "talking cure," it is perhaps not surprising that literary critics have been among the most active in the recent rise of trauma studies. Although some critics, including Dominick LaCapra, argue that "there is no such thing as writing trauma itself if only because trauma, while at times related to particular events, cannot be localized in terms of a discrete, dated experience" (186), others have argued that in the fiction that most faithfully represents the experience of trauma, the texts imitate or manifest its effects at the formal level. "Novelists have frequently found that the impact of trauma can only adequately be represented by mimicking its forms and symptoms," suggests Anne Whitehead, "so that temporality and chronology collapse, and narratives are characterized by repetition and indirection" (3). In a survey of recent literary and critical work on trauma, Michelle Balaev confirms Whitehead's claim. As it is conventionally understood, Balaev reports, the "trauma novel conveys a diversity of extreme emotional states through an assortment of narrative innovations, such as landscape imagery, temporal fissures, silence, or narrative omission—the withholding of graphic, visceral traumatic detail." It is through such narrative innovations, she contends, that authors work to "emphasize mental confusion, chaos, or contemplation as a response to the [traumatic] experience."

In a critical context that often positions narrative innovation as central to representational legitimacy, Birdsell's account of Katherine's youth and her family's massacre might appear hopelessly traditional. Katherine's reliance on a clear, largely linear narrative structure, her careful use of tropes and symbols to create a satisfying narrative arc, and her patient, detailed reconstruction of both the prelude to and the aftermath of the massacre all suggest that the novel falls short of the formal experimentation often expected of trauma fiction. Nonetheless, Freud's central claims regarding the belated temporality of trauma, the gap at the centre of traumatic recall, and its insistence on the role of narrative itself offer compelling insights into the structure of Birdsell's novel. So much so, in fact, that in "Getting It Right: Sandra Birdsell on Writing *The Russländer*," psychotherapist Hazel Loewen notes that she was startled to find how "consistent" the novel is in terms of what she knew "as a therapist about trauma." Loewen goes on to ask Birdsell how she was able to write "such a compelling account of the resolution of trauma." Like Loewen's question, Birdsell's response—that the process of representing "the trauma and how to bring Katya through it was a major challenge"—emphasizes that the novel examines not only the horror of a traumatic event but also the (narrative) process through which its survivor works through its impact.

Although Katherine's narrative appears to be a straightforward, chronological account of her youth, a Freudian understanding of trauma invites a closer examination of the temporal implications of the novel's framing device. Indeed, time is a central trope in the novel, and there are moments when the text seems to tentatively raise a timelessness similar to the one established by *Lost in the Steppe* in support of an ethnic narrative. Much as Dyck's novel presents the paradisiacal preconflict colonies as existing outside time, for example, Katherine remembers the "Golden Years" of the Commonwealth as if "she was living in eternity" (5). "What went on beyond the borders of her Russian Mennonite oasis was not worth noticing," she declares, and she recalls being happy to "dwell safely within the circumference of her privileged world" (6). Her father, Peter, even teaches his children to decipher the time from the position of the sun and the shape of a flower on a water lily, echoing the passage in *Lost* in which Hans and Berend read the time by stacking their hands against the horizon. Where Dyck's passage seeks to lock the Mennonites in this mythic temporality, however, Birdsell's passage shows its decisive end: Peter's lesson is interrupted by Cossack guards announcing an attack on Abram's cattle (100). With the outbreak of conflict, Katherine's experience of time seems to slow, freeze, then break. "When [Katherine] told [Ernest] the story of what happened that day, she began by saying that when Dietrich and his wife left the estate, the rest of the day pas[sed] slowly," Birdsell writes. "That's the way time went, more slowly, when people left the estate" (248). Later, as the events of the fateful night begin to unfold, Katherine notes that "it was as though she was seeing the world from underwater, voices and movements muted and slow" (254). Although her father calls out for her to hurry—"*Schnell!*" he shouts (265)—Katya cannot bring herself to move. When she picks up the narrative sometime later, Katherine notes that, while she had been "far away," the "Old Style calendar had given way to the New Style, the Julian" (271)—as if time itself had been reconstructed by the violence of the Russian Revolution. This is not the timelessness of a paradisiacal origin or the doubled time of the theo-pedagogical. Instead, it marks the traumatic break in Katherine's experience that becomes the source for the belatedness that structures the larger narrative.

Recognizing the belatedness of trauma in *The Russländer* offers a means of understanding Katherine's long silence regarding her experience. "She had known all along that she would one day tell what happened," Katherine explains, "but had delayed telling it until she'd become a widow, until her children settled into middle age and had satisfying lives" (247–48). Although Katherine indicates here that she has made a conscious decision not to share the story of her trauma, there are reasons to question how fully she is in control of her memories of this time. It is not a surprise that she would avoid discussing her family's death, of course, but the lengthy gap between the event and its retelling can also be understood as reflecting what Cathy Caruth has called "the fact of latency" inherent in trauma (*Trauma* 8), showing how the traumatic event is only fully experienced much later, when the victim returns to the experience in order to work through it. Not only does the elderly Katherine share the story of her family's murder for the first time after some eighty years, but she also repeatedly indicates that she was able to understand the significance of those events only much later. This belatedness is manifested in the small phrase "years later," repeated throughout the text. "Years later, Katya would tell her grandchildren" (97); "Years later someone would tell Katya" (99); "Years later Katya would hear the stories" (148); "She would read, years later" (149); "Years later, she would read David Sudermann's letters to her father" (157); and on and on. Unlike the prolepsis in *Lost,* in which the omniscient narrator suddenly leaps forward beyond the present tense of the text to a violence that never arrives within the plot of the novel, even Katherine's flash-forwards remain in the past, indicative of the elderly narrator's halting attempts to retrospectively renarrativize her life through the prism of a traumatic violence foregrounded before her story even begins. This is the belated temporality of the trauma narrative, a move forward in order to grasp the significance of the past, encapsulated in the phrase "years later she would," repeated like a mantra throughout the text.

As one would expect, given that *The Russländer* is presented as Katherine's spoken memories, Birdsell's portrait of the Russian colonies is much less comprehensive or exhaustively detailed than those offered by *My Harp Is Turned to Mourning* and *Lost in the Steppe.* However, Katherine's account of her youth on the Sudermann estate and its immediate surroundings is much more focused and every bit as vivid. That is why it comes as a surprise when Katherine proves unable, or perhaps unwilling, to describe the traumatic event itself. The detail of the narrative builds and its pace slows as the novel reaches the massacre. In the moments immediately prior to the murders, Katherine confidently declares that she is able to "describe Pravda in every detail" (257). With the first slash of the sabres, however, the text of the novel literally stops, leaving an inch of blank space on the page. When the text begins again, the focus has shifted to the framing narrative and the elderly Katherine, a jarring move away from a detailed reconstruction of the events preceding the violence to some eighty years after its effaced climax. Katherine offers only the briefest of summaries of the massacre into her visitor's tape recorder. "When she finished telling the story that day," the novel resumes, "she ended it by saying, After they killed Abram they thought they had to keep on killing until no one was left. They didn't want to leave a witness. They didn't know that the times were such that they could kill without fear of punishment" (265). Although the entire novel is structured around and through this traumatic moment, the event itself arrives nearly as an afterthought, its details almost completely erased, the gap in the text literalizing Katherine's understated refusal or inability to return to the moment of trauma itself.[5] "Well, yes," Katherine continues. "*Na ja*. And so they killed them all" (266).

There are a number of ways to read this important gap at the heart of Katherine's narrative. Perhaps the most obvious is to simply attribute it to a gap in her knowledge. After all, Katherine describes herself as having been dragged away from the scene of the massacre by her sister, Sara, to an underground hiding place. "While I was in the hole in the ground the darkness was like coal and it was as though I had disappeared. I hugged Sara, but didn't feel anything, not her body, or mine," she explains. "I listened for sounds that would tell me what was happening outside, but it was as though that world had ceased to be. The dampness and darkness were overwhelming" (283). In this reading, Katherine fled prior to the massacre itself; the abrupt break in the text simply mimics the complete gap in her knowledge. Similarly, she later claims that "everyone else [...] knew more about what happened that day than she did," since "[m]ost people would have read the account of the massacre in the *Odessaer Zeitung* that her grandparents had kept from her" (313). If this absence, precisely at the novel's dramatic climax, is the result of her fleeing the scene, then it demonstrates the full extent of Birdsell's commitment to the individual perspective and to the limitations that that perspective imposes on the narrative. However, there are hints that Katherine knows more about her family's massacre than she is willing to share at this point. She later admits, for example, that many of the women who survived the colonies' collapse shared the worst details—of how "*[t]hey fried her breasts in a frying pan*" or "*[t]hey did it to her with the barrel of a gun*"—only among themselves. "There was no point in telling Ernest Unger those kinds of things," she says (344), leaving readers to wonder what she has withheld from him as well. What is more, we know the elderly Katherine is aware of at least some of the details of the massacre (if only through her later reading of the *Odessaer Zeitung*), and that she is willing to retrospectively place important details into her account—thus the mantra of "years later" that echoes throughout the text. Yet, at the novel's climax, she neither offers those details nor makes any mention of the article. Why not?

Of course, it is also possible that Katherine *does* offer further details of the violence to Ernest Unger and that there is another implied narrator—the one who describes her scenes with the archivist—who refuses to share these details with the reader. That is, the break in the text can be taken as a break in Katherine's monologue, but it can also be taken as a blank space in Ernest's tape. After all, Ernest rewinds and tapes over a section later in the novel, which Katherine assumes he does to record over the noise of her cuckoo clock, though it is more likely that he wants to erase his own intervention into the narrative, as he just finished offering statistics about the number of Mennonite deaths in the colonies (342). Moreover, after the key gap in the text, the narrative resumes with "[w]hen *she finished telling the story* that day" (265; emphasis added), which seems to imply that readers have not been privy to all that Katherine has told Ernest. But again: why would Ernest, or Birdsell for that matter, refuse to share this all-important section of Katherine's story?

There is, however, another possible explanation for the gap at the centre of the novel. It was Freud who first noted not only how the trauma victim often "cannot remember the whole of what is repressed in him" but also the fact that "what he cannot remember may be precisely the essential part of it" ("Beyond" 602). Readers must decide whether Katherine is fully in control of her memories of that day, or whether Birdsell's decision not to recount the massacre is better understood as reflecting Katherine's inability to "remember the whole of what is repressed" in her. If the latter is accurate, then it helps to explain the starkly psychoanalytic language that Katherine uses to describe her time in the hole—"it was as though I had disappeared," she says, "as though the world had ceased to be" (283)—and her later claim that she "had emerged from the hole fully grown" (310). More significantly, it also helps to explain Birdsell's deeply unorthodox decision to present the novel's climax via the opening newspaper article, for Birdsell needed to find a voice outside Katherine's abbreviated memories to share the details of the massacre.

A Freudian reading of this passage is encouraged by the fact that Katherine and Sara's hiding place is simply the most prominent instance of a pattern found throughout Katherine's narrative, in which something important disappears (usually into the ground), often to return at a later point. On the night of the massacre, for example, when the outcome of the evening is still in doubt, Kolya and Vera, disgruntled Ukrainians who work on the Sudermann estate, return from the garden having dug up the Sudermanns' strongbox. It is only when Pravda sees the safe retrieved from the ground that he calls all of his men into the yard (260). Similarly, the first time that readers see Kolya, he is "emerg[ing] from the dark stairwell" of the estate's cellar (23)—the same cellar that Pravda's men are shown to go into and out of immediately before the massacre (258). Later, Katherine's grandmother retreats to her own cellar rather than answer Katherine's question about whether her sister had been raped before she had been killed; she emerges the next morning with the announcement that "[t]here are some things we don't talk about" (316). There are other examples, as well. When Ernest begins to tell Katherine about other massacres that had occurred in the colonies, he is interrupted by her cuckoo clock: the small wooden door opens, and out leaps a small bird that chirps and then returns to the darkness (342). In the aftermath of the attack, Katherine repeatedly imagines running into her family members, as if they have emerged from their graves, and she suggests that she withdrew "far away" into her mind, only to return several months after the attack.[6] At the novel's close, Ernest reports that Katherine's childhood village has been submerged by the damming of the Dnieper River; Katherine imagines herself floating above her family house and sees them "all in a row in their wooden coffins" (396). Apart from her hiding place, however, the most significant example of this pattern is the estate well, into which the young Katya throws a silver cup she has stolen from the Sudermanns, only to have it retrieved moments before the massacre. This scene is at the heart of my reading of the novel, and I explore it at length below. For now, however, I want to note that Katherine describes the well as a "chasm of damp darkness" (74), a phrase that directly parallels her later description of the "dampness and darkness" of her hiding place during the massacre (283). As a literary trope, this pattern of departure and return can be read as a unifying device. As part of her reconstruction of her past through the prism of the traumatic event, however, it also reads as a Freudian game of *fort-da* (gone-there) that Katherine plays unconsciously. It betrays what Freud calls "an instinct for mastery" over her trauma, which has unconsciously structured her memories as a process of disappearance and reappearance ("Beyond" 600).

In order to illustrate just how fully Katherine's trauma has structured her account, I want to pause over the disproportionate significance that the Sudermanns' small silver cup takes on in her narrative. Understanding the role of the cup in the novel requires us to return, briefly, to the novel's trope of naming, and the representation of identity construction initiated in its opening pages. Significantly, it is the wealthy and privileged Lydia Sudermann who teaches Katya how to write her initials in the novel's first scene. As Katherine comes to recognize the class difference between herself and the estate owner's daughter, however, she becomes deeply disillusioned with Lydia's easy privilege and the community's expectations of her own subservience. In Katherine's reconstruction of her youth, the differences between Lydia's position and her own position in the community, along with the implications that they hold for their opportunities for self-realization, come to be symbolized by the difference in where they write their names. Katya's initials, written on impermanent surfaces such as icing, frost, and snow, are hopelessly transient; Lydia's, in contrast, are prominently engraved on the lip of a small silver cup that Lydia owns but seems to care little about. In a fit of frustration, the young Katya steals the cup and, as noted earlier, throws it into a well on the estate.

Although Katya later claims to be unable to explain to her mother why she threw the cup away, the elderly Katherine's description of her confession makes it clear that the act was the result of her frustrations with her own invisibility in comparison with the prominence of the Sudermanns. "She recalled the impulse, but no longer remembered the reason behind it," we are told. "She remembered the initials she had stamped out on the lake melting as the snow had melted, initials being wiped from a windowpane in spring, initials she'd stitched into the corner of a handkerchief becoming frayed with each washing. She remembered thinking that Lydia's initials on the cup would last forever, for as long as a name chiseled in stone" (186–87). When she throws Lydia's cup into the well, Katherine literally submerges the object that symbolizes her frustrated desires for privilege and permanence, repressing both her envy of the Sudermanns and her anger at the Mennonite community that sustains their privilege. Fittingly, she is forced to repay the Sudermanns for the theft of the cup by completing a lengthy list of menial tasks that serve to reaffirm her low position in the social hierarchy of the Mennonite community.

If Katherine throws Lydia's cup into the well because of her frustrations with the class structure that limits her family, the full significance of this act becomes clear when the cup reappears in her narrative precisely at the moment when the Commonwealth's class structure is violently overthrown. In fact, in Katherine's abbreviated reconstruction of her family's massacre, it appears to be the cup, along with Lydia's initials on the rim—the very feature that Katya herself rails against—that ultimately sparks the fateful violence that kills her family. In Katherine's unlikely account of that day, Pravda raises the cup in order to display the tiny initials to all those scattered around the lawn, and the young Kolya understands the raised cup as a symbol to kill Lydia's father. "Pravda took the cup as it was handed to him, spat on it, and rubbed it against his sleeve," Katherine tells Ernest. "His face opened in a smile of triumph as he lifted it and turned its engraved initials out for all to see. It was then that Kolya swung the shovel, silencing Abram's sputtering with a blow to the side of his head" (264). Given that the cup was easy enough to retrieve—the men take only minutes to find it after the suggestion that there might be valuables hidden in the well—the fact that the Sudermanns had not bothered to retrieve it after Katherine's earlier confession indicates the inordinate significance that it has taken on in her memories. For Katherine, the cup is the key to her entire past; for the Sudermanns, its retrieval was not worth a few minutes of effort. In her memory, however, the violence initiated by the retrieval of the cup is rendered the fulfillment of her fantasies of the Mennonite Commonwealth's destruction.

Once we understand how thoroughly Katherine's trauma has structured her reconstruction of this history, other aspects of the novel begin to fall into place. As I suggested earlier, Paul Tiessen is right to note the novel's critique of the decadence and class stratification of the Mennonite Commonwealth. Given that the world of the novel is explicitly constructed through Katherine's deeply subjective viewpoint, however, the value of that critique is, at best, secondary to what the structure of that critique reveals of her experience. As such, the parodic elements of Katherine's critique—including what Tiessen correctly identifies as the novel's rendering of the Sudermanns' Faith Conferences as "comically grotesque, even freakish or outlandish"—are best recognized as a projection of her anxieties and desires. Such a reading also helps to explain the novel's surprisingly flat portraits of the authority figures in Katherine's life and the frustratingly simplistic binary into which they fall: in an otherwise subtle and complex novel, Katherine's parents, Peter and Marie, are unfailingly generous, honest, and nearly saint-like in their humility, while the estate owners, Abram and Aganetha, are largely static and shallow representations of greed, pretense, and arrogance. Abram, in particular, is presented as unrelentingly rude, violently aggressive, and hopelessly dishonest, and he lacks any redeeming qualities. He rapes and then fires one of the Russian maids, beats his servants, manipulates his children, and openly conspires against the Vogt family. The portrait that Katherine paints of his murder only exaggerates these qualities: in her account, Abram is impossibly stubborn, stupidly barking orders at the men who are about to kill him, calling them "swine," "pieces of dog dirt, snakes, sons of the devil," and so on (262). At one point, Abram shouts at one of his former workers to "go and milk the cows [...] immediately, and tell the others to do likewise," Katherine recalls, "as though the men who had gathered around him were not carrying guns" (261). Tellingly, Abram's death is the only murder that Katherine is willing and able to relate, and she describes the estate owner in darkly comedic terms: he is "sputter[ing]," "quivering," and "swaying," with a "mountain of flesh jiggling beneath his nightshirt"; when his "nightshirt [lifts] up, exposing the shame of his enormous buttocks," one of the men prods him between his legs with the butt of his gun (262). It is Pravda who christens Abram "King Turd" (261), but nothing in Katherine's description of the estate owner, either at his death or earlier in the text, contradicts this title. Reflecting the perspective from which the narrative is constructed, it is only those who survive the massacre—such as Lydia and David Sudermann—who bloom into full characters rather than simple caricatures of the roles that they play in Katherine's reconstruction of her past.

I have turned to trauma theory as a means of demonstrating that the past that Katherine reconstructs through the lens of her family's massacre is clearly shaped by her trauma, along with her guilt at having survived the violence. Her struggle against the limitations imposed on her by the highly stratified world of the Mennonite Commonwealth has resulted in a caricatured version of that world, and her narrative of her past suggests that she holds herself responsible for her family's death. As I suggested earlier, this marks a significant shift from the strains of this narrative that I have explored to this point, moving the mimetic claim away from historical accuracy or mythical origins and toward a subjective, limited portrait of an individual psyche.

Importantly, Birdsell not only demonstrates the subjectivity of individual memory but also thematizes its role in the Mennonites' collective memory. That is, *The Russländer* not only exhibits but also calls attention to a tension between individual trauma and the communal narrative, mining the structures of individual memory while keeping the communal context ever present through the opening newspaper article, the framing narrative of Ernest Unger and the Mennonite archives, and, most obviously, Katherine's descriptions of her frustrations with the larger community into which she was born and raised. However, if such a determinedly subjective account of trauma is to be understood as a strain of collective narrative, what does this suggest about the relationship between individual trauma and communal history? Is it possible to meaningfully expand a psychoanalytic interpretation of Katherine's trauma to understand the repetition of the Russian Mennonite experience across Mennonite Canadian literature more generally? In short, what is the relationship between individual experiences of trauma and the collective contexts in which they circulate?

"Lest the Spirit of the Story Pollute the Air": Trauma and Cultural Identity

In *Unclaimed Experience,* Cathy Caruth offers an expansive interpretation of Freud's work to argue for what she calls "historical or generational trauma" (136). Caruth points out that Freud does appear to suggest, at times, that a community's experience of a traumatic past can be understood in terms analogous to that experienced by the traumatized individual, before slightly redirecting Freud's argument to suggest that "historical or generational trauma is in some sense presupposed in the theory of individual trauma" (136).[7] Michelle Balaev identifies Caruth's work as one of a number of trauma studies holding to what she calls the "contagion theory" of trauma, in which the trauma experienced by an individual or group at some point in the past "can be experienced by an individual living centuries later who shares a similar attribute of the historical group, such as sharing the same race, religion, nationality, or gender, due to the timeless, repetitious, and infectious characteristics of traumatic experience and memory." Importantly, the possibility that trauma can be passed on across generations or to individuals who did not experience the original traumatic event themselves is not restricted to those drawing on Freud. The "learned about" experience of trauma, for example, remains a part of the contemporary clinical definition of trauma, though it is currently the subject of heated debate in preparations for the release of the next *Diagnostic and Statistical Manual of Mental Disorders* (*DSM-V*) in 2013.[8]

The tension between individual and group memories can be mapped in contemporary memory studies as well, though the majority of scholars working in this field take the social foundations of memory as axiomatic. Maurice Halbwachs, the sociologist often cited as the "father" of the contemporary memory boom, is unequivocal in his argument that individual memories are not only conditioned but also given both their structure and their content by their collective contexts. "[T]here exists a collective memory and social frameworks for memory," he writes, insisting that "it is to the degree that our individual thought places itself in these frameworks and participates in this memory that it is capable of the act of recollection" (38). Others, including Jeffrey C. Alexander, have built on Halbwachs's work to suggest that, because trauma is a social phenomenon, it happens not to individuals per se but to cultures as a whole. "Cultural trauma," he writes, "occurs when members of a collectivity feel they have been subjected to a horrendous event that leaves indelible marks upon their group consciousness" (1). For Austin Sarat, Nadav Davidovitch, and Michal Alberstein, the recent "emphasis on social construction and the use of cultural narrative as a means to explain the self" means that "collective identity becomes the unit of analysis and a group that shares an identity such as ethnicity, nationality, gender, or religion is considered as the primary unit that experiences trauma" (7). Although, as we will see, there are others who call into question the legitimacy of such a turn, there are obvious ways in which my study, with its similar focus on the relationship between a violent history, narrative, repetition, and cultural identity, seems to have been taking it for granted.

Although the scholars I have cited in diaspora studies who are working on the concept of a break event rarely draw directly from cultural memory criticism, the argument that a collective imaginary can be structured or "coloured" by a single historical event clearly presupposes that something of the impact of that key experience of displacement can be passed on across generations. Reading *The Russländer* with an eye to the social contexts of Katherine's trauma reminds us that the heavily theological, class-based, and gendered environment that shapes her representation of her past—and provides the vocabulary to express it—was established by the tightly structured Mennonite community into which Katherine was born and raised; that her family is murdered in large part because of their position within a Mennonite cultural-economic structure; that she undertakes a migration to Canada explicitly as a Mennonite; and that, through the archivist, it is the hail, or request, of the Mennonite community that occasions her retelling. Along with the newspaper account that opens the text, and the framing narrative that has Katherine recounting her story for the Mennonite archives, it reminds us that her individual memory of trauma is, at the very least, deeply mediated by the cultural contexts of her experience.

Yet, while Birdsell's novel clearly demonstrates that the individual and her experience of trauma are shaped by the structure of her community, and recognizes how that individual trauma is rendered a communal experience through its representation in shared venues such as newspapers and archives, it also offers a strong caution against the practice of uncritically accepting such experiences as transhistorical markers of communal identity. Not only does Katherine's narrative serve to remind readers of the deeply subjective nature of trauma, Katherine herself also intentionally works against its transfer, refusing to share her story with anyone—not the curious community members in Russia, not even her family in Canada—for nearly a century.[9] Silence, of course, is a common response to trauma, and it has a long and gendered tradition in Mennonite history; these are points that the novel makes clear and, at places, works against: a group of elderly Russländer women in Canada share their stories only among themselves "[w]hen there were no children, no men around to consider" (343). But Katherine's refusal to share her story is motivated at least in part by an effort to prevent her own trauma from being passed on to others, and to stop them from suffering through her pain. At one point, for example, Katherine explains that she decided to delay sharing her story "until her children settled into middle age and had satisfying lives, not wanting to chance harming anyone lest the spirits of the story pollute the air" (248). She later expresses thanks for the seventy-three children and grandchildren that she has in Canada, but never once does she identify a descendant by name, an omission from her narrative that echoes her expressed desire to keep them separate from her traumatic past (396).

Just as importantly, however, Katherine is openly dismissive of her grandchildren's attempts to connect themselves with her difficult history. Noting that her photographs of life in Russia have been taken from her over the years by "offspring of her children suddenly wanting to know their heritage, wanting to be more than Canadian-born fair-skinned people," Katherine scoffs that her grandchildren are instrumentalizing her past out of their desire "to be more exotic, like the people they lived alongside in their modern world, a multitude of different peoples, tongues, and cultures" (126). Katherine's frustrations with her grandchildren's attempts to claim her past not only indirectly adds Birdsell's voice to those of the many writers who have critiqued the exoticism implicit in the Canadian multicultural ideal, it also echoes Dominick LaCapra's warning that the "appropriation of particular traumas by those who did not experience them, typically in a movement of identity-formation,"

makes "invidious and ideological use of traumatic series of events in foundational ways or as symbolic capital" (65).

In Katherine's frustrations, read through LaCapra's warning, we can see
most clearly what is at stake in the novel's caution against the transgenerational extension of trauma. Even if we acknowledge that it is the communal
contexts that provide the vocabulary for the individual experience of trauma,
as well as its expression in memory and narrative, it seems deeply important
not to fully collapse the individual and the collective contexts of an individual's past in the name of cultural memory in the present. If it is true, as
Anne Whitehead suggests, that "collective remembering is not only, or even
primarily, concerned with preserving the past but rather with maintaining
social cohesion and identity" (152), Birdsell's novel invites us to remain aware
of the ways in which collective markers of identity, including terms such as
"Mennonite," are sustained through the ongoing invocation and deployment
of a myriad of individual experiences of trauma as markers of "social cohesion"
in the present. What is more, when we recall the ways in which Mennonite
texts continue to benefit from their circulation as cultural commodities within
the exoticized logic of Canadian multiculturalism, Birdsell's novel can be
read as a warning levelled at readers, writers, and critics alike. Of course, in
returning to the collapse of the Mennonite Commonwealth, Birdsell herself
is working at one of the foundations of Russian Mennonite cultural identity
in Canada. Although I have suggested that the novel engages with this break
event self-consciously and interrogates its assumptions, it remains true that it,
too, relies on, and benefits from, the literary, institutional, and cultural structures that have been built upon this foundational narrative.

There is a sense in which Katherine's concerns with her grandchildren's
attempts to connect with her personal trauma also level a critique at my
study, which, after all, argues that the contemporary Mennonite community
in Canada has adopted what I defined as the "break experience" of the 1920s
migrants as one of its founding narratives. However, to say that *The Russländer*
questions the ethics at play in the transgenerational passage of trauma is not
to say that it denies its transhistorical impact. That is, the critique offered in
The Russländer does not call into question the ongoing, structural effects of
historical traumas, the legacy of which obviously continues to inform and
shape many contemporary communities.[10] After all, the novel's framing
device presents this migration history specifically as an immigration experience: although nearly the entire plot is set in present-day Ukraine, Katherine

is located in her Canadian home, reminding us that many of the Mennonites who live in Canada today do so as a consequence of this particular history. In my reading, what the novel questions is the urge to capitalize on that past pain, as well as the practice of retaining the paradigm of trauma as a way to understand the ongoing impacts of such events. Although the break events of migrant communities are often traumatic—Robin Cohen's examples include "Babylon for the Jews, slavery for the Africans, [and] famine for the Irish" (28)—defining the ongoing impacts and influences of such events as "trauma" risks trivializing the more literal and individual experience of the trauma itself, on the one hand, and unduly restricting the expression of a contemporary community to its traumatic past, on the other. What is more, as I suggested in the introduction, the adoption of the paradigm of trauma for the discussion of entire migrant communities seems to unavoidably contribute to what Smaro Kamboureli calls the "pathologization of the diasporic subject" (personal interview). As I have found in reading the various strains of the Russian Mennonite migration narrative, undeniably traumatic histories can just as easily be remembered and reconstructed outside a trauma paradigm. Moreover, many Russian Mennonites in Canada feel no connection at all to the former colonies in Ukraine, presuming that they are even aware of them. The appointment of the Commonwealth's collapse as an originary moment for Mennonite Canadian literature is, we must remember, an act of literary criticism, so the cautions offered by *The Russländer* against the deployment of individual trauma in the name of collective identity—that is, to paraphrase Julia Spicher Kasdorf, the dangers of writing as "we" in relation to past suffering (*Body* 162)—are nowhere more relevant than to critics themselves.

One way to counter, or at least mitigate, the depersonalization of individual experiences in communal narratives of trauma might be to return to the work of Paul Ricoeur, who argues that Halbwachs and those who follow his lead "cross an invisible line, the line separating the thesis 'no one remembers alone' from the thesis '[the individual is] not an authentic subject of the attribution of memories'" (*Memory* 122). Drawing on Halbwachs's concession that "it is individuals as group members who remember," Ricoeur insists on a distinction between the *function* of memory, which might be unavoidably communal, and the *attribution* of memory, which is unavoidably individual. The splitting of the self from the self's work of remembering, or the "I" from the "I remember," is, he insists, an often overlooked moment that has led to the confusion between individual and collective memory. Although language not only fundamentally shapes our experience of the world but is itself also fundamentally social—in an example apropos to Birdsell's novel, Ricoeur notes that our names are given to us by others (*Memory* 129)—the expression of memory itself is always already to be distinguished from some other notion of the individual self, however nebulous that "self" might be.

For Ricoeur, this question of *attribution,* of shifting from a focus on the communal function of memory to the individual to whom a given memory is attributed, opens toward a larger discussion of historiography and forgetting. For my purposes, however, it opens an opportunity to consider the ethics of deploying individual experience in the name of maintaining cultural identity, of respecting the specificity of traumatic experience without denying its collective contexts or its ongoing importance for a cultural identity in the present. Indeed, the first line of Katherine's account in *The Russländer* marks precisely this shift, splitting, as I noted earlier, the speaker into both subject and object. The novel begins with a declaration of memory that is at once an example of remembering, a meta-critical recognition of the process of remembering *as* remembering, and a distinction between the individual who remembers and the collective context in which her act of memory occurs. Katherine not only remembers learning how to write her name, but she also remembers remembering this lesson, and she notes that it somehow marked a split between herself and her position in the community. Given what we have uncovered regarding the central role of naming and inscription in the novel, it is worth recounting the novel's opening passage again: "She would always remember the awe, the swelling in her breastbone when she'd first seen her name written, Lydia guiding her hand across a slate. When she had learned to make her name she began to put herself forward, traced K.V. in lemon polish on a chair back, through frost on a window, icing on a cookie. K.V. Which meant: Me, I. Which was, Her" (5). Here, in the opening passage of her account, Katherine calls attention to what we might call the "attributability" of her story. In the shift from "Me, I" to "Her," we see Katherine emphasizing the (self-) attributive moment of language, remembering that the process of being named is not only a moment of self-awareness but also a moment in which she becomes more attuned to her role in the community.

So, yes, we ought to recognize that the notion of a fully autonomous, sovereign individual subject is a fiction largely constructed by language and our social contexts, and that these communal contexts shape how individuals experience events *as* events, giving structure to our memories and vocabulary to our descriptions. However, we must also acknowledge that violent events are originally inscribed on specific bodies and specific minds, to whom their memories remain attributable in a primary and important sense. That is to say, if trauma itself is an unavoidably social experience, then it remains imperative that we respect that the violence that precipitates it is inflicted on individual bodies, on the "Me, I," even as it almost immediately shifts into "Her" within the social context of the collective.

Conclusion

In Chapter 2, I suggested that the theo-pedagogical narrative offered in Al Reimer's *My Harp Is Turned to Mourning* generalizes the violence of the Rußländer experience by overlaying it with the martyrdoms of the sixteenth century and the eschatological violence of a coming apocalypse, a move that invites contemporary readers to reconsider the theology of violence and suffering in the present moment. In *The Rußländer*, this communal function of the violence of the Russian Mennonite experience is confronted with a portrait of individualized trauma. Birdsell reveals a reciprocal but unequal relationship between the individual's memories of trauma and their communal contexts, offering a historical narrative shot through the prism of individual experience. The novel does not suggest that the individual experience somehow transcends the communal narrative or that the individual memory can ever move outside the social frameworks of its production. Rather, its intervention is to call attention to the processes by which the trauma of the individual is rendered a communal experience—including its representation in shared venues such as newspapers, churches, and archives—and to ask its readers to consider what is at stake in this process.

Despite its insistence on the specificity of the traumatic experience, the novel makes no attempt to resolve the tension that it poses between collective and individual narratives. Not only does Birdsell begin the novel with that most communal of documents, the newspaper, her decision to have Katherine recount her story to Ernest Unger for the archives ensures that Katherine's deeply personal narrative is never free of the spectre of its communal reception. If, as Derrida insists, the archive "marks [an] institutional passage from the private to the public" (2), then Katherine's account is, as we would expect, unavoidably marked by this passage: not only does Katherine share her story for the archives, but she also concedes that she has learned the details of her family's murder through her own archival research (313), and that she has even translated some of the Sudermann diaries and letters for the archives in Winnipeg (342). The belatedness of trauma and the historical focus of the archive are not as incongruent as they might appear at first glance, either, for as we saw in Chapter 3, the underlying structure of an archive returns to the past in the service of the present. We saw a clear example of the archival urge in the ethnic narrative, but if Dyck's *Lost in the Steppe* is implicitly archival, quietly amassing a collection of documents and details as evidence of a Mennonite ethnicity, Birdsell's novel takes up the Mennonite archival urge as a trope, troubling its structure and inviting a consideration of its larger implications. Where *Lost* raises the spectre of a coming trauma to legitimate its archiving gesture, *The Russländer* insists on the primacy of the trauma itself, and calls attention to the dangers of voyeurism and appropriation implicit in the urge to draw on the individual story in the construction of a transhistorical collective narrative.

Near the end of the novel, there is a brief final exchange between Katherine and Ernest that crystallizes Birdsell's interrogation of the communal use of individual experience. Ernest interrupts Katherine's narrative to share a set of statistics demonstrating the extent of the Mennonite loss across the Commonwealth. Paralleling the death list of the opening newspaper article, his statistics provide both the context of and a striking contrast to the personal nature of Katherine's narrative. Yet, as her response makes clear, his collective focus, already implicit in the archival urge that has motivated his visit, stands as something of a threat to her individual experience. "He had been to the archives," Katherine thinks, "[he] had read the stories which, in the end, all sounded the same" (342). Given that she is just finishing recording her story for the archives, her comment reminds us of the ways in which the communal narrative depersonalizes the history that it mobilizes in the name of collective identity. Importantly, Katherine responds to Unger's statistics by turning the focus on the archivist himself. "Just what do you hope to get from my story?" she asks (342). As it turns out, what Unger hopes to get out of her story is not really her story at all, but rather a community of readers that stretches across generations. He is collecting the "stories of the Russländers," he answers, "told in their own voices, for future generations" (342). What is more, the very structure of the novel imitates and emphasizes the collective context for Katherine's story and broadens Unger's question to implicate us, its audience. Although Birdsell is less explicit about the novel's archival structure than, say, Weier is in *Steppe*, she quietly presents the novel itself as an archival fond, with recipe cards, unsent letters, and newspaper articles inserted into Katherine's account.[11] Indeed, *The Rußländer* positions its readers as visitors to the Mennonite Heritage Centre in Saskatchewan, listening to a recording of Katherine's interview and flipping through a box labelled "The Rußländer." And so Katherine's question for Unger extends beyond the page directly to us, the eager readers of the Rußländer story. Just what do we hope to get from this story?

Chapter 5

The Strain of Diaspora:
The Blue Mountains of China *and the Meta-Narrative*

Early in Rudy Wiebe's *The Blue Mountains of China* (1970), an elderly Mennonite man named Franz Epp and his young Canadian relative, John Reimer, are visiting in a small Mennonite village in the Paraguayan jungle. Franz is surprised by John's request to hear the story of how their families fled out of the Soviet Union in 1929. It might be possible to forget that story in Canada, Franz suggests, but in Paraguay it is all they talk about. "Here what else have we to remember?" he asks. "Or talk about? The one big thing" (65). When Franz begins to retell the story, however, his memory fails him. As he tries to explain a "thing" that he saw, or felt, as the Mennonites waited in Moscow for permission to emigrate, he concedes that he "can't say 'this and this and so and so' is exactly like it was" (67).[1] His frustration in retelling the story is worth quoting at length:

> When you keep thinking so long of one thing, after a while you can't
> be certain whether you actually saw it like that, then, right from
> the start, or whether that little time so long ago has foreshortened
> in your mind, the understanding you got from later when most of
> it happened shifting to earlier in time as you remember it, your
> remembrance sort of organizing itself in a more logical way as you
> keep thinking over the years. That as you think over the years this
> central—thing—gets more and more meanings, like a sponge soak-
> ing all your memories into it and leaving nothing, just it. (67–68)

Given Franz's uncertainties, the reader might expect his story to be marked by false starts, corrections, and generalizations, but the remaining twenty pages of the chapter present his account in uninterrupted, intricately detailed prose, showing the reader that if Franz has trouble remembering anything, he certainly can *tell* his story as if "'this and this and so and so' is exactly like it was." Still, his initial hesitation is significant, for not only has Franz insisted on the centrality of the dispersal story to his Mennonite community—"what else have we to remember?" he asks—but also he concedes that it continues to take on more meanings as time passes, demonstrating how the retelling of the "one big thing" in the community's history is subject to the twin processes of repetition and revision. Franz's retelling, as we will see, is just one of several versions of their escape from Moscow that circulates in the novel, and each time the story is told it is slightly different in its details and significantly different in its implications. In this chapter, I read *Blue Mountains* as a meta-narrative that returns to the Russian Mennonite migration story self-consciously, problematizing its role as a central narrative in a larger diasporic Mennonite community.

If the theo-pedagogical and ethnic narratives share the assumption that the Mennonites in Russia constituted a clearly definable, largely homogeneous community, and if the trauma narrative requires the reader to focus on the individual experience within that community, the meta-narrative of *Blue Mountains* moves toward a much broader and more disparate portrait of a global Russian Mennonite diaspora. As a collection of loosely connected stories of innumerable characters settled across the world bound together by a dense network of overlapping but incommensurable histories, *Blue Mountains* is sufficiently complex and ambitious to present something of the vast heterogeneity of the Russian Mennonite migrant experience. In the process, it directly challenges the concept of an identity built upon a communal narrative, suggesting that a cultural identity is maintained not by relying on a shared past that underpins the differences of the present but through and because of difference itself. Revealing (and, at times, revelling in) the function of difference within the Russian Mennonite migration narrative, *Blue Mountains* seeks to challenge Mennonite identity itself, ultimately calling for a new form of community in the novel's closing pages.

"A Stranger Shape of Novel"

Over the first four chapters of this study, I have focused primarily on what might be considered monologic narratives, or novels that, while often encompassing numerous protagonists and multiple plotlines, nonetheless work to establish a singular version of a complex past. This process is facilitated, I have suggested, by the ordering power of narrative, that process of selection and ordering that imposes an artificial sense of structure on its subject in order to render it coherent and meaningful. Wiebe's *Blue Mountains*, however, moves away from the monologic structure of these other strains. Like Weier's *Steppe*, the multiple or "polyphonic" narrative of Wiebe's novel structurally parallels the larger collection of texts retelling the Russian Mennonite migration narrative. However, where a meta-narrative such as Weier's largely contains the implicit critique of its polyphonic voice by presenting its many stories as the compilation of a single character's research, Wiebe's novel resolutely refuses to ground its narrative in a single character, location, or perspective.

Originally intended as a collection of short stories, *Blue Mountains* is a patchwork of narratives in which each chapter relates only in part to the overarching story of a community's dispersal. Even when laid out as straightforwardly as possible, its many characters, locations, and experiences can be overwhelming. The novel follows the circuitous migrations of five families for nearly a century across four continents. First, Isaak Friesen's family, which includes his daughter, the deeply religious Frieda Friesen, leaves Russia for Canada in 1883 and relocates to Paraguay in 1927. Esther, Frieda's daughter, eventually returns to Canada to marry the wealthy Dennis Willms, and they have a daughter named Irene. Second, Isaak's brother, Jakob Friesen, is a wealthy estate owner in Russia who attempts to flee from the Mennonite colonies after losing his *hof* and his only son, also named Jakob, in the post-revolutionary violence. Although the elder Jakob is arrested in Moscow and spends a decade in a Siberian labour camp before finding his way to Canada at the novel's end, his wife and three daughters succeed in reaching Paraguay in 1929. Third, Samuel Reimer's family also migrates from the Soviet Union to Paraguay in 1929 before moving on to Canada, where Samuel's two sons feel called by God to renew their fledgling Christian faith in strange ways: Samuel (Jr.) hears God's voice ordering him to proclaim peace in Vietnam, and John, following his discussion with Franz in Paraguay, returns to Canada and carries a large wooden cross across the country. Fourth, the young

Elizabeth Driediger flees to Paraguay with the Friesen and Reimer families; while her parents remain in Paraguay, Elizabeth ultimately moves to Canada (via Argentina) and becomes a professor of linguistics. And fifth, David Epp's family flees the Soviet Union by heading not west but east, through China. David, however, leaves his young family and returns to the Soviet Union in the hope of helping other Mennonites escape, knowing that it will likely cost him his life. His brother, Franz, who had emigrated out of Moscow, reaches Paraguay, where he lives to share his emigration story with John. The novel closes in Canada, with many of these characters coming together for a fragile and fleeting reunion.

Despite the obvious challenges that attend a story with so many characters, settings, and eras, Wiebe makes little effort to aid the reader in keeping them apart. There are, for example, two characters named Samuel Reimer, three named David Epp, and no fewer than five named Jakob Friesen.[2] Four of the novel's key characters change their names, with three of them deliberately disguising their identities.[3] There is a list of principal characters that precedes the text, but, as Zailig Pollock observes, it is "confusing, both because of its format and because, for the sake of completeness, it is cluttered with many characters who play little or no role in the book" (71). Pollock is being kind; the list is so hard to follow that it is tempting to read its inclusion as ironic. Consider, for example, the first entry: "Jakob (III) and Isaak Friesen: identical twin grandsons of Jakob (I) who founded the Karatow *hof* after re-settling from Chortitza, the Ukraine, where the Friesens had come in 1789 from Danzig; born Karatow 1859; Jakob deceased there in 1919, Isaak in Manitoba 1933." In a single entry, Wiebe covers nearly a century and a half, gesturing to two international mass migrations and identifying four locations on two continents. He uses the German term *hof* to describe the Friesens' estate, and only the most knowledgeable readers could locate Chortitza on a map of Ukraine, given that the former Mennonite colony is now part of the city of Zaporizhia, its Mennonite name long having been abandoned. What is truly baffling, however, is that neither of the entry's characters makes an appearance in the book. In fact, of the twenty-seven individuals identified by name in the six entries of the opening character list, only fifteen participate directly in the action of the novel. No wonder, then, that the journal *Essays on Canadian Writing* took the remarkable step of publishing an eight-page annotated genealogy of the book's characters. Pollock, the compiler, suggests that "perhaps no other Canadian novel encompasses as wide a range of experience," and he presents the extensive genealogy as "a way of making [it] more approachable" (70).

For many readers, the novel itself seems to offer little by way of clarification. The chapters are set in various locations around the world, yet many of them begin without any setting, temporal, or character cues, so readers are often well into a character's story before they have enough contextual details to comprehend in which decade, or on which continent, the action is taking place—not to mention who the characters are and how they are related to the action or characters of the preceding chapters.[4] Not surprisingly, critics have suggested that the novel "seems to have been devised to discourage ordinary readers" (Spriet 68). Eva-Marie Kröller calls the novel "one of the most challenging in Canadian literature" and thinks it necessary to assure readers that, though complex, its organization "is by no means random" (274), while David L. Jeffrey calls the novel "probably the most demanding novel English speaking Canada has yet produced" (186). When asked about the novel's dizzying complexity, however, Wiebe himself responds dryly: "I'm not for speed readers" (qtd. in Keith, *Voice* 2).

On the one hand, the formal complexity of *Blue Mountains* shows it to be a product of its time. Published in 1970, the novel follows in the wake of the modernist texts of the 1960s, a point that Andrew Gurr underscores when he suggests that Wiebe was working out of the tradition of the modernist short story (159). And, in fact, the novel is self-conscious about its position within Canadian literature's modernist tradition: Wiebe cites from a poem by John Newlove in the novel's epigraph; includes a passage from Sheila Watson's *The Double Hook*;[5] and offers an extended critique of Leonard Cohen's *Beautiful Losers* (219–20). On the other hand, its fragmented structure can also be understood as a thematization or illustration of the difficulties of attempting to portray a people who are, as Magdalene Falk Redekop writes, "paradoxically gathered together for us by the realistic portrayal of their dispersion" (103). In fact, in a lengthy author's note to the New Canadian Library edition of the novel (2008), Wiebe suggests as much himself, explaining that it was his visits with Mennonites in Paraguay that "dared [him] into a stranger shape of a novel, a form where the basic human mud of the stories [he] found would remain what it was: unarranged, flung together, sprawling" ("Origins" 298).

Far from simply reflecting a high modernist desire to "make it new," then, the novel's challenge to order, coherence, and stability seems to reflect, or even manifest, something of the shattering experience of migration itself. It demonstrates how, in James Clifford's words, "experiences of unsettlement, loss, and recurring terror produce discrepant temporalities [and] broken histories" (263). This is not to suggest, of course, that narrative complexity is somehow inherently or exclusively diasporic; rather, when used to represent diaspora, it both echoes and conveys the fragmentation of the communities that it represents. Like the theo-pedagogical and ethnic narratives, the mimetic aim of the meta-narrative remains on a community's (broken) history, but Wiebe's novel does so fully aware of the limitations of such a project— particularly of the dangers of nostalgia and hagiography. Given the reciprocal relationship that I have been assuming between the narrative form and the formation of communal identity, Wiebe's decision to make "narrative itself the problem" (Ferris 79) seems to strain against the ordering power of narrative and thereby challenge the very concept of a collective Mennonite identity. Although Wiebe has suggested that the history of the Russian Mennonites determined the form of the novel—"If you're going to have a novel about a people who are scattered all over the continents of the world throughout an entire century [...] you can't write a third-person, central-intelligence novel," he tells an interviewer (Twigg 285)—the novels considered in the earlier chapters of this study have demonstrated that this story can, indeed, be rendered in a more straightforward form. As Al Reimer suggests, the "deliberately disjunctive form" of *Blue Mountains* appears to reflect "Wiebe's view of the collective Russian Mennonite world as less purposeful, coherent, and homogenous than it traditionally assumed itself to be" (*Mennonite Literary Voices* 26). The scattered narrative that Wiebe uses to portray the Mennonites as a diasporic community, then, underscores the extent to which the linear narrative structures of *My Harp Is Turned to Mourning* and *Lost in the Steppe* have, in their function of imposing order and structure onto the history of the Mennonites, been working in support of the totalizing claims of the theo-pedagogical and ethnic narratives, both of which imagine the Mennonite community as satisfyingly distinct, complete, and coherent.

The Threads of Diaspora

In the novels that I have considered thus far, Canada has been at best the teleological endpoint of a migration that includes only two points: southern Russia and Canada. In both *My Harp Is Turned to Mourning* and *Out of the Storm*, Canada is relegated to the epilogues, literally separated from the larger narratives. Despite being positioned by its framing narrative as a story told in Winnipeg, *The Rissländer* also barely manages to arrive on Canadian soil: apart from Katherine's brief description of departing from the train in the Prairies on the novel's final page, all the reader is shown of Canada is the inside of her apartment and the view of the parking lot afforded by her window. And *Lost in the Steppe* never manages to arrive on Canadian soil at all.

Within the context of the Russian Mennonite migration narrative, the multi-national scope of *The Blue Mountains of China* levels an important challenge to the position of Canada as simply a "landing pad" for the Mennonite migrants. In Wiebe's novel, Canada is just one stop in an ongoing process of migration, and not a particularly promising one at that. In his portraits of Mennonites from across the diaspora—from the traditional and deeply religious Frieda Friesen in Paraguay to the worldly and assimilated Dennis Willms in Canada, from the disillusioned Jakob Friesen (IV) in Russia to the naive young Elizabeth Driediger on the boat crossing the Atlantic—Wiebe insists on the heterogeneity of the wider Russian Mennonite community. Indeed, in placing these competing, and often conflicting, stories beside each other and deferring the desire to smooth their differences into a single, overarching narrative, *Blue Mountains* reminds readers of the important differences commonly effaced in communal narratives of the past. As Penny Van Toorn writes, the novel's disparate chapters form "a fragmented, multi-voiced, historical narrative which encodes the plurality of the Mennonites' experience of the past" (67–68). The key point for me, however, is not simply that Wiebe has made an effort to show a variety of perspectives within the larger Mennonite community—Reimer and Birdsell do likewise—but rather that he does not suture those differences into a clear narrative that takes for granted the stability of the community as its ultimate referent. Although the novel's "complex structure of individual narratives and their cross-references to each [offers] a description of the Mennonite diaspora" (Korkka 24), the sheer complexity of *Blue Mountains* asks whether an identity based in part upon a shared history of ongoing migration—shared both as a commonly lived experience and as a story passed on to others—is really strong enough to bind these disparate experiences together in a fashion that constitutes a "community" in any meaningful sense of the term.

As we have seen, Wiebe does nothing to downplay the challenge of maintaining a sense of community across widely different contexts. A close reading of the novel, however, reveals a meticulous use of subtle familial, historical, and cultural cues that constructs an intricate network of relations that links the text's many characters, spaces, and narratives.[6] Some of the links among the stories function at the level of theme, so that the portrayal of the Canadian millionaire Dennis Willms, for example, takes on its full meaning as a class critique of the global Mennonite community only when read alongside the story of Jakob Friesen (IV), the wealthy Russian estate owner. Similarly, the physical challenges of being poor in the Paraguayan jungle are tempered in contrast to the spiritual challenges of living in comfort in Canada. Catching other connections, however, requires a closer reading. To take just one representative example, consider what is required to understand the implications of Frieda's son, a Kanadier living in Paraguay, falling in love with the newly arrived Russländer, Susie Friesen. Readers must have the genealogy of the novel at their fingertips to catch the significance of Frieda's passing comment that Susie's grandmother "had been my father's brother's [...] wife" (176). Failing that, they need to recognize Susie's family story—a father and a brother taken by the GPU, a grandmother who refuses to leave—to realize that her marriage to Johann reunites the families of the estranged Friesen twins, Jakob and Isaak. It is only by recognizing that Frieda's new daughter-in-law is her cousin's daughter that readers can appreciate the significance of the mistakes that Frieda makes in her account of Susie's past. Frieda's comment that Susie's family "had always been poor," for example, shows that the humbled Mrs. Friesen has not told anyone of her family's former wealth and status in the Russian colonies. Her newfound humility is significant for what it suggests about how the collapse of the Mennonite Commonwealth resulted in a widespread renegotiation of class difference in the larger Mennonite community, the significance of which is underlined by the marriage of a Kanadier and Russländer. Finally, Frieda's assumption that Susie's father "must be now long dead" (176) takes on its tragic poignancy only if readers realize that her father is Jakob (IV), whom they have already seen alive but suffering in Siberia, dreaming of his family in Paraguay (134). Despite the obvious disjuncture that characterizes the novel and the important differences between each story, tracing the connections that implicitly tie them together allows readers to draw a portrait of a larger diasporic community.

A close reading of the novel also reveals that the dearth of clear temporal markers at the opening of many chapters masks what turns out to be a largely linear retelling of the 1920s migration narrative. In fact, with the notable exception of Frieda's four chapters (1, 3, 6, and 10), the story—though, as I will explore later, not the plot—of the novel progresses chronologically. Chapter 2 is the story of Jakob (IV), a glimpse of Mennonite life in the Soviet Union as the colonies fall apart in the late 1920s. Franz's story of escaping Moscow is Chapter 4, which shows the fate of Jakob's family and the progression of the Mennonites on their way out of their "Russian" homeland in 1929. Chapter 5 is Elizabeth's story, which relates their migration out of the USSR via boat, and Chapter 7 is Anna's story, which shows their arrival in Paraguay. Chapters 8 and 9 show the Mennonites who remained in the USSR (Jakob [V] languishing in Siberia; David Epp leading villagers fleeing via China), while Chapters 11 and 12 show, through the stories of the Reimer brothers, the Mennonites settling in both Canada and Paraguay. The final chapter, set in Canada in 1967, reunites, momentarily, many of the Mennonites who fled together in the novel's second chapter.

Although the novel presents a complex narrative structure that troubles any straightforward reading of the larger Mennonite community, then, the threads that link one character to the next succeed in constructing a tenuous community that exists across continents and decades, even placing it in a coherent (if submerged) linear temporal structure. The fact that Wiebe does nothing to emphasize any of these connections, however, forces the reader to consciously participate in the novel's construction of meaning, to recall the relevant details, and to weave them into something approximating a coherent whole. As Pollock writes, "[a]ll the characters in the book are engaged in, or engaged in avoiding, acts of remembrance, and, if we are to understand them and their struggles, *we* must remember, too" (70). Although there is a sense in which readers always undertake this weaving, the complexity of *Blue Mountains* demands that they consciously work to narrativize the text, and thereby to add yet another layer of narrative to the novel. The question remains, however, whether all of these narratives are sufficient to maintain the community that they rather tenuously construct.

"After the Break": Difference and Repetition

To this point, I have been suggesting that the vast differences among the many characters and settings in *The Blue Mountains of China* are linked through a network of details that reveals the underlying unity of the Mennonites as a diasporic community. Simply the fact that these stories are collected together and given a single title seems to encourage such a reading, and Wiebe has placed enough connecting details to reward it. Yet it seems important to recognize that, without an artifice of some sort—here not only the cultural identity of the Mennonites but also the material form of the text—that invites readers to search at length for the common threads that can then be woven into something like a shared identity, the characters and events described in the novel would remain stubbornly distinct and hopelessly disconnected. In fact, the process of repetition that characterizes the novel's complex narrative suggests that the Mennonite identity being constructed in the novel emerges not in spite of the differences that dominate the text, but precisely because of them.

To understand the function of difference in the construction of diasporic identity, I want to return to what J. Hillis Miller identified as the Nietzschean tradition of repetition, in which identity is constructed in a "world based on difference" and in which repetitions are understood as the "ungrounded doublings which arise from differential interrelations among elements" (6). Where novels working out of the Platonic tradition of repetition, such as *My Harp* and *Lost*, claim to represent the past "as it really was" in order to support what they posit to be the primary significance of the historical community and the meaning of its collapse, novels in the Nietzschean tradition of repetition, such as *Blue Mountains* and *Steppe*, destabilize the process of representation as part of their problematizing of the concept of communal identity itself. It is true that Wiebe seems to lose his nerve on this point as the novel comes to a close, but before we get to the final chapter it is worth first exploring what is at stake in the larger novel's engagement with the overlapping concepts of narrative, repetition, and identity.

In "Cultural Identity and Diaspora," one of the foundational essays in contemporary diaspora studies, Stuart Hall suggests that there are two versions or positions of cultural identity, the first of which is easily recognizable as indicative of the first two strains examined in my study, the second of which helps to explore the strain that I am considering here: "The first position defines 'cultural identity' in terms of 'one true self,' hiding inside the many other, more superficial or artificially imposed 'selves,' which people with a shared history and ancestry hold in common. Within the terms of this definition, our cultural identities reflect the common historical experiences and shared cultural codes which provide us, as 'one people,' with stable, unchanging, and continuous frames of reference and meaning, beneath the shifting divisions and vicissitudes of our actual history" (234). As Hildi Froese Tiessen ("Artist" 228) and Ann Hostetler ("Cultural" 42) have noted, this understanding of cultural identity is clearly the dominant, if unspoken, assumption behind many discussions of the Mennonite community and its literary culture. Suggestions that literature is able to relay "the heart and soul, the universal essence of Mennonite ethnic experience," as Al Reimer claims of Arnold Dyck's work ("Introduction," *Collected Works* 3: 6), are transparent appeals to this first form of cultural identity. Although critical work drawing on Hall's essay often disparages this version of cultural identity as being essentializing and naive, Hall himself does not dismiss it, recognizing that it "offer[s] a way of imposing an imaginary coherence on the experience of dispersal and fragmentation, which is the history of all enforced diasporas" (235). As his example from the African diaspora demonstrates, this form of identity is often spatialized in the form of a mythic geography of origin. "Africa, the name of the missing term," Hall writes, is "the great aporia, which lies at the center of our cultural identity and gives it a meaning which, until recently, it lacked" (235). Although the example is from a context that is obviously irreducibly different from the Russian Mennonite experience, Hall's first form of cultural identity gives me reason to pause anew over the ways in which the narrative arc of *order, chaos,* and *flight* that characterizes the Mennonites' 1920s migration narrative implicitly position the Russian experience as an origin for the Mennonite community in Canada. When novels begin their renderings of the community's migration narrative with the glories of the Commonwealth in Russia, they affirm that landscape as an originary point, as a "mythic geography of origin" that serves to ground that community both literally and figuratively.

Blue Mountains, however, complicates this narrative arc. Although its representation of the Russian experience does start in the Commonwealth, it begins *after* the collapse of the colonies; there is no return to the so-called Golden Years that would colour this originary landscape in nostalgia. More important, however, is the fact that Wiebe's novel does not begin with the Russian story at all. Instead, it begins with the story of Frieda Friesen, a Kanadier woman whose father immigrated from Russia half a century before the Commonwealth's collapse, who was born in Canada, and who now lives in Paraguay. Working against the practice of folding all of Russian Mennonite history into the Russländer narrative—the logic wherein the 1920s story is taken as the "tragic curve of all Mennonites" (Reimer, "Coming" 263) and the "foundation for a new marking of the past by Mennonite refugees" (Urry, "Memory" 39)—Wiebe's reintroduction of the Kanadier story into the 1920s experience insists on the deep internal differences often effaced in the process of accepting Russia as the "great aporia" at the heart of the Mennonite community. Frieda's story reminds readers that, if the Russian experience occasionally threatens to overdetermine the community's larger narrative, Russian Mennonite identity both precedes and exceeds the boundaries drawn by its reliance on this break event. In refusing to allow the Russian experience to project an imaginary coherence onto all the Russian Mennonites across the diaspora—and by refusing to replace it with any other experience—Wiebe risks losing the community's coherence altogether. Indeed, much of the novel's complexity and incoherence, I suggest, can be read as a direct result of his refusal to ground Mennonite identity in Hall's first form of cultural identity.

Against this first notion of a shared essence that underlies all superficial differences, Hall posits another version of cultural identity. "This second position," he writes, "recognizes that, as well as the many points of similarity, there are also critical points of deep and significant *difference* which constitute 'what we really are'; or rather—since history has intervened—'what we have become'" (236). Since claims of "one experience, one identity" can never be made about cultural communities in general, and diasporic communities in particular, with any degree of precision, Hall concludes that cultural identities must always be understood as "'becoming' as well as 'being'" (236). Suggesting that this second notion of identity better explains the experience of diaspora, he insists on "a conception of 'identity' which lives with and through, not despite, difference; by *hybridity*. Diaspora identities," he writes, "are those which are constantly producing and reproducing themselves anew, through transformation and difference" (244). Reading the splintered narrative of *Blue Mountains* through the lens of this second form of cultural identity reveals the ways in which the novel presents the contrasts among the Mennonites of Canada, Russia, and Paraguay not as barriers to a Mennonite cultural identity but as the differences that constitute it.

Hall turns to Jacques Derrida's concepts of *différance* and *trace* to illustrate the way that the "meaning" or "essence" of a cultural identity manages to signify while being deferred, and suggests that any understanding of a stable or even recognizable identity "depends on the contingent and arbitrary stop—the necessary and temporary 'break' in the infinite semiosis of language" (240). Hall's reading sheds further light on the function of the break event in communal narratives: rather than serving as a direct reference to a historical event in a well-defined communal history, here the break becomes the (not entirely "arbitrary") moment in which the repetition of differences is frozen just long enough to stop the chain of deferral and establish a referent that can ground a communal identity. In this reading, the referent for the various strains of the migration narrative is not a historical event at all, but rather a highlighted trace of the ongoing process of its deferral. "The past continues to speak to us," Hall writes, "[b]ut it no longer addresses us as a simple, factual 'past,' since our relation to it [...] is always-already 'after the break'" (237).

Hall's essay, as I noted earlier, is a foundational text in both diaspora studies and cultural studies, and its central claims—that cultural identity is best understood not as an essence but as an interplay of difference, that it is marked by hybridity and constant revision—are well established in Canadian critical discourse. Indeed, "diaspora" itself has become a central term in Canadian literary studies over the past two decades, as critics have argued that the logic of official multiculturalism reifies static, essentialized notions of identity that do not reflect the fluidity of diasporic identities. However, I want to argue that the critique enabled by Hall's work retains a fresh significance in the context of my study for at least two reasons. First, as I have suggested, identifying a text as reflecting a diasporic identity takes on a new significance when it is set against a collection of novels retelling the same communal story using alternative models of migration and dramatically different narrative structures. Since individuals in a diaspora can always imagine their communities otherwise—as exiles, immigrants, nomads, and so on—critics must consider what is at stake not only in how a diasporic community is represented, but also whether the community is represented as a diaspora at all. Second, if Hall's essay is regularly invoked for its recognition of how diasporic identity is characterized by hybridity and transformation, the larger implications of his insistence on difference as the source of communal identity often go overlooked. While it might be true that the literary representations of diasporic communities are often characterized by cultural hybridization, the widespread adoption of hybridity as the privileged and empowered marker of diasporic identity can overshadow the fact that, inasmuch as all diasporas by definition seek to maintain shared memories and histories across time and space, they are defined at least as much by what they (attempt to) retain as they are by their fluidity and hybridity. In diaspora, the process of hybridization through difference is always lived in tension with what we might call the community's insistence on the same, which draws on Hall's "first" form of cultural identity. As Hall points out in a much less discussed passage of the essay, without this "dialogic relationship," a cultural identity loses the coherence necessary for it to be recognizable.

In much the same way, the argument that diasporic experience results in fractured narratives has become a well-worn critical trope, to the point that Laura Moss recently levelled a moratorium on such a finding, announcing that it has lost its political efficacy because of its repetition (24). The efficacy of such critiques, however, must be judged not by the repetition of the claim (which presumably works to establish its validity if not its novelty) but by its function within the particular contexts of its operation. Although *Blue Mountains* is certainly not alone in using a disjointed narrative to demonstrate both the fractured nature of diasporic identities and the fragile bond of the concept that works to tie them together, it is more unique in the way in which it uses this disjointed narrative to call the efficacy and ethics of the diasporic bond into question. Wiebe's rendering of the Mennonite diaspora ultimately presents the "imaginary coherence" that it projects onto the community as yet another totalizing gesture that does not accurately reflect the difference that characterizes the individuals it claims to represent.

To explore the tensions among repetition, difference, and identity more closely, I want to follow Miller one step further by turning to Gilles Deleuze. Deleuze argues that, while philosophers from Plato onward have laboured to grasp things "in themselves" and relegated the notion of difference to a transitory position between "things," it is difference itself that is primary. Identity, he suggests, is but the by-product of a repetition that can return only difference. In a key passage in *The Logic of Sense* (2004), Deleuze describes two competing understandings of identity: "Let us consider two formulas: 'only that which resembles differs' and 'only differences can resemble each other.' These are two distinct readings of the world: one invites us to think difference from the standpoint of a previous similitude or identity; whereas the other invites us to think similitude and even identity as the product of a deep disparity. The first reading precisely defines the world of copies or representations; it posits the world as icon. The second, contrary to the first, defines the world of simulacra; it posits the world itself as phantasm" (299). These two ways of reading the world are clearly echoed in Hall's two forms of identity (though Hall's essay attempts to position them in a dialogic relationship, whereas, for Deleuze, they are mutually exclusive). While it is true that a given identity can never be fully and identically replicated, and so what would return in its repetition is always slightly different, this is not Deleuze's primary insight here. For Deleuze, the differential structure of identity means that "the accretions and deletions" that I have identified as marking the negotiation or debate of communal identity through a repeated narrative are not, in fact, differences *within* a communal identity at all. Since repetition, however construed, can only ever return difference, communal identity is better understood as the product of that debate, rather than its subject.

Deleuze's work shows how Wiebe's novel, which explicitly decentres the Russian experience even as it focuses on it, manages to present a cultural identity through a deeply disjointed and disparate text. From a Deleuzian perspective, the multiple narratives of the novel do not reflect an "ideal of showing all sides" (L. Weaver 20) or "all sides taken separately'" (Redekop, "Translated" 103), and they certainly do not "reveal essential aspects of the Mennonite quest" (Keith, *Epic Fiction* 6). These implicitly Platonic readings seem to read the novel's multiple narratives as offering a set of perspectives on a single "true" or "essential" Mennonite identity. Through Deleuze, however, we can see not only that there is no "true" or "essential" Mennonite identity against which each of the competing snapshots offered in *Blue Mountains* can be measured, but also that the very possibility of Mennonite identity is constructed by the differences among these portraits. "All identities," Deleuze suggests, "are only simulated, produced as an optical 'effect' by the more profound game of difference and repetition" (*Difference* ix). Whether it is the collection of stories that makes up Wiebe's novel or the larger body of texts that makes up the various narrative strains in this study, each retelling or story contributes to a larger Russian Mennonite identity not because it adds yet another iteration of the same story to the pile, then, but precisely because it does not.

Meta-Narrative and Time

I began this chapter by tracing the complexity of the first twelve chapters of *The Blue Mountains of China* at some length, including the way that Wiebe exaggerates the differences between each chapter by withholding setting, temporal, or character cues, thereby refusing to immediately ground the characters or narrative by appeals to their place in a larger constructed identity. Because it is clear that the characters in the novel understand themselves to share a cultural identity that transcends national and generational boundaries, I highlighted the network of largely hidden connections between characters and chapters that can be understood as the threads that hold together the novel's portrait of a Mennonite diaspora. Through Hall and Deleuze, however, it becomes clear that to focus on teasing out the latent connections between chapters is to risk missing the implications of the massive and obvious differences between them. Following Deleuze's shift from an understanding of repetition in which "only that which resembles differs" toward an understanding in which "only differences can resemble each other," I want to suggest that the novel encourages readers to interrogate the assumption of an underlying unity of identity beneath the differences of each chapter, and to recognize the ways in which that identity itself is the product of these differences.

The repetitive structure of *Blue Mountains* can be understood as exemplifying what Deleuze calls the "optical 'effect'" by which repetition and difference construct identity. The disparate chapters appear to be united through the repeated markers of their shared identity, yet a closer reading shows the ways in which this repetition points not to a common source but to the "world of simulacra" (Deleuze, *Logic* 299). To take one seemingly benign example, consider the repeated place and character names in the novel. Wiebe shows that as the Russian Mennonites have dispersed around the globe, they have often used the same names for their villages wherever they settle. "[W]herever Mennonites had lived," his narrator explains, "whether in Canada or as far back as story and strong memory could depend on Russia, there had always been such village names: Gartental, Blumenau, Rosenfeld, Friedensruh" (116). After establishing repeated character and place names, Wiebe builds upon these repetitions by staging parallel scenes in which similarly named characters move through these similarly named settings. Although the actual characters and contexts are different, Chapters 2 and 3 show a man named Jakob Friesen (IV in Chapter 2, V in Chapter 13) released by the GPU and returning to his family estate in Gnadenfeld, Russia, only to find his family gone and the farm irrevocably changed; Chapters 4 and 12 both tell the stories of someone named Samuel Reimer (Sr. and Jr.) attempting to leave his home country (Russia, Canada) in response to violence (Russian Revolution, Vietnam War). Chapters 9 and 11 both show a man named David Epp (II, III) on a lonely highway (one in China, the other in Paraguay) struggling to live out a genuine faith, while Chapters 2 and 10 both show opportunistic Mennonite men (Jakob IV, Dennis Willms) unscrupulously capitalizing on the spoils of World War I, after their countries (Russia, Canada) have exempted them from fighting for reasons of conscience.

It is possible, as Eva-Marie Kröller shows, to read this type of internal repetition as an affirmation of the community identity at the expense of the individual. "The recurrence of names may be exasperating, but such confusions of identity are symptomatic of a culture which places little store in an individual bereft of her people," she writes. "Mennonites have rarely been afforded the luxury of a safe and stable homeland, and yet they maintain a sense of belonging and family cohesiveness over long periods of separation" (275). Through Deleuze, however, one can see this echo chamber of repetition not simply as the product of a shared identity but also as the simulacrum of its internal difference. What is more, Wiebe insists on the importance of these differences by showing, on a structural level, the confusion that results from assuming their transferability. In Chapter 2, for example, the GPU arrives at the Friesen *hof* and demands to see the "kulak" Jakob Friesen (IV), only to have his son announce, truthfully, "I'm Jakob Friesen" (18). Although they initially insist on the difference—"Not you, you ass!" (19)—they ultimately take the son (Jakob Friesen [V]) in his father's place. The incommensurability behind this mask of similarity haunts the father for the remainder of his life. Similarly, the repeated place names that seem to point to a shared psychogeography quickly become a simulacrum that unravels, rather than supports, a distinct identity. Take, for example, the fact that the Mennonites emigrating from Canada to Paraguay decide to name their new village Schoenbach before anyone has visited the site (116). The incongruity between the name itself, which means "beautiful river," and the desolate plot of desert to which it is given, underscores the distance between signifier and signified in the discourse of communal identity. "[T]he village name simply named again their thoughtless faith," the narrator explains. "A thoughtful man hauling his family through the cactus brush [...] would have cried, or laughed, at such a name" (117). In fact, the novel makes clear that the names of such communities are nearly empty of significance—"Each word was a place; it contained no word context for anyone; it was," the narrator announces (116)—demonstrating how communal markers lose their referentiality in repetition and become markers of little more than the idea of identity. Like my earlier attempt to insist on the links among characters, settings, and chapters in the name of a diasporic identity, any attempt to draw ultimate meaning from these superficial similarities in names is to ignore the obvious incommensurability of their referents, and the world of differences that cannot be effaced through a simple insistence on the same.

The destabilizing repetition that functions at the level of place and character names also functions at the level of the 1920s narrative itself. Take, for example, the passage with which I opened this chapter, in which Franz tells

John the story of their families' escape from the Soviet Union via Moscow. This specific story gets repeated throughout the novel, and a few more details are necessary to understand the function of its repetition. In November 1929, Franz explains to John, his family fled the Mennonite colonies in the dead of night and travelled to Moscow. Elizabeth's father, Helmut Driediger, had devised a plan for the thousands of Mennonites who had descended on Moscow to sign a mass petition pleading for permission to emigrate to Canada and to threaten that, if permission was not granted, they would all gather at Red Square and "starve to death before the eyes of all the world" (82). Franz's job was to collect signatures from the Mennonites who were quietly hiding in rooms around the city and to deliver the petition to the Soviet officials. One night, however, the GPU arrived at the apartment where the Epp and Friesen families were staying, and they hauled Jakob (IV) out into the night. When John's father, Samuel (Sr.), cruelly praised God for answering his personal prayers for safety, Franz's father rebukes the man's selfishness, retorting, "I think Mrs. Friesen was praying, too" (80). It becomes clear, at this point, that it is not that John had never heard the story of his parents' flight out of Moscow before, but rather that he had never heard *this* version, the one in which his family's safety comes at the cost of another man's freedom. Franz's retelling of this history causes John to reconsider his relationship to the larger Mennonite community, and precipitates a crisis of conscience that proves central to the novel's conclusion.

Franz's retelling of his experience in Moscow is only one of many iterations of this story in the novel, and Wiebe draws attention to the repeated story *as a story* by showing it being told and retold by nearly everyone with a connection to the event—as well as by some without any connection at all: Samuel (Jr.), already born and in Moscow with his parents in 1929, tells his version of this story to his pastor in Canada (211–12); Jakob (IV) shares the story of his arrest with Elizabeth when the two meet on a plane late in the novel (230) and another part of the story with an unnamed prisoner in Siberia (133–38); Elizabeth tells the young Canadian Mennonite, Irene, the story of her and her father's participation in the flight from Moscow (254); and John, Samuel's son, recounts the story to Jakob (IV) near the novel's end, unaware of Jakob's (IV) sensitive role in it (267). Even the Kanadier Frieda Friesen retells this story as part of the account of how her daughter came to marry a Russländer (176). But if each of these retellings of this particular moment in the 1920s migration demonstrates how the community is able to retain a sense of cohesion across decades and continents, Wiebe also shows how, in their more immediate meanings, they remain irreducibly different. For Franz, who recalls his own dangerous part in the migration plan, it is a story of his own bravery and his father's quiet faith; for Samuel (Jr.), who remembers his father's selfishness, and his brother John, who hears of it from Franz, it is a story of cowardice; for Elizabeth, it is a story of her father's wisdom and the background of her cosmopolitanism; for Jakob (IV), it is a story that recounts his betrayal of his only son. Again, there may be only one history, but there are many stories.

Although the retold story signifies differently for each of those who participated in the history that it recounts, these differences collapse into the return of the superficial "same" for those Mennonites who later adopt the flight from Moscow as a part of their heritage. John says that the Mennonite children in Canada rarely hear about this story—but how seriously can we take this claim, coming, as it does, in a Canadian novel?—while Franz suggests that, in Paraguay, it is the "one big thing." "Here the youth hear it all over," Franz explains. "Just a little while ago on the street in Zentrale I heard a boy, maybe sixteen, say to his friend, 'But in Russia *we* did it *this* way!' He knew all about Russia, and irony. At sixteen. Here they hear too much about Russia" (65). The youth in Paraguay, much too young to have been in the Mennonite Commonwealth themselves, have turned the Mennonites' Russian story into an ironic marker of parental nostalgia that nonetheless works to affirm a common identity of which they understand themselves to be a part. Against the backdrop of difference represented by the story as it functions for Franz, John, Sam, Elizabeth, Jakob, and Frieda, the story appears to have lost its differential quality and has begun to participate in the larger Mennonite simulacrum of character and place names, whereby the story's ultimate referent is not a shared history at all, but simply the communal identity in itself.

Given the correlation between narrative and time, it is little surprise to find that the novel's interrogation of narrative includes a corresponding interrogation of temporality. Earlier I suggested that, though one of the immediate experiences of reading *Blue Mountains* is a temporal disorientation, the story of the Mennonites' 1920s migration actually appears to structure the novel into a largely linear, chronological narrative. The operative word, it turns out, is *appears*. As Penny Van Toorn points out, the "narrative in *Blue Mountains of China* repeatedly turns back on itself, despite the forward-moving chronological progress of the historical narrative" (96). Much as the network of obscure details or superficial similarities should not blind readers to the lived disunity of the diaspora, the coherent linear temporality offered by the key migration narrative should not blind them to the fractured and shifting temporality of the characters' lived experiences. That is, it is solely the 1920s story that projects a coherent, linear temporality onto the novel and its characters; the novel's plot, which includes the time of the lived experiences of the characters retelling the story, fluctuates dramatically. For example, while the story that Franz tells John about the Mennonites in Moscow in 1929 (Chapter 4) is chronologically in order between the account of Jakob (V)'s return to the *hof* (Chapter 2) and Elizabeth's account of their migration to Paraguay (Chapter 5), the date that Franz actually tells this story to John in the Paraguayan jungle is many decades later. In much the same way, if we refuse to excise the four chapters of Frieda's story in the name of textual coherence and a unified cultural identity, the chronology offered by the 1920s story falls apart further. Frieda's remembrances, which include experiences set in several countries over half a century, show an alternative temporality within the Mennonite community that is never fully integrated into the diasporic identity constructed in the novel. Again, it is only by emphasizing the retelling of the 1920s story—the projection of this key story over the varying lived realities of the novel's many characters—that the larger imagined community gains a sense of coherence through linear, temporal progression.

The way in which the coherent temporality of the novel is revealed to have been invested in the artifice of the Mennonite Commonwealth is elegantly embedded in the first pages of the novel's representation of the colonies' collapse. On his return to his abandoned and ransacked Mennonite *hof*, Jakob (V) notes that the family's Kroeger clock—which I identified earlier as a quintessential marker of the Russian Mennonite experience—has stopped, its hands frozen to mark the exact moment of the attack: nine minutes after eleven (20, 35). Jakob draws up the weights to restart the clock, but he neglects to set the pendulum swinging, and it still reads nine after eleven when a Russian takes it as part of the collectivization process (43). Without the structure and steady progression of the orderly Russian Mennonite world, Jakob's chapter dissolves into a broken stream-of-consciousness narrative that ends with his death.

Although *Blue Mountains* offers a portrayal of a diasporic, transnational community, then, its emphasis on the massive differences that function to build that cultural identity calls its cohesion into question. Although the characters of the novel return repeatedly to the markers of the community, including the 1920s narrative itself, in an effort to ground themselves in an overarching cultural identity, it is only the process of returning itself that works to maintain its stability. The tension between the shared communal identity and the differences that threaten to break it apart reaches its apex in the novel's final chapter, in which many of the central characters come together for a brief moment of unity that, I will argue, ultimately serves to emphasize their differences. Yet, if the Deleuzian lesson of *Blue Mountains* is that "[a]ll identities are only simulated, produced as an optical 'effect' by the more profound game of difference and repetition" (*Difference* ix), the very un-Deleuzian lesson offered by the novel's final chapter is that there is a new form of communal identity that is able to transcend this illusion. Perhaps not surprisingly, it does so by asking one to "think different" (269).

On the Way

After twelve chaotic chapters emphasizing the differences and distances between characters and problematizing the concept of communal identity, the final chapter of *The Blue Mountains of China* arrives as a surprise. John is carrying a large wooden cross across Canada, spurred into action by his father's selfish spirituality and his brother's sudden death. Elizabeth and Jakob (IV), who meet by chance on a plane from Toronto to Calgary and promptly discover their shared past, decide to drive out and meet John after stumbling across a newspaper article tracing his strange journey. While the two are chatting with John on the side of the Trans-Canada Highway, Dennis Willms (now Williams) and his family happen to be driving by in their Cadillac, and they stop as well. Together they have a meal on the shoulder of the highway, speaking in Low German as they chat and unravel their shared history of migration and their common relatives. Given the formal experimentation that characterizes the earlier chapters, it is hardly surprising to find that the chapter has been roundly criticized. Ina Ferris calls it "a striking reversal of method and perception" (83), while Penny Van Toorn says that it changes "a polyphonic history into a monologic trial" (69). Indeed, it is difficult to deny that the novel's denouement feels out of place in a text that is otherwise so innovative.

To the extent that the novel maintains—one might even say contains—its disparate and competing voices as the heterogeneity of a diasporic community, the conclusion can be read as a confirmation of an undercurrent that has been latent throughout the text. The reassertion of narrative coherence parallels the reunion of these Mennonite characters, and, even when the largely linear, coherent prose of the chapter begins to fragment into a cacophony of voices during their brief reunion, it serves to show how the fragmentary and partial portraits of these characters throughout the novel are, in fact, part of a single conversation. Similarly, the shared language, history, and kinship ties seem to affirm a distinct identity that lies beneath the differences that have dominated much of the text. Indeed, Wiebe even writes that a "sudden oneness, like a still lap of heat on a breezy day," comes across the group (251). The novel's final chapter, then, appears not only to recognize but also to confirm the persistence of a diasporic Mennonite identity that arises through the interplay of repetition and difference of the preceding chapters.

It does not, however, ultimately endorse that identity. In spite of the community members' shared markers of identity, the chapter offers no promise that the links that have bound the community thus far will be sufficient to keep it together. It is John Reimer's decision to carry the cross that brings these characters together, remember, and Reimer is strongly critical of the Mennonite community, roundly condemning Dennis's wealth, Elizabeth's arrogance, and the children's complacent, commerce-based worldview. Moreover, their moment of unity takes place on a highway, in a language that the children cannot speak, and with key characters missing. After the police arrive and break up their meeting as a safety hazard, all but Jakob promptly leave John alone on the highway. Most telling of all, however, is the conversation between the young John and the elderly Jakob in the novel's final two pages, where John levels a stinging criticism of what might be called a diasporic Mennonite imaginary. "You know the problem with Mennonites?" he asks. "They've always wanted to be Jews. To have land God had given them for their very own, to which they were called; so even if someone chased them away, they could work forever to get it back. Wherever they got pushed, or they pull themselves, they try to prove to themselves they are building that land" (271). Against this land-based communal identity, John argues that "Jesus just said, 'I'm going to make a place ready for you and then I'll come and get you. You wait'" (272). Hildi Froese Tiessen rightly points to the final pages of *Blue Mountains*, including this passage, as evidence that the novel critiques the idea of a Mennonite diaspora ("'Well'"). However, she has twice referenced this passage as a part of a larger argument that "the religion and cultural orientation, the conflicted projection of imagined homelands in Mennonite writing, [...] would suggest that the term diaspora might very well remain a troubled term for Mennonites and critics of Mennonite writing" ("'Well'"; see also "What Remains" 12). Yet the passage's critique of a diasporic Mennonite identity is that it runs counter to the religious foundations of Anabaptism, not that it does not exist. Indeed, as John makes clear, the critique is necessary precisely because it is so common for Russian Mennonites to imagine themselves in diasporic terms. The exchange between Jakob and John that immediately follows the passage above—"They came close in Russia," Jakob responds; "Closest there, I think. Unfortunately," John answers (272)—reflects back on the larger novel, in which many of the Mennonites hang on to the Russian experience in precisely the fashion that John is critiquing.

Another way to understand the unifying gesture at the novel's close, however, is to recognize it as a call for the Mennonites to release this diasporic identity and imagine themselves into a new form of religious community. After all, John not only criticizes the other Mennonites in this passage, he also preaches to them, rebuking them for their superficial focus on wealth or academic knowledge and explicitly calling on them to repent. Jesus was "on earth to lead a revolution! [...] a revolution for social justice" (257), he says, going on to invite his Mennonite visitors to join what he calls a "Jesus society" (258). In fact, Van Toorn reads the novel's conclusion as projecting a divine, or theological, order onto the novel, which she sees less as a "reversal" of the larger text than a "revelation" of its underlying religious message (69). It is a reading implicitly encouraged by Ervin Beck, who convincingly demonstrates that John's preaching in the final chapter is a direct engagement with "The Original Revolution," a sermon by Mennonite theologian John Howard Yoder. Calling John a "unifying device," Beck shows that his sermon is, in fact, deeply indebted to Yoder's essay—to the point that parts of it are nearly word-for-word quotations ("Politics").[7] Importantly, the Jesus society advocated by John is not an attempt to restore the "true" (i.e., theological) meaning of Mennonite identity. Although several of his claims might be recognizable as having their roots in Anabaptism (as we would expect, given its connection to Yoder's work), he makes no direct reference to either Mennonites or Anabaptism in his sermon—just as the novel provides no indication that there was a "purer" or "more proper" earlier period of Russian Mennonite identity to which they might return. For this reason, I would resist Beck's conclusion that the final chapter unifies the novel by "show[ing] how all prior Mennonite experience bears fruit, finally, in the public peacemaking and church-renewing activities of John Reimer" ("Politics"). To the contrary, it seems far from clear that "*all* prior Mennonite experience" has borne fruit in the novel, and, if there is a church being renewed in the closing pages, it is not defined by Mennonite parameters in any recognizable way. Rather than "renewing" it, John mocks the "many different directions of the Mennonite church," saying that "all of them [are just] making sure they stay alive, [with] no significant difference between many of them" (256). In fact, the only passage of scripture that he cites in his sermon—where Mary notes that "the Mighty God has [...] stretched out his mighty arm and scattered the proud people with all their plans" (257)—seems to implicitly render the diasporic movement of the Mennonites a divine punishment for their arrogance.

Far from redeeming the Mennonite community through an appeal to the purity of its religious past, John's vision of a Jesus society posits a surprisingly Deleuzian demand on its members in asking them to be open to an entirely different form of thought. In order to join this new movement, one needs "a new attitude toward everything, toward everybody. Toward nature, toward the state in which you happen to live, toward women, toward slaves, toward all and every single thing," John insists. "Because this is a Jesus society and you repent, not by feeling bad, but by *thinking different. Different*" (258). Indeed, as Magdalene Falk Redekop writes, the new society that John announces is characterized by a "constant willingness to be diminished [and an] openness to difference and change" ("Translated" 116). This is not to suggest that John's Christian vision is strictly Deleuzian, of course, but rather to point out that the novel's surprising conclusion attempts to locate a transcendent possibility in the very function of difference that it has also recognized as the fragile foundation of cultural identity.

Although Wiebe's novel examines, and attempts to place aside, an imagined Mennonite identity based on the Russian experience in favour of a Jesus society not bound by shared historical narratives, it also demonstrates just how thoroughly enmeshed the Mennonites are in such stories—nicely illustrating Stuart Hall's claim that "[i]dentities are the names we give to the different ways we are positioned by, and position ourselves within, the narratives of the past" (236). That is, for all its critique of the idea of a cultural identity that spans territory and time, for all its insistence on individual voices and divergent experiences, *Blue Mountains,* like each of the novels in this study, ultimately rewrites and reinscribes the Russian experience as the break event for Canadian Mennonites, constructing a "collective protagonist" out of that community even as it calls that community into question (Korkka 24). As I noted in the introduction and reiterated in the chapter on Birdsell's *The Rossländer*, any engagement with a foundational communal narrative—even the writing against it—ultimately serves to affirm its importance. This is why, in Myrna Kostash's critique of the representation of the Russian (i.e., Ukrainian) experience in Mennonite Canadian literature, her imaginary Mennonite correspondent insists that the only way to break the hold of a narrative is not to correct or critique it but to refuse to write it, to simply ignore it altogether. "But you do not think that all stories must be told," she writes. "It is the only way out of myth, you say—this leave-taking without story or significance" (145). Even if, as Kostash goes on to suggest, such logic is the privilege of those whose stories are already well accounted for, it is true at least in this respect: there is no literary or critical engagement with a communal narrative of a break event that is not immediately and simultaneously redeployed in its group-defining role. It is possible to redefine its parameters, perhaps, but it turns out you simply cannot write your way out of a communal story.

Conclusion

In a novel that structurally parallels the larger body of novels repeating the Russian Mennonite narrative, it seems fitting that Wiebe closes by opening onto yet another retelling of the 1920s story. In the cacophony of conversation taking place during the novel's passing moment of unity along the Trans-Canada Highway, Wiebe inserts a snippet of Elizabeth's brief exchange with Irene, the daughter of the wealthy Dennis Willms. The reader is given just enough of their conversation to know that Elizabeth is retelling the story of how she and her family escaped from the Soviet Union by boat when she was roughly Irene's age (251–54). Having already read Elizabeth's story several times by this point, and having seen the violence that precipitated their narrow escape, readers should immediately recognize that Irene completely misunderstands the story that she hears, and that Elizabeth allows the young Canadian to shape her difficult past into a more positive story:

> "...in Moscow and went on a big ship all the way to South America?" Irene's eyes shone. "That Latin music!"
>
> "The orchestra wasn't exactly the Tijuana Brass," said Elizabeth dryly, and Irene flicked a look. "I was a little younger than you now." Elizabeth shifted quickly with a smile. "And I had some fun.

Especially crossing the equator—"

"Oh, I've read about that, they throw everybody for the first time in the ocean, oh, it'd just be the supremes, traveling on a luxurious ship, to Brazil and Rio and Capulco!"

Smiling, Elizabeth did not correct her. (254–55)

The look that Irene gives Elizabeth prompts her to change course, even though both must know that the story she is telling is losing her intended meaning. When Irene interrupts to say that she has heard that passengers on cruise ships take celebratory swims at the equator, Elizabeth's story has been turned nearly inside out, for the young Elizabeth *did* fall off the boat and into the ocean near the equator during their migration, but it was an accident, and she nearly drowned. The story of the break event, it seems clear, is still being told. But what it will come to mean, and whether it will be sufficient to bind an imagined community together, remain to be seen.

Conclusion

On Reading Migration in Canadian Literature

I began this book by briefly drawing on diaspora studies to build an argument about key migrations functioning as break events, but I quickly moved away from diaspora as a critical frame in an effort to trace the wider range of ways in which Mennonite Canadian literature has imagined the 1920s migration experience. The critical lexicon of displacement, I suggested (which includes not only *diaspora* but also related concepts such as *nomad, exile,* and *immigrant*), must be recognized as both sociological terms of classification and critical models of interpretation. That is, in literary studies, such concepts function in both descriptive and prescriptive modes. While the former is always an act of interpretation, in the latter they risk projecting their own framing assumptions onto histories that can, and often are, imagined otherwise. Although the Mennonites' 1920s migration is clearly presented as a diaspora narrative in Wiebe's *The Blue Mountains of China,* for example, it is the only novel in this study to imagine a Mennonite community beyond a strict Canada-Ukraine binary. Dick's *Out of the Storm* presents the same history as an exodus narrative, in which a benevolent God facilitates an escape from the colonies to Canada, while Birdsell's *Children of the Day,* which picks up the narrative of *The Russländer* and explores the impact of the Vogt family massacre upon Sara's family in Canada, offers a narrative of immigration. Dyck's *Lost in the Steppe* only briefly considers a flight to "America," but, when set within this repeated narrative, its nostalgia for a lost world reads as a narrative of exile. Rather than attempt to respond to the various rewritings of the community's break event exclusively through the central tropes of contemporary diaspora studies, I have worked to disaggregate the larger communal narrative into its various strains of emphasis. The result, I hope, is a methodology that loosely reflects the "mode of thinking" for which Iain Chambers calls in *Migrancy, Culture, Identity*: one that "is neither fixed nor stable, but […] open to the prospect of a continual return to events, to their re-elaboration and revision," while tracking the way in which "[h]istory is harvested and collected, to be assembled, made to speak, re-membered, re-read and rewritten" (3).

Although *Rewriting the Break Event* is primarily an exploration of a single history rewritten across Mennonite Canadian fiction, then, it can also be understood as an extended search for a methodology that actively estranges the conventions of critical engagements with migration literature in Canada. This self-conscious emphasis on methodology, along with my insistence on the importance of historicizing the emergence of Mennonite Canadian literature as a body of literature in order to better understand its shape and function, places my study firmly within what Smaro Kamboureli has recently identified as the "steady shift" in Canadian literary studies "toward a foregrounding of the situational and material conditions that influence the production of Canadian literary texts" ("Introduction" 1). Although I devoted substantial space in the introduction and first chapter to situating Mennonite writing within the institutionalization of Canadian literature, I went on to narrow my focus to close readings of individual texts. I will close this study with some final comments on rewriting the collapse of the Mennonite colonies, but I would first like to briefly locate my study back within the field of contemporary Canadian literary studies and, in particular, within Canadian diaspora studies.

As an effort to engage with minoritized bodies of literature while recognizing, in practical and critical terms, the heterogeneity that is masked by large ethnic, religious, or racialized titles, this study participates in a larger reconsideration of such terms that is currently under way in Canada.[1] I worry, along with Laura Moss, about the enduring trend of "interpreting texts based more upon who wrote them rather than what is written" (19), and about what she sees as contemporary postcolonial critics' poor habit of "reading fractally," or taking a single text as sociologically representative of the whole community (21). Along with critics such as Roy Miki, however, I remain reluctant to fully release titles such as "Asian Canadian literature" or "Black Canadian literature" or, in the case of this study, "Mennonite Canadian literature." It is true, as I argued in the introduction, that these are categories of convenience that do not correspond to any clearly defined collections of texts or communities and that, used uncritically, can limit literary discussions and tokenize authors. But because literature does not exist in a vacuum and because there is no neutral ground to which we might retreat—as if the larger concept of "Canadian literature" is somehow free from politics, or as if an ambiguously universal "literature" is not clearly structured along political, economic, racial, and national lines—they remain imperfect but powerful tools for engaging the social, political, and cultural aspects of literary texts. Given the ongoing function of race and racialization in Canada, the politics of bodies of literature minoritized on the basis of ethnicity will differ in important ways from those minoritized through the process of racialization; understanding and unpacking these differences require a methodological attention to the emergence, history, and ongoing function of such categories. When we forget that a term such as "Mennonite literature" is a critical construct with its own histories and politics, it is easy to fall into celebratory essentialisms that pigeonhole and short-change all involved: texts, authors, and readers. Used critically, however, by scholars willing to recognize and wrestle with the histories and politics inscribed within it, it retains its value as enabling important discussions on the circulation of literary texts in Canada.

A wider effort of tracing break events across Canadian literature has already begun as well, albeit under different terminology. Lily Cho, for example, has used a series of recent essays to begin a reading of Asian Canadian literature by focusing on the role of indentured labour. In "The Turn to Diaspora," Cho announces her effort to inject "back into the discussion the role of indenture as a formative event for contemporary Asian diaspora" (22). "Contrary to understanding indenture as an event in the past," she continues, "I suggest that Asian indenture is [...] formative of the present" (22). Similarly, in "Asian Canadian Futures: Diasporic Passages and the Routes of Indenture," she declares that "a rigorous exploration of the politics and culture of indenture and its aftermath needs to be at the centre of Asian Canadian literary studies" (183). Naming less a single historical moment than a set of conditions resulting in varied and complex histories, "indentured labour" becomes, for Cho, a privileged point of entry through which to mark the connections and contradictions of Asian diasporic communities both within and beyond Canada. In fact, Cho advocates for a consideration of diaspora in such a way that "enables connections" not only within complex and diverse diasporic communities but also *across* diasporas. Accordingly, much of her recent scholarship has been dedicated to establishing a "relationship between indenture and slavery, between Asian Canadian and black Canadian communities" ("Asian Canadian Futures" 191; see also "Underwater" 193). For Cho, then, a focus on indenture within the framework of diaspora enables a number of related but distinct turns: it offers an important point of entry into contemporary Asian Canadian diasporic culture and literature; it enables connections among diasporic communities in Canada; and it facilitates the mapping of a network of migrations and identifications that exceeds the national frame.[2]

Cho's work reflects the shifting ground of contemporary Canadian literary studies, on which diaspora has emerged as a key critical concept for a widespread reconsideration of the "cultural grammar" of the nation-state (Kim, McCall, and Singer). It is true, as Kamboureli notes (with a nod to Jonathan Kertzer), that it is "a national pastime for Canadianists to 'worry the nation'" ("Introduction" 5), but this pastime has recently returned with a renewed urgency and a critical difference. The turn of the millennium was marked by a number of high-profile pronouncements about the death of the nation-state and the suggestions about the irrelevancy of critical modes working at the intersection of culture and nations, including postcolonialism.[3] As Kamboureli and I argue in the preface to our collection *Shifting the Ground of Canadian Literary Studies*, however, the "widespread reassertion of 'national interests' in relation to issues of 'security' that followed the attacks on the World Trade Center on 11 September 2001, along with the collapse of the world's financial markets in 2008, has shown that pronouncements of the triumph of global capital and the corresponding death of the nation-state were hopelessly rash" (xii). The reassertion of the nation, however, has not been a straightforward return. As Canadian literary critics such as Kit Dobson and Jeff Derksen have shown, the relationship between nation and literature is now best understood not in opposition to the globalizing forces of contemporary capital but as a key avenue or scale within its broader logic.[4] Far from relegating nation-based critiques to the dustbin of history, then, the force of globalization has occasioned a rearticulation of trans- or non-national concepts through the nationalizing rubric of postcolonialism. In Canadian literary criticism, this has meant that while diasporic critique has occasionally been theorized as a means of working outside the claims of the nation, it has more often functioned as an extension of postcolonialism's long-standing critical engagement with the nation-state. Rinaldo Walcott's bold pronouncement that "self-conscious diasporic affiliations offer a way out of the mess that modern nation-states represent for black peoples" (20), for example, quickly gives way to the more localized insistence that "[d]iaspora sensibilities use the nation to make ethical claims and demands for social justice," that they "speak to nations' limitations" and demand that "nations be remade" (23). Similarly, many diasporic critiques by Canadian cultural and literary critics—from single-authored studies such as Walcott's *Black like Who? Writing Black Canada* and Kamboureli's *Scandalous Bodies* to edited collections such as *Cultural Grammars of Nation, Diaspora, and Indigeneity in Canada* (Kim, McCall, and Singer) and *Narratives of Citizenship: Indigenous and Diasporic Peoples Unsettle the Nation-State* (Fleischmann, Van Styvendale, and McCarroll)—are primarily levelled at and explicitly framed by the nation, rarely working to trace extensive connections to larger international diasporic communities. Ostensibly a trans- or even anti-national concept, in Canadian literary studies, diaspora has often been circumscribed by the national contexts of its expression, part of the larger critical project of worrying the nation.

Understanding the national(izing) context for Canadian diaspora studies is key to understanding why Mennonite Canadian literature fits rather uneasily within its frame. Although Cho encourages critics to seek connections across diasporic communities, for example, she goes on to caution strongly against what she sees as the indiscriminate use of diaspora as a critical frame. Even as she insists that she does not "wish to declare the limits" of the field or "claim it for anyone or anything," she also insists that critics must allow "the genealogy of [diaspora] to guide its application" and that it must "be understood within the long history of the term and within specific conditions of possibility" ("Turn" 12). Although it is not immediately evident what those conditions might be, they quickly become clear: Cho insists that diaspora, properly understood, "emerges from deeply subjective processes of racial memory," and she declares that she "want[s] to reserve diaspora for the underclass" ("Turn" 15, 19). Elsewhere she draws on the work of Richard Fung to make her claim clearer still. "[T]he study of diaspora in Canada," she suggests, "is [...] grounded in the specificity of racial formations" ("Underwater" 204).

In the context of Canadian literary studies, in which diaspora has emerged primarily through postcolonial studies and retains an attendant focus on race and racialization, a consideration of Mennonite literature as diasporic runs counter to the dominant critical discourse in part because of the "whiteness" of Mennonite identity.[5] Just as Daniel Coleman and Donald Goellnicht insisted that Mennonites ought not to be placed alongside "authors of Asian,

African, or Aboriginal descent" in Canadian literary studies as part of their argument that "some differences are more different than others," Cho's insistence that "not all elsewheres are equal" challenges the notion of a Mennonite Canadian diasporic literature or text ("Diasporic" 99, 100). However, given her gloss of the broadest, most geo-political meaning of the term—"almost everyone seems to agree that diaspora, in its most basic sense, refers to a scattering of peoples who are nonetheless connected by a sense of a homeland, imaginary or otherwise," she writes ("Turn" 12)—there seems little question that Canada's Russian Mennonites are, or at least have been, unproblematically diasporic.[6] The challenge, then, becomes negotiating the particular critical histories and contemporary contexts in which the relationship between the terms "Mennonite" and "diasporic" become contentious, and to recognize, along with critics like Kamboureli and Jennifer Bowering Delisle, the ways in which discussions of white diasporas in Canada remain implicated in the racialized politics of the field.[7] A consideration of Mennonite texts within diaspora studies, moreover, may help to reassert religion as a key element in the field. As Melina Baum Singer has recently noted, the racialized logic of diaspora studies in Canada has managed to "de-link" itself nearly completely from the term's foundational connection to Jewish identity, relegating Jewish diasporic experience to the field's "etymological *past*" (99). "[R]eligious differences have been downplayed in the redrawing of the construction of Canadian nativism," she writes, before accurately suggesting that, "in the post-9/11 North American political landscape, there is surely a renewed urgency to consider the play between religion, race, and home/land shaping white and non-white forms of belonging in Canada" (105). Informed by a long history of mass migrations, a complex interplay between theo/eschatological and geographical notions of homeland, and a contested relationship between ethnicity and religion, Mennonite literature productively interrogates the implicit boundaries of diaspora studies in Canada—even as the "genealogy of [diaspora studies'] emergence" in Canada places a productive pressure on the field of Mennonite literary studies, as well.

Part of the project of *Rewriting the Break Event* has been an effort to gently estrange the conventions of critical engagements with migration fiction in Canada. Just as Caren Kaplan writes that "[t]o question travel […] is to inquire into the ideological function of metaphors in discourses of displacement" (26), an examination of the Russian Mennonite migration narrative unavoidably opens an inquiry into the genealogy of critical terms in Canadian literary critique. To be clear, however, the methodology that I have developed here has emerged directly from my engagement with a very specific geo-political history and a particular literary tradition. As such, there is no question that it would need to be adapted, rather than simply adopted, to prove useful outside the immediate context of Mennonite Canadian writing. Nonetheless, I am hopeful that a focus on the narrative strains of a break event offers a valuable method of gathering together a body of texts that engages with important historical events without relying solely on the assumed biological markers of their authors. I am hopeful that by acknowledging the diversity of ways in which the community is imagined—and by taking it seriously enough to explore these differences at length through readings that attend closely to both the content and the structure of the texts themselves, along with the ongoing impacts of their social, political, and institutional contexts—we might gain new insights into the form and function of migration literature in Canada.

Midway through John Weier's *Steppe*, the narrator looks back with exasperation over the many pages that he has accumulated as part of his research into the Mennonite Commonwealth. "The story comes in bones and ruins, in shards and fragments, from a thousand sites and sources," he writes in his journal. "I search. Sometimes I discover" (3.1). Researching and writing this book has been a similar experience for me. It seems that in nearly every Mennonite journal, academic study, or novel that I open I stumble across another shard, another fragment, of the larger story about the Mennonites in Russia. And, like Weier's narrator, I have to concede that "[m]y theory of ruins and fragments is incomplete" (3.8). Of course, the incompleteness of this story is at the heart of my thesis, for it is through its repetition that this story has helped to imagine, debate, and sustain a particular form of Mennonite identity in Canada. The extent that I am correct in my thesis is the extent to which I can expect that this story, along with the task of tracing it through Canadian literature, will remain perpetually unfinished.

Perhaps it is not entirely surprising, then, that the authors whose work I have examined at length here have proven unwilling, or perhaps unable, to leave the stories of their novels behind. Sandra Birdsell, for example, wrote a formal sequel to *The Russländer*, continuing with the story of the Vogt sisters' experience in Canada in her next novel, *Children of the Day*. Like her sister Katherine, Sara tries to keep the story of her family's massacre from her Canadian family, but her daughter proves haunted by what Ross Chambers might call the "orphaned memory" of her grandparents' murder. The novel's portrait of an intergenerational transmission of trauma stands in notable contrast to Birdsell's emphasis on the individual experience in *The Russländer*. Al Reimer, Arnold Dyck, and Rudy Wiebe, meanwhile, have all taken the more unusual step of returning to write additional chapters for their novels. And, as with Birdsell's *Children*, these additional chapters not only extend the narratives of their respective novels but also revise the originals in significant ways. In 1998, for example, the literary executors of Dyck's estate in Germany published *Hochfeld: Ein Steppendorf im Bürgerkrieg: Ukraine 1918/19*, a lengthy additional section (perhaps better considered a sequel) to *Lost in the Steppe*. Although there is reason to question how thoroughly the novel represents Dyck's own vision,[8] *Hochfeld* provides an account of early Anabaptist history, along with a detailed exploration of the violence of the Commonwealth's collapse—both elements carefully avoided by the first five books or sections of his novel. Similarly, Reimer returned to the narrative of *My Harp Is Turned to Mourning* twenty-three years after its publication with "Mennonite Firebirds," the closing short story of his recent collection *When War Came to Kleindarp* (2008). This story, as the title implies, suggests a Canadian rebirth of the artistic vision that Wilhelm found but lost in the collapse of the Commonwealth. In "Mennonite Firebirds," the educated Wilhelm and Clara have managed to foster a small community of Mennonite artists who remain true to their faith, appearing to quietly affirm the migration that his earlier novel called into question. Finally, Wiebe returned to the narrative of *Blue Mountains* a full forty years after its original publication, adding a chapter entitled "Finally, the Frozen Ocean" to a recent collection of short fiction. Among the surprises in Wiebe's chapter is that the communal identity that appears to be so fragile in the closing pages of *Blue Mountains* continues to be intact decades later: the wandering John Reimer ultimately marries the naive Irene Williams, for example, while the elderly Elizabeth Driediger has returned to Ukraine, where she stumbles across a relative of Jakob Friesen (IV). The uniformity with which these novelists have returned to publish additional chapters to their novels illustrates the powerful position that the 1920s migration experience continues to hold in the imagination of the Mennonite community in Canada. What is more, it attests to the relentless processes of revision and reinvention that characterizes the nar-ration of break events more generally. These authorial returns are certainly remarkable, yet, if the foundational assumptions of this study are accurate, they should not come as a surprise.

I opened this book by noting that Weier's *Steppe* opens with this ques-tion: "Is this the beginning?" Near the end of the novel, his narrator offers an answer. "Stories don't begin, they never end," he writes in his journal (4.13). And in the closing pages, just after he has arrived in Ukraine and has begun wandering through the ruins of the former Commonwealth, he returns to this thought with a point that I will adopt as my closing lines. "Nothing ever ends," he insists. "I hope it stays that way. A story, once started, runs in all di-rections, takes a million shapes. It lives in blood and bone, in mind and matter. One story builds another story" (5.15).

Notes

Introduction: On Rewriting Migration in Canadian Literature

1   Unless otherwise noted, all references to Cohen's *Global Diasporas: An Introduction* are taken from the first edition (1997).

2   A few more detailed notes on nomenclature are necessary. In addition to the Russländer and Kanadier Mennonites, there have been more recent waves of Mennonite emigration out of Russia, including, notably, following World War II. These Mennonites are also conventionally included in the term "Russian Mennonites" but are rarely discussed directly in the novels that I take up here. For a more detailed discussion on the term "Russian Mennonite," see the section "Mennonites in Russia, Russian Mennonites," in Chapter 1 of this study. Given my focus on this particular aspect of Russian Mennonite history, my discussion of Mennonite identity in Canada does not extend to the Swiss Mennonites, who are prominent in southern Ontario. Although the Russian and Swiss Mennonites share a related theological tradition, their histories—literary and otherwise—differ substantially. Finally, though it is important to recognize that the Mennonite colonies were built on Russian territory and were destroyed as part of the Soviet Union, that land is now part of Ukraine, and the local population retained a strong sense of themselves as Ukrainian throughout the time of the Mennonite Commonwealth. I will try to be historically accurate in using "Russia" when referring to this area during the time of the Commonwealth, the "Soviet Union" or "USSR" when referring specifically to the period between 1922 and 1929, and "Ukraine" when referring to it today. As a general rule, however, I will adopt "Russia" and "Russian Mennonite" as terms that, already in circulation, demonstrate how the events in question have had impacts well beyond the particulars of their histories. Although there is a sense in which my use of these terms works to affirm their logic, I am hopeful that the larger project, which aims to interrogate their circulation, mitigates this process. I further examine what is at stake in some of these conventions later in this Introduction and in Chapter 1.

3   Although I lean heavily on the sociological tradition of diaspora studies for the vocabulary of the "break event," I should note my discomfort with some of its more rigid prescriptions for the field. In particular, Cohen's desire to establish a neat taxonomy for diaspora studies—complete with "ideal types"—strikes me as limiting in its implications. What is more, the "surprise" (151) that Cohen concedes in finding value in postmodern critiques of diaspora is more than undercut by the paternalism that saturates his engagement with it throughout. Although I appreciate his emphasis on the break event, my discussion of a Russian Mennonite diaspora, undertaken in my chapter on Rudy Wiebe's *The Blue Mountains of China*, will draw on a different stream of diaspora criticism.

4   Although it would take me too far afield here, I have explored the notion of founding violence elsewhere. See Zacharias, "'And Yet'" and "'Some Great Crisis.'"

5   On this point, I want to acknowledge and thank Jade Ferguson, whose questions
     on the appropriateness of diaspora studies as a blanket approach for Mennonite
     literature pushed me to consider the larger implications of what I am calling the
     "discourses of displacement." I explore this question further in the Conclusion.

6   For a brief discussion of this historical process, see Urry, "Memory."

7   Although Smucker is commonly considered a Canadian writer due to the success
     of her novels *Underground to Canada* (1977) and *Days of Terror* (1979), it is worth
     noting that she wrote *Henry's Red Sea* in 1955, over a decade before she emigrated
     from the United States.

8   Perhaps the most arresting pieces in *Tongue Screws and Testimonies* are Ian
     Huebert's "Views from a Pond" ink drawings, which reimagine a key image from
     the *Martyrs Mirror* in which Dirk Willems reaches back to rescue his pursuer, who
     has fallen through the ice of a frozen river. Huebert redraws the image, imitating
     the etched lines of the original while changing its central details: in one piece,
     Willems sits and contemplates his pursuer rather than helping him; in another,
     Willems hides behind a soldier who is pointing a gun at the pursuer; in a third,
     Willems is presented as Mickey Mouse with a fishing rod.

9   See Chatterjee; and Bhabha, "DissemiNation," in *The Location of Culture*.

10   Al Reimer's "The Print Culture of the Russian Mennonites 1870–1920" offers a
     valuable overview of Mennonite literacy in Russia, while Harry Loewen's "'Can
     the Son Answer for the Father?' Reflections on the Stalinist Terror" offers a brief
     but compelling discussion of several Mennonite authors in the former colonies
     who "welcomed the new era, expressing admiration for Lenin, singing the praises
     of Communist achievement, and protesting against oppression in capitalist
     countries" (82). James Urry's "The Reading Worlds of Russlaender and Kanadier
     Mennonites: Print, Libraries, and Readers in the Origins of Mennonite Creative
     Writing" establishes and explores the role of literacy and book culture in early
     Mennonite settlements in Canada. Urry speculates that "the fact that Mennonites
     have been writers, printers, publishers, as well as builders and users of libraries
     and keen readers for a long period" may "be of significance" to "the flowering of
     Mennonite writing in modern times" (143).

11   Wiebe's work (including her unpublished dissertation, "Restorying in Mennonite
     Canadian Writing: Implications for Narrative Inquiry,"), is much more
     narratological, and more focused on personal stories, than my own, and we focus
     on different authors. Although these and other methodological differences lead
     Wiebe to different conclusions than my own, her emphasis on the "restorying"
     of Mennonite narratives parallels my own interest in rewriting and serves as a
     valuable confirmation of the importance of repetition and narrative in Mennonite
     literature.

12   The phrase "Mennonite miracle" was coined by Andris Taskans, the (non-
     Mennonite) editor of *Prairie Fire*, a Winnipeg-based literary journal, and has
     often been repeated by critics and in popular discourse (quoted in Walker, "In
     Country"). A recent example is episode eighty-five of the CBC's *Words at Large*
     radio program. Entitled "The Mennonite Miracle: A Separation of Faith and
     Writing," the hour-long program consisted of a wide-ranging discussion between
     the host, Michael Enright, and authors David Bergen, Sandra Birdsell, and
     Miriam Toews.

13   Indeed, I was part of an intensive workshop, held at Penn State University in 2013, dedicated to reconsidering the long-standing critical assumptions regarding a tight relationship between Mennonite identity and Mennonite/s Writing.

14   For an exploration of many of these varied forms and functions of repetition, see Moraru.

15   For a discussion of archetypes in the context of Mennonite literature, see Beck's "The Signifying Menno: Archetypes for Authors and Critics."

16   I mean "strain" as a "thread" or "stream" (*Oxford English Dictionary* 3:1a), of course, but I also want to invoke its meanings as "ancestry" (*OED* 1:6a); as the use of a sieve, in which much is let through but some is retained (*OED* 2:1a); and as "pressure" or "effort," even to the point of breaking (*OED* 2:4a)—all meanings that I see as related to the construction and negotiation of communal identity.

17   Here I am adapting the distinction made by David Couzens Hoy in his recent study *The Times of Our Lives: A Critical History of Temporality* (2009). Hoy is careful to define temporality as "time insofar as it manifests itself in human existence," rather than as "subjective time" or "experienced time," on the ground that terms such as "subjectivity" and "experience" are themselves at issue (xiii). For the purposes of my study, however, it is sufficient to emphasize that my claims about time in these novels are, strictly speaking, claims about temporality—the human experience or mediation of time—rather than time itself.

18   Kroeger's book is fascinating not only because of its careful accounting of the history and mechanics of the Kroeger clocks but also because of his collection of "Amazing Clock Stories": 65 of the book's 166 pages are dedicated to the stories attached to more than 60 individual clocks.

19   These clocks are commonly called Kroeger clocks because the Kroeger family was the most prominent of the Mennonite clockmakers. Other significant Mennonite clockmakers of this period include Peter Lepp, Kornelius Hildebrand, and the Mandtlers (see Kroeger, *Kroeger Clocks* 58–60).

20   In *Mennonite Literary Voices Past and Present,* Al Reimer anticipates these findings by noting "the kind of community-centered, committed Christian writing Ruth called for is not what we are getting from Mennonite writers in the Russian-Mennonite tradition" (59).

21   Of course, questions of literary quality, or even literariness, are themselves complex. I will not be able to address this point at any length here, but I want to emphasize that while there is certainly a substantial range in the "quality" of novels I consider in this study, each of the four primary texts I examine at length is well worthy of study both for its particular interpretation of Mennonite history, and for the compelling and complex ways in which it represents that past—as I expect will become clear in the chapters that follow.

22   The replacement of "literature" with "writing" productively broadens the scope of the field, as does the inclusive gesture implicit in the term "Mennonite/s," which allows that all writing by Mennonites is pertinent to the field. As useful as such a move might be, it also risks simply transferring the difficult debate about what constitutes Mennonite literature away from individual texts and onto the biographies of their authors. Just as importantly, inclusion of the forward slash (which Gundy tellingly removes) indicates that critics continue

to conceive of "Mennonite writing" as constituting a distinct body of texts. As such, the homogenizing and limiting implications that I will locate in the title "Mennonite literature" might be productively estranged by the critical use of the term "Mennonite/s writing," but they are not fully resolved.

· 23 Critics have gestured, at times, in this direction. Harry Loewen, for example, mentions in passing that Mennonite artists and writers in Canada were "greatly aided financially by the government's policy of multiculturalism and its various arts programs" ("Mennonite Literature" 569), as does James Urry ("Memory" 41). Hildi Froese Tiessen, as I noted earlier, has also noted a connection between Mennonite writing and multiculturalism in Canada. My point, however, is that the implications that this context holds for Mennonite writing have not been sufficiently explored.

24 For an examination of the relationship between the policy framework of multiculturalism and the formation of Canadian literature, see Smaro Kamboureli's *Scandalous Bodies: Diasporic Literature in English Canada* (especially "Sedative Politics," 81–130) and her introduction to the first edition of *Making a Difference: Canadian Multicultural Literatures in English*. There is a wealth of material examining the impact of multiculturalism on the reception of minoritized literatures; see Bannerji; Miki, *Broken Entries;* and Mukherjee; also see key essays by Karpinski; and Padolsky. For examinations of the institutionalization of Canadian literature more generally, see Cavell; and Kamboureli and Miki.

25 According to Paul Litt, the Massey Report is so widely connected with the emergence of Canada's state-sponsored cultural production that "it has come to serve as something of a creationist myth for Canadian cultural nationalists," in which "the essentials of the parable are simple: before Massey, barbarism; after Massey, civilization" (5). Such a narrative, he argues, ignores the long history of debate over the validity of state intervention into Canadian culture (19). For a range of assessments of the Canadian government's ongoing regulation of culture, see, in addition to Litt, Dowler; Globerman; and Ostry.

26 Barry Cameron expresses a widely held view when he writes that "[t]he full institutionalization of Canadian literature as a recognizable and relatively autonomous discourse did not take place until the mid-to late 1960s, when it became thoroughly inscribed in both the agenda of Canadian publishers and the curriculum of Canadian university departments of literature" (124). Similarly, T.D. Maclulich argues that "[a]cceptance of the idea that Canadian writing could be more than the eccentric hobby of a few otherwise sane professors can be dated with some precision to the years from 1959 to 1965" (19). Maclulich goes on to identify Carl F. Klinck's *Literary History of Canada*, published in 1965 with a sizable grant from the Canada Council, as another marker in the emergence of Canadian literature, calling it the "definitive imprimatur of respectability to the academic study of Canadian writing" (19). Robert Lecker agrees, suggesting that, with its publication, "the institution called Canadian literature was born" (656–657). Ironically, *Literary History of Canada* includes Northrop Frye's famous "Conclusion," in which Frye announces that there is still no national literature in Canada.

27 Although I am critical of the deployment of ethnicity within the report, I should note that the commission was remarkably self-aware of the dangers of the concept.

Book IV, for example, insists that "[w]hat counts most in our concept of an 'ethnic group' is not one's ethnic origin or even one's mother tongue, but one's sense of belonging to a group, and the group's collective will to exist" (14). The authors take steps to avoid the type of essentializing that many critics have suggested has been the result of Canada's multicultural ideal. They explicitly (if perhaps naively) refuse to ascribe any biological significance to the terms "people," "race," and "ethnic group" (13), for example, and note their preference for the term "cultural group" rather than "ethnic group," on the grounds that the "adjective 'ethnic' is ambiguous at best, and often appears to be more or less synonymous with 'foreign'" (20). In fact, they explain that use of the term "other" in the much-maligned title of Book IV (*The Cultural Contributions of the Other Ethnic Groups*) was meant to signify that, though people of British and French descent constituted the overwhelming majority in Canada, the commission considered them to constitute "ethnic groups" as well. Nonetheless, the term "other" in the title has more commonly been read as indicating the supplementary nature of non-British or -French communities in Canada.

28   A few examples of critics engaging Mennonite literature as a form of ethnic writing include William H. New's entry on "Ethnicity and Race and the Politics of Reading" in the *Encyclopedia of Literature in Canada*; Steven Tötösy de Zepetnek's "Selected Bibliography of Theoretical and Critical Texts about Canadian Ethnic Minority Writing"; Enoch Padolsky's "Canadian Ethnic Minority Literature in English" (363, 377); Joseph Pivato's *Echo: Essays on Other Literatures;* Linda Hutcheon's *Splitting Images: Contemporary Canadian Ironies* (19, 53–54); and Jars Balan's *Identifications: Ethnicity and the Writer in Canada* (67–87). Mennonite writers were also featured prominently in two of the most significant anthologies of multicultural literature of the 1990s: Linda Hutcheon and Marion Richmond's *Other Solitudes: Canadian Multicultural Fictions* (1990), which includes an interview and a short story by Rudy Wiebe, and Smaro Kamboureli's *Making a Difference: Canadian Multicultural Literatures in English* (1996), which includes work by Rudy Wiebe, Sandra Birdsell, Patrick Friesen, and Armin Wiebe.

29   See also Hostetler's "The Unofficial Voice: The Poetics of Cultural Identity and Contemporary U.S. Mennonite Poetry," esp. pages 35–36.

30   Here I am adapting a comment made by Julie Rak at the TransCanada 3: Literature, Institutions, Citizenship conference (2009), where she suggested that religion is often racialized in Canadian literary criticism.

31   These anthologies are Camille Haynes's *Black Chat: An Anthology of Black Poets* (1973); John P. Miska's *The Sound of Time: Anthology of Canadian-Hungarian Authors* (1974); Tomi Nishimura's *Maple: Poetry by Japanese Canadians with English Translations* (1975); Liz Cromwell's *One out of Many: A Collection of Writings by 21 Black Women in Ontario* (1975); Abraham Boyarsky and Lazar Sarna's *Canadian Yiddish Writings* (1976); Pier Giorgio Di Cicco's *Roman Candles: Anthology of Poems by Seventeen Italo-Canadian Poets* (1978); the Asian Canadian Writers Workshop's *Inalienable Rice: A Chinese and Japanese Canadian Anthology* (1979); and Naín Nómez's *Chilean Literature in Canada/Literatura Chilena en Canadá* (1982). For a fuller account, see Robert Lecker's exhaustive *English-Canadian Literary Anthologies: An Enumerative Bibliography*, and Judy Young's "Canadian Literature in the Non-Official Languages: A Review of Recent Publications and Work in Progress."

32   The irony of Wiebe's claim is doubled for readers who know that, until recently, Canadian Mennonites commonly used the term "the English" to refer to anyone not directly of Mennonite heritage. "In the community where I grew up," Wiebe explains elsewhere, "the English were not only something else, they were *everything* else" ("Write Speaking" 27).

33   Here I am gesturing to an essay by author David Elias in a recent issue of *Rhubarb* magazine in which he discusses the "currency" of his Mennonite identity at some length.

34   See especially Chapter 2, "Sedative Politics," and Chapter 3, "Ethnic Anthologies."

35   Of course, this is precisely what Coleman himself does in his more recent work, in which he positions Mennonites with Jews, Caribbeans, and Somalis as representing a shared chronotope of diasporic displacement ("Contented Civility" 233). My point here is not to catch Coleman in a contradiction but to suggest that, as his own work makes clear, there are ways to cautiously connect and compare across racialized boundaries.

36   Notably, this concern is not fully unique to Canadian Mennonites. American poet Julia Spicher Kasdorf, for example, notes that "[t]he temptation of writing as 'we' has never been greater for Mennonite and other minority or ethnic American authors," at least in part because "[m]ulticultural enthusiasts and scholars are eager to endorse [such] texts" (*Body* 161). Nonetheless, it is uniquely pertinent in Canada, where the full force of state policy supports the critical discourse of multiculturalism.

37   Of course, I would count this study among those critical works that benefit from the exoticization of Mennonite culture and literature in Canada.

Chapter 1

Mennonite History and/as Literature

1   According to Noon Park, "Amid the sectarian bloodshed of 16th century Western Europe, Christians executed on heresy charges numbered approximately 5000, of which roughly 2000 to 2500, 40 to 50%, were Anabaptists" (55).

2   I take this emphasis on the impact of the Russian bureaucracy from James Urry's essay "Time and Memory: Secular and Sacred Aspects of the World of the Russian Mennonites and Their Descendants."

3   See Adolf Ens's *Subjects or Citizens? The Mennonite Experience in Canada, 1870–1925* for a discussion of the debate regarding the status of non-baptized Mennonites in Canada during World War I. The "Mennonite Identification Certificates" that the federal government began issuing in 1918 show that the government required an authorized minister of the Mennonites to confirm that the bearer was a Mennonite by both faith and kinship (Ens, Appendix 6). As Frank H. Epp writes, the threat of conscription in Canada made it "obvious that the Mennonites felt compelled to define as Mennonites all those who were part of the community, thus confirming the ethnic definition" ("Mennonite Experience" 29).

4   Along with Hutterites and Doukhobors, Mennonites were deemed "[u]ndesirable, owing to their peculiar customs, habits, modes of living, and methods of holding property, and because of their probable inability to become readily assimilated to assume the duties and responsibilities of Canadian citizenship within a reasonable time after entry" (qtd. in Epp, *Mennonites* 407). See Order-in-Council PAC, Record Group 2, 1, 923, 1 May 1919; 1204, 9 June 1919.

5   Rudy Wiebe's inclusion of the story of Jacob Friesen IV in *The Blue Mountains of China* (1970) is notable as one of the few novels focusing on the 1920s experience to meaningfully address those Mennonites unable—or unwilling—to leave Russia.

6   For a brief summary of the similarly competing interpretations of earlier Anabaptist history, see Redekop and Steiner (6–8). See also Synder; and A.E. Weaver.

7   Kroetsch suggests that Mennonite writing is marked by "a story of the fall from a golden age (the departure from an ideal world somewhere in the past which was apparently in Russia, somewhere, in the late 19th century)" and that it shows "all the narrative implications of this: that this is a worse place, that we are in decline, that things are going from good to bad" (225). Although he seeks to contrast this narrative of exile from Russia to what he calls "another and competing story, the story that we left something bad and have come to a garden" (225), I would argue that these two "competing" stories are better understood as two interpretations of the same historical narrative of migration.

8   *Watermelon Syrup* was left unfinished by Annie Jacobsen when she died in 2005. At Jacobsen's request, the novel was revised by Jane Finlay-Young, who relied on Di Brandt for editorial support.

9   On the function of the migration narrative in Toews's award-winning novel, see Wiebe, "Miriam Toews'."

Chapter 2

Gelassenheit or Exodus: *My Harp Is Turned to Mourning* and the Theo-Pedagogical Narrative

1   Gundy makes clear that he does not mean that "Mennonite writing" is necessarily disengaged from theological concerns. Nonetheless, that he thinks it necessary to draw such a distinction at all is indicative of the rather low standing of religious literature even within Mennonite critical discourse. Although a distinction between "Mennonite literature" and "Mennonite writing" might be useful for Gundy's essay, the concept of "Mennonite literature" circulates much too widely, at least in the Canadian context, to be redefined this narrowly. It seems confusing to offer a definition of Mennonite literature that would explicitly exclude work by Rudy Wiebe, Sandra Birdsell, or Di Brandt.

2   For the purposes of this study, I understand *faith, religion,* and *theology* to be closely related, but not synonymous, terms, as per the following definitions in the *Oxford English Dictionary: faith* refers to the "spiritual apprehension of divine truths, or of realities beyond the reach of sensible experience or logical proof" (3.c), that are held within, but not completely overdetermined by, the collective context of a *religion,* which refers to a "particular system of faith" (4.a), or its organized, institutionalized structure, including church leaders and traditions. The institution

of religion is again separate from, but based upon, a *theology*, or "particular theological system" (1.b) or doctrinal tradition—in the case of Mennonites, an Anabaptist understanding of Christianity. These distinctions, though slight, are implicitly insisted upon in these novels, where the authority of an individual faith drawing on a shared theological tradition makes possible a critique of the established religious structure.

3   The spelling of the name of the second major Mennonite colony varies between these novels, appearing both as Molochnaya (*My Harp*) and as Molotschna (*Out*).

4   Reimer's title is taken from Job's lament: "My harp also is turned to mourning, and my organ into the voice of them that weep" (Job 30:31); Dick's title is taken from the pronouncement, "[a]nd the Lord God spoke to Job from out of the storm" (Job 38:1).

5   Janz's repeated demands that the Russian authorities "set our people free" (39, 223) are clearly meant to be an echo of Moses' demands to Pharaoh, and the novel refers to the migration as an "exodus" (302) and Canada as "the promised land" (345, 401). Midway through the novel, Dick makes the connection explicit when she has Janz pray for the Lord "to make a way for thy people here in this Egypt to again cross the sea to freedom" (223).

6   The habit of connecting Mennonite migration, peoplehood, or suffering to Jewish history is common in Russian Mennonite literature. At times, the connection is presented as an implicit equation, as in Dick's *Out* or in Harry Loewen's long poem "The Land," which intertwines the Jewish exodus from Egypt with the Mennonite flight from Russia. More commonly, however, this connection is interrogated—or at least questioned—even as it is raised as a standard trope in Mennonite cultural thought. In Sandra Birdsell's *Children of the Day*, a young Mennonite girl mistakes photos of the Jewish Holocaust as photos of her family's massacre in Russia; in Birdsell's *Night Travellers*, a Mennonite grandfather begins a lesson on "HOW GOD LED HIS PEOPLE OUT OF THE LAND OF EGYPT" but instead offers a set of stories about the Mennonites' migration out of Russia (122). In David Waltner-Toews's *One Foot in Heaven*, the young Abner Dueck initially agrees with his father's insistence on the "similarities of Jews and Mennonites," only to have his friends call it into question (65–67). The narrator in Weier's *Steppe* asks "[w]ho am I really, some kind of wandering Jew?" and wonders if he might be the grandson of a Jewish woman whom he sees across an alley. "Read me your genes," he writes. "Teach me your skin. [...] Your family and mine, I think we might have mixed metaphors in Russia" (3.11). Rudy Wiebe explores the Mennonite-Jewish connection in *The Blue Mountains of China*, while more recently the narrator of David Bergen's *The Matter with Morris* spends much of the novel longing to be Jewish.

7   Dick names Katya's massive family estate Succoth, for example, which seems to align it with the Egyptian place of the same name near the start of the Israelites' flight (Exodus 12, 13). But Succoth Estate is also described in the novel as Eden (22, 179) as well as Sodom (319), a confusion of biblical parallels for the Russian colonies echoed in the novel's description of Canada, which is at once a Promised Land in the Exodus paradigm, a postlapsarian wasteland in the Genesis paradigm, and a direct contradiction to the Job paradigm. These confusions are nicely encapsulated by the description of the Mennonites crossing the Atlantic en route

to Canada, in which the wake of their boat is described as "a parting of the Red Sea" behind them—opening the way back to the collapsed Commonwealth rather than the way in front of them toward Canada (399).

8   The representation of Makhno's love for Katya, the Mennonite daughter of his former employer, reflects what Myrna Kostash calls the novel's "political economy of cross-cultural desire" (168). As Kostash points out, Katya's perfection and purity have as their binary opposites the lustful and perverse Ukrainian servant, Marusya, who presides over the Bocks' massacre. Women in *My Harp*, Kostash suggests, are "sluts or mothers," depending on whether they are Ukrainian or Mennonite (169).

9   As an explicit warning against the accumulation of wealth, the invocation of James 5 in this context risks presenting the violence suffered by the Mennonites in Russia as a form of divine punishment and thus justifying Makhno's actions. "Now listen, you rich people, weep and wail because of the misery that is coming upon you," it reads. "You have lived on earth in luxury and self-indulgence. You have fattened yourselves in the day of slaughter" (James 5:1, 5). I will return to the problems that such a passage holds for the novel's larger theology shortly, but here I want to simply note it as another example of the novel's willingness to allow the biblical narrative to critique Mennonite history.

10 As I will discuss in greater detail in the next chapter, this temporal shift also facilitated a larger shift in the Mennonites' self-understanding away from a religious minority and toward an ethnic community, establishing what Urry calls an "issue of origin and identity clearly outside the bounds of the sacred" ("Time" 20).

11 The six sections relating the events of this date are as follows: an overview of the political situation among Makhno's men, the Red and White Armies, and B.B. Janz's efforts to secure passage for a Mennonite migration (366–68); Wilhelm's participation in the defence of Colonists Hill and his decision to flee home (368–72); Jacob Loewen's fateful decision to alter the route of his family's flight from the colony (372–73); Erdmann Lepp's attempts to justify the Mennonites' self-defence units to a Red Army commander (374–76); and Nikolai's witnessing of Makhno's grief on coming upon the Loewens' corpses (376–78).

12 Sandra Birdsell, for example, uses Psalm 23 as an ordering trope in *The Russländer*, invoking it repeatedly (39, 241) and adopting its central images as section titles ("1. In Green Pastures"; "2. In the Presence of Enemies"; "3. Surely Goodness and Mercy"). However, if the novel recognizes the importance of religion to the Mennonite community of this period, it does not present a theological interpretation of their experience.

13 See, for just one example among many, Aron A. Toews. The introduction suggests that "[t]he story of the Anabaptists, especially in its early stages, was mainly written with tears and blood. It has repeated itself in the last decades, especially in the case of the Mennonites in Russia" (4). For critical assessments of what Daniel J. Hess calls the "martyr complex" (29), see Urry, "Time and Memory."

Chapter 3

Dreaming *das Völklein: Lost in the Steppe* **and the Ethnic Narrative**

1   This included a decade at the *Steinbach Post* (1924–36), an illustrated monthly magazine *Mennonitische Warte* (1936–40), an annual journal *Warte-Jahrbuch* (1943–44), and the *Mennonitische Auslese* (1951).

2   In *Daut Jeburtsdach*, his final (and never produced) play, an extended Mennonite family gathers together from around the world to celebrate their patriarch's seventy-fifth birthday. Although the elderly man would like everyone to speak to him in German, it is impossible: the family members from Ukraine speak Ukrainian; those from South America speak Spanish; and the Mennonites from Canada speak only English. In a heavy-handed allegorical warning about what the demise of German is doing to Mennonite identity, the patriarch has a heart attack and dies when a family member argues that Mennonites ought to give up on their Germanic heritage. See also Dyck's short story "*Nicht seine Schuld*" (in Volume 4 of his *Collected Works*) which, according to Gerhard K. Friesen, "implies that the loss of a linguistic and cultural heritage is tantamount to murdering one's ancestors" (138).

3   On Canadian Mennonites and National Socialism, see Redekop, "Roots"; and Urry, "*Mennostaat*." On Urry's controversial comments, see his essay "Fate, Hate, and Denial: Ingrid Rimland's *Lebensraum!*" as well as the *Mennonite Quarterly Review*'s official apology, along with several letters to the editor, in the following issue.

4   See, for example, Epp and Peters (3); Hadley (199); and Loewen ("Canadian-Mennonite Literature" 79).

5   See, for example, Berend's monologue on how wind motors, horseless carriages, and airplanes will transform the family farm "someday" (157–58).

6   For a recounting of Rimland's *Lebensraum!* trilogy, see Urry, "Fate."

7   This claim certainly rings true when Mennonite historians suggest that the Mennonites in Russia were "[s]et against a vast sea of Russian peasantry [... and so] experienced themselves as a Germanic people of superior breeding and culture" (Epp, "Problems" 283), much as it does in Dyck's novel.

8   As I noted earlier in the chapter, Froese suggests that the novel would appeal to "the exiled Mennonite who with Dyck would relive his/her own childhood in just such a village" ("*Lost*" 148).

9   In a footnote, Henry D. Dyck explains that the "family calendar" for the Mennonites in Russia was "[a] kind of almanac which carried short stories and anecdotes besides information on days of the week and month of the new calendar year, facts about the heavens, tides, etc." (159). James Urry positions "calendar time" as an experiential middle ground between the sacred timeless time and the "profoundly secular" clock time on the grounds that through the names of days and months, through holy days, and so on, the calendar retains "its links to sacred concerns in the past" ("Time" 5).

10   In a chapter fittingly entitled "No Longer a Child," Abraham Friesen writes of what he calls the "educational explosion" in the larger Mennonite Commonwealth in the first decade of the twentieth century (39).

Chapter 4

The Individual in the Communal Story: *The Rußländer* and the Trauma Narrative

1   Birdsell has called the newspaper clipping "a kind of family tree [to] assist readers in sorting everyone out" (Birdsell, Loewen, and Thomas).

2   See Keefer; and Mierau, whose comments on *The Rußländer* are part of his review of Birdsell's *Children of the Day.*

3   The novel's representation of this period certainly flattens a complex history, but it is self-conscious of the limitations that come from an individual perspective. Birdsell repeatedly inserts the framing narrative—the elderly Katherine recounting her story to Ernest Unger for the Mennonite archives—into Katherine's account, reminding readers that the novel's historical referents are being routed through an individual's memory. Similarly, she establishes the political limitations of her protagonist early on, having Katherine admit her narrow perspective on the first page: she had learned "through inference and the attitudes of people around her," readers are told, that "what went on beyond the borders of her Russian Mennonite oasis was not worth noticing" (5–6). Moreover, the references to Bhabha stones throughout the novel stand as reminders of the earlier inhabitants of the land on which the Commonwealth was built.

4   This process is traced by Freud in "Remembering, Repeating, and Working-Through," in which he notes that "[a]s long as the patient is in the treatment he cannot escape from this compulsion to repeat; and in the end we understand that this is his way of remembering" (150).

5   Here I am talking about the gap in information rather than the break in the text. Although the line break is not unique to this moment—Birdsell uses it throughout the novel to indicate a change in venue or time—it nonetheless serves as a literalization of the gap where the novel's central event would otherwise be.

6   "Six months following the massacre of her family she was still far-away," Birdsell writes. "She's not here yet. She's far-away and doesn't have much to say" (271).

7   Although Freud is often invoked in arguments for the extension of individual trauma to a larger community, he wrote relatively little on the topic. In his controversial *Moses and Monotheism*, he connects individual and communal experiences of trauma (or what he calls "the problem of traumatic neurosis and that of Jewish Monotheism") on the basis of shared investment in "*latency*"—an observation that he himself calls "an afterthought" after noting their "fundamental difference" (109–10). See also Freud, "Group Psychology" (627).

8   On the proposed changes for trauma in the *DSM-V*: "The most controversial aspect of the *DSM-IV* A1 Criterion is 'learning about' the traumatic exposure of a close friend or loved one. Some have recommended elimination of this part of the criterion because, they argue, it opens the door too wide for qualifying traumatic events. However, there is good evidence that PTSD does occur among people who have learned about the homicide, gruesome death, grotesque details of rape, genocide, or violent abuse of a loved one. As a result, our proposed *DSM-V* A Criterion retains the 'learned about' category but has attempted to narrow the list of qualifying events to reduce ambiguity and forensic misrepresentations" (Friedman).

9   Katherine remembers with disgust the pestering of Franz Pauls, her former tutor, who begged for details of the massacre because (her grandmother suspects) he wanted to know if Lydia was raped (316).

10   *Children of the Day*, a sequel to *The Russländer* set entirely in Canada, tells the story of Katherine's sister and her Métis husband. As the novel makes clear, the massacre in Ukraine continues to haunt the Vogt family's grandchildren in Canada.

11   The American edition of the novel emphasizes its archival structure, stylizing the heading of the opening newspaper article in gothic text, as if it was clipped from the newspaper itself, and including a map of the colonies.

Chapter 5

The Strain of Diaspora: *The Blue Mountains of China* and the Meta-Narrative

1   Wiebe leaves the "thing" somewhat ambiguous. Franz first sees the "thing" as his family waits to escape to Canada via Moscow, and, given that he describes it as "something you don't want to think about but is always in the back of your head" (68), I read the "thing" in this passage as representing the community's confusion over and sorrow at the collapse of the Commonwealth and, perhaps more importantly, guilt over having been among the few who fled and escaped the violence. This reading is supported by the fact that Franz refers to the migration as the "one big thing" that they have to "talk about" (65) and that he says it "has been following us ever since" (86), as well as the fact that the novel privileges those Mennonites who, like David Epp, refuse to place their safety over that of their neighbours who are unable to leave the suffering.

2   Samuel Reimer Sr. is named Balzer in Franz's story; his son Samuel Jr. later attempts to proclaim peace in Vietnam. David Epp (I) is Samuel Reimer Sr.'s cousin and the father of David Epp Jr., who returns to the Soviet Union after leading his family safely across the Amur. His son, the third David Epp, becomes a missionary in Paraguay and the subject of Chapter 11. Jakob Friesen (I) founded the Karatow *hof* taken over by his son, Jakob (II). Jakob (III), twin brother to Isaak, is murdered on the estate in 1919, but his son Jakob (IV) manages to flee to Moscow before being arrested by the GPU (Soviet secret police) and exiled to Siberia. Jakob (V) is arrested in his father's place, later returning to the *hof* to find that his family has fled to Moscow without him.

3   Fritzchi becomes Frieda, Dennis Willms becomes Dennis Williams, Liesel Driediger becomes Elizabeth Cereno, and Samuel Reimer is called Balzer.

4   In fact, many of the stories and characters are not grounded at all, but are on the move: Chapter 5 is set exclusively on a boat somewhere in the Atlantic; Chapter 9 follows a caravan of Mennonites fleeing by foot somewhere on the border between the USSR and China; and Chapter 11 takes place entirely on a jeep somewhere in the Paraguayan desert. The setting for the novel's concluding chapter is split in two: the first half takes place on a plane flying somewhere above Canada, while the second half unfolds on the side of the Trans-Canada Highway, somewhere in Alberta.

5   John recites a line that he says is spoken by Coyote in "a novel [he] read": "I have set his feet on soft ground; I have set his feet on the sloping shoulders of the world" (270). The passage is from Watson's *The Double Hook* (134).

6   Although I worry that Van Toorn searches too much for the "infallible guide to [Wiebe's] position" (77), her study offers an excellent passage-by-passage account of how Wiebe crosses various characters' stories so that the meaning of each becomes clear only when read in juxtaposition to the others.

7   Noting that Yoder and Wiebe became close friends in the mid-1960s when they were both teachers in Elkhart, Indiana, Beck reveals that the short poem recited by John (258) was originally written by Wiebe as an attempt to adapt Yoder's essay for use in a sermon that Wiebe gave on several occasions, entitled "Jesus Christ, Revolutionary."

Conclusion
On Reading Migration in Canadian Literature

1   For example, the wide-ranging reconsideration of "Asian Canadian" as a representational category includes *Asian Canadian Studies*, a special issue of *Canadian Literature*; Beauregard; Cho; Goellnicht; Miki, *Broken Entries* and *In Flux*; Ty and Verduyn; and Wah. Important reconsiderations of "Black Canadian" as a representational category include Chariandy; Clarke; and Walcott.

2   Cho is not the only Canadian critic drawing on diaspora to make connections across racialized lines. See also Christine Kim's discussion of "[i]nterdiasporic connection" in her recent essay "Racialized Diasporas, Entangled Postmemories, and *The Letter Opener*" (187). "Diasporic intimacy," Kim suggests, "is critically important as it repositions individuals and communities in relation to various forms of diasporic and racialized loss, helps us finds [sic] more hopeful ways of interpreting such stories, and encourages the formation of new social and psychic attachments" (188).

3   In their influential study *Empire*, for example, Michael Hardt and Antonio Negri suggest that global capital has become such a force that "even the most dominant nation-states should no longer be thought of as supreme and sovereign authorities" (xi). Hardt and Negri argue that, since the nation and its imperializing logic was the central object of postcolonialism's original critique, postcolonial critics have "fail[ed] to recognize adequately the contemporary object of critique" and are now "pushing against an open door" (136,138).

4   Dobson insists on the falsity of the "nation/globe dichotomy" and unpacks the process through which "literary writing has become both a part of the construct of the nation and a commodity for exchange in a time when international trade agreements have become interested in including culture within their scope" (208, 207). See also Derksen's ongoing work on the relationship between globalization and national cultural production, including his essay "National Literatures in the Shadow of Neoliberalism."

5   As David Chariandy observes, for those drawing on postcolonialism, the "turn to diaspora" is often understood as being "simultaneously [...] a turn to race." Vinder S. Kalra, Raminder Kaur, and John Hutnyk go further, suggesting that the "two

terms in the phrase, 'white diaspora', almost seem antithetical" (105). For scholars tightly connecting postcolonial and diasporic critiques in Canadian literary criticism, see Chariandy, "Postcolonial Diasporas"; Fleischmann, Van Styvendale, and McCarroll ("Introduction"); and Kim and McCall. For a critical discussion of "diaspora studies as a sub-genre linking postcolonial and globalization studies" (702) more generally, see Brydon.

6   It is not uncommon for Russian Mennonites to be considered in terms of diaspora. Robin Cohen, for example, briefly discusses Mennonites as an exemplary case of religious diaspora in the second edition of his *Global Diasporas* (151). See also Coleman; Sneath; A. Weaver; N. Wiebe; and Zacharias.

7   Kamboureli's *Scandalous Bodies: Diasporic Literature in English Canada* attends closely to the processes of racialization in Canada while exploring diaspora across racial and ethnic lines. Delisle, whose work draws on diaspora theory to explore Newfoundland out-migration, cautions against "equating 'diaspora' with 'racial minority' in Canada," suggesting it is necessary to recognize whiteness as a form of racialization and thus to work against its naturalized privileges (77).

8   In a brief review article, Reimer reports on the elusive chapter/novella's "intriguing" history: after being caught up for more than a quarter-century in a debate over divorce proceedings, several sections of the once-complete manuscript went missing. To Reimer's eye, the final document seems to have been amended by a family member not fully sympathetic to Dyck's tone or his usual "'Mennonite' High German." Although the final document is of interest, Reimer concludes that it represents a manuscript that is an "incomplete and collaborative one at best" (221).

Works Cited

Alexander, Jeffrey C. "Toward a Theory of Cultural Trauma." *Cultural Trauma and Collective Identity.* Ed. Jeffrey C. Alexander, Ron Eyerman, Bernard Giesen, Neil J. Smelser, and Piotr Sztompka. Berkeley: University of California Press, 2004. 1–30.

Anderson, Alan B. "The Sociology of Mennonite Identity: A Critical Review." Redekop and Steiner 193–201.

Anderson, Benedict. *Imagined Communities: Reflections on the Origin and Spread of Nationalism.* Rev. ed. New York: Verso, 2001.

... And When They Shall Ask: A Docu-Drama of the Russian Mennonite Experience. Dir. John Morrow. David Dueck Films, 1984.

Arnason, David. "A History of Turnstone Press." Tiessen and Hinchcliffe 212–22.

Asian Canadian Studies, special issue of *Canadian Literature* 199 (2008).

Asian Canadian Writers Workshop. *Inalienable Rice: A Chinese and Japanese Canadian Anthology.* Vancouver: Powell Street Revue, 1979.

Balaev, Michelle. "Trends in Literary Trauma Theory." *Mosaic* 41.2 (2008): n. pag. *Academic OneFile.* Web. 1 Jan. 2011.

Balan, Jars. *Identifications: Ethnicity and the Writer in Canada.* Edmonton: Canadian Institute of Ukrainian Studies, 1982.

Bannerji, Himani. *The Dark Side of the Nation: Essays on Multiculturalism, Nationalism, and Gender.* Toronto: Canadian Scholars Press, 2000.

Barthes, Roland. "The Death of the Author." 1968. *The Norton Anthology of Theory and Criticism.* Ed. Vincent B. Leitch. New York: W.W. Norton, 2001. 1466–70.

——. "The Reality Effect." 1968. Trans. Richard Howard. *Novel: An Anthology of Criticism and Theory, 1900–2000.* Ed. Dorothy J. Hale. Malden: Blackwell, 2006. 229–34.

Beachy, Kirsten Eve, ed. *Tongue Screws and Testimonies: Poems, Stories, and Essays Inspired by the Martyrs Mirror.* Waterloo, ON: Herald Press, 2010.

Beauregard, Guy. "The Emergence of 'Asian Canadian Literature': Can Lit's Obscene Supplement?" *Essays on Canadian Writing* 67 (1999): 53–76.

Beck, Ervin. "The Politics of Rudy Wiebe in *The Blue Mountains of China.*" *Mennonite Quarterly Review* 73 (1999): n. pag. Web. 5 Jan. 2011.

——. Rev. of *My Harp Is Turned to Mourning,* by Al Reimer. *Mennonite Quarterly Review* 52 (1988): 90–91.

——. "Rudy Wiebe and W.B. Yeats: Sailing to Danzig and Byzantium." *ARIEL: A Review of International English Literature* 32.4 (2001): 7–19.

_____. "The Signifying Menno: Archetypes for Authors and Critics." Roth and Beck 49–67.

Bender, Harold S. "The Anabaptist Vision." 1942. N. pag. *Mennonite Church USA Archive.* Web. 5 July 2010.

Benjamin, Walter. *Illuminations: Essays and Reflections.* Trans. Harry Zohn. Ed. Hannah Arendt. New York: Schocken Books, 1968.

Bergen, David. *The Age of Hope.* Toronto: HarperCollins, 2012.

_____. *The Matter with Morris.* Toronto: HarperCollins, 2010.

_____. *A Year of Lesser.* Toronto: HarperCollins, 1996.

Bhabha, Homi. *The Location of Culture.* 1994. New York: Routledge, 2004.

Birdsell, Sandra. *Children of the Day.* Toronto: Random House, 2005.

_____. *Katya: A Novel.* Minneapolis: Milkweed Editions, 2004.

_____. *Night Travellers.* Winnipeg: Turnstone Press, 1982.

_____. *The Russländer.* Toronto: McClelland and Stewart, 2001.

Birdsell, Sandra, with Hazel Loewen and Joan Thomas. "Getting It Right: Sandra Birdsell on Writing *The Russländer.*" Interview. 2002. N. pag. Web. 20 Sept. 2010.

Blodgett, E.D. "Ethnic Writing in Canadian Literature as Paratext." *Signature: A Journal of Theory and Canadian Literature* 3 (1990): 13–27.

Boyarsky, Abraham, and Lazar Sarna, eds. *Canadian Yiddish Writings.* Montreal: Harvest House, 1976.

Brandt, Di. *Dancing Naked: Narrative Strategies for Writing across Centuries.* Stratford: Mercury, 1996.

_____. *questions i aked my mother.* Winnipeg: Turnstone Press, 1987.

Braun, Connie T. "Silence, Memory, and Imagination as Story: Canadian Mennonite Life Writing." *CMW: Centre for Mennonite Writing Journal* 1.3 (2009): n. pag. Web. 20 Aug. 2010.

_____. *The Steppes Are the Colour of Sepia: A Mennonite Memoir.* Vancouver: Ronsdale, 2008.

Brydon, Diana. "Postcolonialism Now: Autonomy, Cosmopolitanism, Diaspora." *University of Toronto Quarterly* 73.2 (2004): 691–706.

Butler, Kim D. "Defining Diaspora, Refining a Discourse." *Diaspora* 10.2 (2001): 189–219.

Cameron, Barry. "English Critical Discourse in/on Canada." *Studies on Canadian Literature: Introductory and Critical Essays.* Ed. Arnold E. Davidson. New York: Modern Language Association of America, 1990. 124–43.

"Canada Tries to Bar Pro-Nazi View on Internet." *New York Times* 2 Aug. 1998. Web. 1 May 2010.

Canada. Canadian Multiculturalism Act. Second Session, Thirty-Third Parliament, 35–37 House of Commons, 12 July 1988. Ottawa: Canadian Government Publishing Centre, 1988.

_____. Constitution Act, 1982 (Canadian Charter of Rights and Freedoms.) Web. http://laws-lois.justice.gc.ca/eng/Const/page-15.html

Canadian Literature, special issue of *Literature and Theology* 16.2 (2002).

Caruth, Cathy, ed. and introduction. *Trauma: Explorations in Memory*. Baltimore: Johns Hopkins University Press, 1995.

_____. *Unclaimed Experience: Trauma, Narrative, and History*. Baltimore: Johns Hopkins University Press, 1996.

Cavell, Richard. "Introduction." *Love, Hate, and Fear in Canada's Cold War*. Ed. Richard Cavell. Toronto: University of Toronto Press, 2004. 3–34.

Chambers, Iain. *Migrancy, Culture, Identity*. New York: Routledge, 1994.

Chambers, Ross. "Orphaned Memories, Foster-Writing, Phantom Pain: The *Fragments* Affair." *Extremities: Trauma, Testimony, and Community*. Ed. Nancy K. Miller and Jason Tougaw. Urbana: University of Illinois Press, 2002. 92–112.

Chariandy, David. "Black Canadas and the Question of Diasporic Citizenship." Fleischmann, Van Styvendale, and McCarroll 323–46.

_____. "Postcolonial Diasporas." *Postcolonial Text* 2.1 (2006): n. pag. Web. 18 Nov. 2009.

Chatterjee, Partha. "Anderson's Utopia." *Diacritics* 29.4 (1999): 128–34.

Cho, Lily. "Asian Canadian Futures: Diasporic Passages and the Routes of Indenture." *Canadian Literature* 199 (2008): 181–201.

_____. "Diasporic Citizenship: Contradictions and Possibilities for Canadian Literature." *Trans.Can.Lit.: Resituating the Study of Canadian Literature*. Ed. Smaro Kamboureli and Roy Miki. Waterloo: Wilfrid Laurier University Press, 2007. 93–109.

_____. "The Turn to Diaspora." *Topia* 17 (2007): 11–30.

_____. "Underwater Signposts: Richard Fung's *Islands* and Enabling Nostalgia." Kim, McCall, and Singer 191–205.

Clarke, George Elliott. *Odysseys Home: Mapping African-Canadian Literature*. Toronto: University of Toronto Press, 2002.

Clifford, James. "Diasporas." *Routes: Travel and Translation in the Late Twentieth Century*. Cambridge, MA: Harvard University Press, 1997. 244–77.

Cohen, Leonard. *Beautiful Losers*. 1966. Toronto: McClelland and Stewart, 2003.

Cohen, Robin. *Global Diasporas: An Introduction*. Seattle: University of Washington Press, 1997.

_____. *Global Diasporas: An Introduction*. 2nd ed. London: Routledge, 2008.

Coleman, Daniel. "From Contented Civility to Contending Civilities: Alternatives to Canadian White Civility." *International Journal of Canadian Studies* 38 (2008): 221–242.

Coleman, Daniel, and Donald Goellnicht. "Race into the Twenty-First Century." *Essays on Canadian Writing* 75 (2002): n. pag. Web. 5 Feb. 2010.

Cromwell, Liz, ed. *One Out of Many: A Collection of Writings by 21 Black Women in Ontario.* Toronto: Wacacro Production, 1975.

Culler, Jonathan. "Anderson and the Novel." *Diacritics* 29.4 (1999): 20–39.

Currie, Mark. *About Time: Narrative, Fiction, and the Philosophy of Time.* Edinburgh: Edinburgh University Press, 2007.

De Fehr, William, et. al., eds. *Harvest: Anthology of Mennonite Writing in Canada: 1874–1974.* Winnipeg: Centennial Committee of the Mennonite Historical Society of Manitoba, 1974.

de Zepetnek, Steven Tötösy. "Selected Bibliography of Theoretical and Critical Texts about Canadian Ethnic Minority Writing." *Canadian Ethnic Studies* 28.3 (1996): 210–23.

Deleuze, Gilles. *Difference and Repetition.* 1968. Trans. Paul Patton. New York: Columbia University Press, 1994.

_____. *The Logic of Sense.* 1969. Trans. Constantin V. Boundas. New York: Continuum Books, 2004.

Delisle, Jennifer Bowering. "A Newfoundland Diaspora? Moving through Ethnicity and Whiteness." *Canadian Literature* 196 (2008): 64–81.

Derksen, Jeff. "National Literatures in the Shadow of Neoliberalism." Kamboureli and Zacharias 37–63.

Derrida, Jacques. *Archive Fever: A Freudian Impression.* Trans. Eric Prenowitz. Chicago: University of Chicago Press, 1995.

Di Cicco, Pier Giorgio, ed. *Roman Candles: Anthology of Poems by Seventeen Italo-Canadian Poets.* Toronto: Hounslow, 1978.

Dick, Janice L. *Calm Before the Storm.* Waterloo: Herald, 2002.

_____. *Eye of the Storm.* Waterloo: Herald, 2003.

_____. *Out of the Storm.* Waterloo: Herald, 2004.

Dobson, Kit. *Transnational Canadas: Anglo-Canadian Literature and Globalization.* Waterloo: Wilfrid Laurier University Press, 2009.

Doerksen, Victor G. "From Jung-Stilling to Rudy Wiebe." *Mennonite Images: Historical, Cultural, and Literary Essays Dealing with Mennonite Issues.* Ed. Harry Loewen. Winnipeg: Hyperion Press, 1980. 197–208.

_____. "In Search of a Mennonite Imagination." *Journal of Mennonite Studies* 2 (1984): 104–12.

_____. "Recalling a Past Generation: Some Observations of German-Canadian Mennonite Writing." *Journal of Mennonite Studies* 8 (1990): 146–55.

Doerksen, Victor G., et al., eds. *Collected Works of Arnold Dyck.* 4 vols. Steinbach: Derksen, 1985–90.

Doerksen, Victor G., and Harry Loewen, eds. *Collected Works of Arnold Dyck.* Vol. 1. Steinbach: Derksen, 1985.

Dowler, Kevin. "The Cultural Industries Policy Apparatus." *The Cultural Industries in Canada: Problems, Policies, and Prospects.* Ed. Michael Dorland. Toronto: James Lorimer, 1996. 328–46.

Dueck, Dora. *This Hidden Thing.* Winnipeg: Canadian Mennonite University Press, 2010.

Dunham, Mabel. *The Trail of the Conestoga.* 1924. Toronto: McClelland and Stewart, 1973.

Dyck, Arnold. *Collected Works of Arnold Dyck.* Ed. Victor G. Doerksen et al. 4 vols. Steinbach: Derksen, 1985–90.

———. *Daut Jeburtsdach.* Doerksen et al. 4: 219–96.

———. "Die Neue Weltmacht." Doerksen et al. 4: 33–47.

———. *Hochfeld: Ein Steppendorf im Bürgerkrieg: Ukraine 1918/19.* Uchte, Germany: Sonnentau Verlag, 1998.

———. "Life as a Sum of Shattered Hopes: Arnold Dyck's Letters to Gerhard J. Friesen (Fritz Senn)." Trans. and ed. Gerhard K. Friesen. *Journal of Mennonite Studies* 6 (1988): 124–33.

———. *Lost in the Steppe.* 1944–48. Trans. Henry D. Dyck. Steinbach: Derksen, 1974.

———. *Two Letters, the Millionaire of Goatfield, Runde Koake.* Trans. Elisabeth Peters. Steinbach: Derksen, 1980.

Dyck, E.F. "The True Colours of Plain Speech." *Books in Canada* Oct. 1988: 19–22.

Dyck, Mrs. Henry D. Preface. *Lost in the Steppe,* by Arnold Dyck. Steinbach: Derksen, 1974. iv–vi.

Dyck, Sarah, ed. *The Silence Echoes: Memoirs of Trauma and Tears.* Kitchener: Pandora Press, 1997.

Elias, David. "If I Am a Mennonite Writer..." *Rhubarb* 30 (2012): 7–10.

Ens, Adolf. *Subjects or Citizens? The Mennonite Experience in Canada, 1870–1925.* Ottawa: University of Ottawa Press, 1994.

Epp, Frank. "Two Essays." De Fehr et al. 1–6.

Epp, Frank H. *Mennonite Exodus: The Rescue and Resettlement of the Russian Mennonites since the Communist Revolution.* Altona: D.W. Friesen, 1962.

———. "The Mennonite Experience in Canada." *Religion and Ethnicity: Essays.* Ed. Harold G. Coward and Leslie S. Kawamura. Waterloo: Wilfrid Laurier University Press, 1978. 21–36.

———. *Mennonites in Canada, 1786–1920: A History of a Separate People.* Toronto: Macmillan, 1974.

———. "Problems of Mennonite Identity: A Historical Study." *The Canadian Ethnic Mosaic: A Quest for Identity.* Ed. Leo Driedger. Toronto: McClelland and Stewart, 1978. 281–94.

Epp, George K., and Elisabeth Peters, eds. *Collected Works of Arnold Dyck.* Vol 4. Steinbach: Derksen, 1985.

Epp, George K., and Heinrich Wiebe, eds. *Unter dem Nordlicht: Anthology of German-Mennonite Writing in Canada.* Winnipeg: Mennonite German Society of Canada, 1977.

Erb, Paul. "An Artistic Explosion." *Festival Quarterly* 1.1 (1974): 5.

Erb, Peter C. "Critical Approaches to Mennonite Culture in Canada: Some Preliminary Observations." Loewen and Reimer 203–11.

"Faith." Def. 3.c. *Oxford English Dictionary Online.* 2000. Web. 4 Oct. 2010.

Ferris, Ina. "Religious Vision and Fictional Form: Rudy Wiebe's *Blue Mountains of China.*" *Mosaic* 11.3 (1978): 79–85.

Fleischman, Suzanne. *Tense and Narrativity: From Medieval Performance to Modern Fiction.* Austin: University of Texas Press, 1990.

Fleischmann, Aloys N.M., Nancy Van Styvendale, and Cody McCarroll. "Introduction." Fleischmann, Van Styvendale, and McCarroll 3–24.

Fleischmann, Aloys N.M., Nancy Van Styvendale, and Cody McCarroll, eds. *Narratives of Citizenship: Indigenous and Diasporic Peoples Unsettle the Nation-State.* Edmonton: University of Alberta Press, 2011.

Foucault, Michel. "Nietzsche, Genealogy, History." Trans. D.F. Bouchard and Sherry Simon. *Language, Counter-Memory, Practice: Selected Essays and Interviews.* Ed. D.F. Bouchard. Ithaca: Cornell University Press, 1980. 139–64.

Francis, E.K. *In Search of Utopia: The Mennonites in Manitoba.* Altona: D.W. Friesen, 1955.

——. *Interethnic Relations: An Essay in Sociological Theory.* New York: Elsevier, 1976.

——. "The Russian Mennonites: From Religious to Ethnic Group." *American Journal of Sociology* 54.2 (1948): 101–07.

Franz, J. Winfield. *The Waterloo Mennonites.* Waterloo: Wilfrid Laurier University Press, 1989.

Freud, Sigmund. "Beyond the Pleasure Principle." 1920. Gay 594–626.

——. "Group Psychology and the Analysis of the Ego." 1921. Gay 627–28.

——. *Moses and Monotheism.* Trans. Katherine Jones. Hertfordshire: Garden City Press, 1939.

——. "Remembering, Repeating, and Working-Through." *The Standard Edition of the Complete Psychological Works of Sigmund Freud.* Vol. 12. Trans. and ed. James Strachey. London: Hogarth, 1955. 147–56.

Friedman, Matthew J. "PTSD Revisions Proposed for *DSM-5*, with Input from Array of Experts." *Psychiatric News* 21 May 2010. Web. 29 Nov. 2010.

Friedmann, Robert. "Gelassenheit." *Anabaptist Mennonite Encyclopedia Online.* 1955. Web. 17 Jan. 2013. www.gameo.org/encyclopedia/contents/G448.html.

Friesen, Abraham. *In Defense of Privilege: Russian Mennonites and the State before and during World War I.* Winnipeg: Kindred Press, 2006.

Friesen, Gerhard K. Rev. of *The Collected Works of Arnold Dyck,* by Arnold Dyck. *Journal of Mennonite Studies* 9 (1991): 136–39.

Friesen, Patrick. *The Shunning.* Winnipeg: Turnstone Press, 1980.

Froese, Edna. "*Lost in the Steppe:* Portrait of an Acceptable Artist." *Journal of Mennonite Studies* 16 (1998): 142–62.

———. "To Write or to Belong: The Dilemma of Canadian Mennonite Storytellers." PhD diss., University of Saskatchewan, 1996.

Frye, Northrop. "Conclusion to a *Literary History of Canada.*" 1965. *The Bush Garden: Essays on the Canadian Imagination.* Concord: Anansi, 1995. 215–53.

Funk Wiebe, Katie. "A Tale of Seduction." Loewen, *Why* 324–36.

Gay, Peter, ed. *The Freud Reader.* New York: W.W. Norton, 1989.

Giesbrecht, Herbert. Rev. of *My Harp Is Turned to Mourning,* by Al Reimer. *Journal of Mennonite Studies* 4 (1986): 254–58.

Globerman, Steven. *Cultural Regulation in Canada.* Montreal: Institute for Research on Public Policy, 1983.

Goellnicht, Donald. "A Long Labour: The Protracted Birth of Asian Canadian Literature." *Essays on Canadian Writing* 72 (2000): 1–41.

Grekul, Lisa. *Leaving Shadows: Literature in English by Canada's Ukrainians.* Edmonton: University of Alberta Press, 2005.

Gundy, Jeff. Rev. of *The Steppes Are the Colour of Sepia: A Memoir,* by Connie Braun. *Conrad Grebel Review* n.d.: n. pag. Web. 27 Apr. 2012.

———. *Walker in the Fog: On Mennonite Writing.* Telford: Cascadia, 2005.

Gurr, Andrew. "Blue Mountains and Strange Forms." *Journal of Commonwealth Literature* 17 (1982): 152–60.

Hadley, Michael L. "Education and Alienation in Dyck's *Verloren in der Steppe:* A Novel of Cultural Crisis." *German-Canadian Yearbook* 3 (1976): 199–206.

Halbwachs, Maurice. *On Collective Memory.* 1941, 1952. Trans. and ed. Lewis A. Coser. Chicago: University of Chicago Press, 1992.

Hall, Stuart. "Cultural Identity and Diaspora." 1990. *Theorizing Diaspora: A Reader.* Ed. Jana Evans Braziel and Anita Mannur. Alden: Blackwell, 2003. 233–46.

Harder, Hans. *No Strangers in Exile.* 1934. Trans. and expanded Al Reimer. Winnipeg: Hyperion Press, 1979.

Hardt, Michael, and Antonio Negri. *Empire.* London: Harvard University Press, 2001.

Haynes, Camille, ed. *Black Chat: An Anthology of Black Poets.* Montreal: Black and Third World Students Association, 1973.

Hess, Daniel J. "Where Does the Train Lead? A Review of *And When They Shall Ask.*" *Festival Quarterly* 29 (1984): 29.

Hiebert, Paul. *Sarah Binks.* 1947. Toronto: McClelland and Stewart, 1995.

Hildebrand, Isbrand. "The Pickup at the Post Office." De Fehr et al. 97–98.

Hinz, Evelyn. "What Is Multiculturalism? A 'Cognitive' Introduction." *Mosaic* 29.3 (1996): vii–xii.

The Holy Bible. NIV. Nashville: Holman, 1986.

Hostetler, Ann. "Bringing Experience to Consciousness: Reflections on Mennonite Literature, 2004." *Journal of Mennonite Studies* 23 (2005): 137–50.

———. "The Unofficial Voice: The Poetics of Cultural Identity and Contemporary U.S. Mennonite Poetry." Roth and Beck 31-48.

Hoy, David Couzens. *The Time of Our Lives: A Critical History of Temporality.* Boston: MIT, 2009.

Huggan, Graham. *The Postcolonial Exotic: Marketing the Margins.* New York: Routledge, 2001.

Hutcheon, Linda. *Splitting Images: Contemporary Canadian Ironies.* Toronto: Oxford University Press, 1991.

Hutcheon, Linda, and Marion Richmond, eds. *Other Solitudes: Canadian Multicultural Fictions.* Toronto: Oxford University Press, 1990.

Jacobsen, Annie, with Jane Finlay-Young and Di Brandt. *Watermelon Syrup.* Waterloo: Wilfrid Laurier University Press, 2007.

James, William Closson. *Locations of the Sacred: Essays on Religion, Literature, and Canadian Culture.* Waterloo: Wilfrid Laurier University Press, 1998.

Janzen, Waldemar. "More Comments on Reimer's Novel." Rev. of *My Harp Is Turned to Mourning,* by Al Reimer. *Mennonite Reporter* 16.9 (1986): 10.

Jeffrey, David L. "A Search for Peace: Prophecy and Parable in the Fiction of Rudy Wiebe." Keith, ed., 179–201.

Jensen, De Lamar. *Reformation Europe: Age of Reform and Revolution.* Lexington: D.C. Heath, 1981.

Kalra, Virinder, Raminder Kaur, and John Hutnyk. *Diaspora and Hybridity.* London: SAGE, 2005.

Kamboureli, Smaro. "Canadian Ethnic Anthologies: Representations of Ethnicity." *ARIEL: A Review of International English Literature* 25.4 (1994): 11–52.

———. "Introduction. Shifting the Ground of a Discipline: Emergence and Canadian Literary Studies in English." Kamboureli and Zacharias 1–36.

———. *Making a Difference: Canadian Multicultural Literatures in English.* 2nd ed. Don Mills: Oxford University Press, 2007.

———. Personal interview. 14 Jan. 2009.

———. *Scandalous Bodies: Diasporic Literature in English Canada.* Don Mills: Oxford University Press, 2000.

Kamboureli, Smaro, and Robert Zacharias. "Preface." Kamboureli and Zacharias xi–xviii.

Kamboureli, Smaro, and Robert Zacharias, eds. *Shifting the Ground of Canadian Literary Studies.* Waterloo: Wilfrid Laurier University Press, 2012.

Kamboureli, Smaro, and Roy Miki, eds. *Trans.Can.Lit: Resituating the Study of Canadian Literature.* Waterloo: Wilfrid Laurier University Press, 2007.

Kaplan, Caren. *Questions of Travel: Postmodern Discourses of Displacement.* Durham: Duke University Press, 1996.

Karpinski, Eva C. "Multicultural 'Gift(s)': Immigrant Writing and the Politics of Anthologizing Difference." *Literary Pluralities.* Ed. Christl Verduyn. Peterborough: Broadview Press, 1998. 111–24.

Kasdorf, Julia Spicher. *The Body and the Book: Writing from a Mennonite Life: Essays and Poems.* University Park: Pennsylvania State University Press, 2009.

———. "The Making of Canada's 'Mennonite' Writers." *Festival Quarterly* 17, 2 (1990): 14–16.

Kearney, Richard. *On Stories.* London: Routledge, 2002.

Keefer, Janice Kulyk. "Paradise Lost in Russia, Found in Manitoba." Rev. of *The Russländer,* by Sandra Birdsell. *Globe and Mail* 29 Sept. 2001: D17.

Keim, Albert. *Harold S. Bender, 1897–1962.* Scottdale, PA: Herald, 1998.

Keith, W.J. *Epic Fiction: The Art of Rudy Wiebe.* Edmonton: University of Alberta Press, 1981.

Keith, W.J., ed. *A Voice in the Land: Essays by and about Rudy Wiebe.* Edmonton: NeWest, 1981.

Kim, Christine. "Racialized Diasporas, Entangled Postmemories, and *The Letter Opener.*" Kim, McCall, and Singer 171–89.

Kim, Christine, and Sophie McCall. "Introduction." Kim, McCall, and Singer 1–18.

Kim, Christine, Sophie McCall, and Melina Baum Singer, eds. *Cultural Grammars of Nation, Diaspora, and Indigeneity in Canada.* Waterloo: Wilfrid Laurier University Press, 2012.

Kirtz, Mary K. "Old World Traditions, New World Inventions: Bilingualism, Multiculturalism, and the Transformation of Ethnicity." *Canadian Ethnic Studies/Études ethniques au Canada* 28.1 (1996): 8–21.

Klaassen, Walter. *Anabaptism: Neither Catholic Nor Protestant.* Waterloo: Conrad, 1973.

Klassen, Sarah. "Everyman's Story." Rev. of *My Harp Is Turned to Mourning,* by Al Reimer. *Prairie Fire* 7.4 (1986–87): 57–60.

———. *Journey to Yalta.* Winnipeg: Turnstone Press, 1988.

Klinck, Carl F. *Literary History of Canada: Canadian Literature in English.* Toronto: University of Toronto Press, 1965.

Konrad, Anne. "Why the Soviet Mennonite Story Remains Unfinished." *Christian Living* (April–May 2000): 4–8.

Korkka, Janne. "Making a Story that Could Not Be Found: Rudy Wiebe's Multiple Canadas." *Tales of Two Cities: Essays on New Anglophone Literature.* Ed. John Skinner. Turku, Finland: University of Turku Press, 2000. 21–35.

Kostash, Myrna. *The Doomed Bridegroom: A Memoir.* Edmonton: NeWest, 1998.

Krahn, Cornelius. "Literature, Russo-German Mennonite." 1957. *Global Anabaptist Mennonite Encyclopedia Online.* Web. 10 Feb. 2011.

Krahn, Cornelius, and Ervin Beck. "Clocks." *Global Anabaptist Mennonite Encyclopedia Online*. 1989. Web. 29 April 2013. http://www.gameo.org/encyclopedia/contents/C58ME.html

Kraybill, Donald B. "Gelassenheit." *Concise Encyclopedia of Amish, Brethren, Hutterites, and Mennonites*. Baltimore: Johns Hopkins University Press. 93.

_____. "Modernity and Identity: The Transformation of Mennonite Ethnicity." Redekop and Steiner 153–72.

Kroeger, Arthur. *Hard Passage: A Mennonite Family's Long Journey from Russia to Canada*. Edmonton: University of Alberta Press, 2007.

_____. *Kroeger Clocks*. Steinbach: Mennonite Heritage Village (Canada), 2012.

Kroeker, Wally. *An Introduction to the Russian Mennonites*. Intercourse, PA: Good Books, 2005.

Kroetsch, Robert, et al. "Closing Panel." Tiessen and Hinchcliffe 223–42.

Kröller, Eva-Marie. "Afterword." *The Blue Mountains of China*. 1970. By Rudy Wiebe. Toronto: McClelland and Stewart, 1995. 273–78.

Kuester, Martin. "From Personal Anecdote to Scholarly Field of Research: A European's View of Canadian Mennonite Writing." *Journal of Mennonite Studies* 28 (2010): 151–65.

LaCapra, Dominick. *Writing History, Writing Trauma*. Baltimore: Johns Hopkins University Press, 2001.

Landa, José Ángel García. "Narrating Narrating: Twisting the Twice-Told Tale." Pier and Landa 419–51.

Lecker, Robert. *English-Canadian Literary Anthologies: An Enumerative Bibliography*. Teeswater: Reference, 1997.

Lindquist, N.J. "Canadian Authors: Preserving History through Fascinating Stories." *Maranatha News: Canada's Christian Newspaper* 15 Dec. 2006. Web. 20 Apr. 2010.

Litt, Paul. *The Muses, the Masses, and the Massey Commission*. Toronto: University of Toronto Press, 1992.

Loewen, Harry. *Between Worlds: Reflections of a Soviet-Born Canadian Mennonite*. Kitchener: Pandora Press, 2006.

_____. "'Can the Son Answer for the Father?' Reflections on the Stalinist Terror." *Journal of Mennonite Studies* 16 (1998): 76–90.

_____. "Canadian-Mennonite Literature: Longing for a Lost Homeland." *The Old World and the New: Literary Perspectives of German-Speaking Canadians*. Ed. Walter E. Riedel. Toronto: University of Toronto Press, 1984. 72–93.

_____. "Leaving Home: Canadian-Mennonite Literature in the 1980s." *Canadian Review of Comparative Literature* 16 (1989): 687–99.

_____. "Mennonite Literature in Canadian and American Historiography: An Introduction." *Mennonite Quarterly Review* 73.3 (1999): 557–70.

_____. "The Land." Loewen and Reimer 117–24.

Loewen, Harry, ed. *Mennonite Images: Historical, Cultural, and Literary Essays Dealing with Mennonite Issues.* Winnipeg: Hyperion, 1980.

_____. *Road to Freedom: Mennonites Escape the Land of Suffering.* Kitchener: Pandora Press, 2000.

_____. *Why I Am a Mennonite: Essays on Mennonite Identity.* Kitchener: Herald, 1988.

Loewen, Harry, and Al Reimer, eds. *Visions and Realities: Essays, Poems, and Fiction Dealing with Mennonite Issues.* Winnipeg: Hyperion, 1985.

Loewen, Helmut-Harry. Rev. of *My Harp Is Turned to Mourning,* by Al Reimer. *Border Crossings* 20 (1986): 56–57.

Loewen, Jacob A., and Wesley J. Prieb. "The Abuse of Power among Mennonites in South Russia, 1789–1919." *Power and the Anabaptist Tradition.* Ed. Benjamin W. Redekop and Calvin Wall Redekop. Baltimore: Johns Hopkins University Press, 2001. 95–114.

Loewen, Royden. "The Poetics of Peoplehood: Ethnicity and Religion among Canada's Mennonites." *Christianity and Ethnicity in Canada.* Ed. Paul Bramadat and David Seljak. Toronto: University of Toronto Press, 2008. 330–64.

_____. "Text, Temporality, and Transcultural Identities: Writing Mennonite History." Paper presented at the Narrating Mennonite Canada: History and/as Literature Colloquium. TransCanada Institute, Guelph, 27 Feb. 2009. Web. 14 Sept. 2010.

_____. "Trains, Text, and Time: The Emigration of Canadian Mennonites to Latin America, 1922–1948." In *Place and Replace: Essays on Western Canada.* Ed. Adele Perry, Esyllt W. Jones, and Leah Morton. Winnipeg: University of Manitoba Press, 2013. 123–138.

Loewen, Royden, and Steven M. Nolt. *Seeking Places of Peace. Global Mennonite History Series: North America.* Intercourse, PA: Good Books; Kitchener: Pandora Press, 2012.

Lohrenz, Gerhard. *Storm Tossed: The Personal Story of a Canadian Mennonite from Russia.* Winnipeg: Christian Press, 1976.

Maclulich, T.D. "What Was Canadian Literature? Taking Stock of the CanLit Industry." *Essays on Canadian Writing* 30 (1985): 17–34.

Mennonite Committee on Human Rights. "Submission to: The Canadian Museum for Human Rights." Accessed online via Canadian Mennonite University. 7 June 2012.

Mierau, Maurice. "Mennonites. Métis. Massacre. Marvelous." Rev. of *Children of the Day,* by Sandra Birdsell. *Globe and Mail* 17 Sept. 2005: D8.

Miki, Roy. *Broken Entries: Race, Subjectivity, Writing.* Toronto: Mercury, 1998.

_____. *In Flux: Transnational Shifts in Asian Canadian Writing.* Edmonton: NeWest Press, 2011.

Miller, J. Hillis. *Fiction and Repetition: Seven English Novels.* Cambridge, MA: Harvard University Press, 1982.

Mishra, Vijay. "The Diasporic Imaginary: Theorizing the Indian Diaspora." *Textual Practice* 10.3 (1996): 421–47.

Miska, John P., ed. *The Sound of Time: Anthology of Canadian-Hungarian Authors.* Lethbridge: Canadian-Hungarian Authors' Association, 1974.

Moraru, Christian. *Rewriting: Postmodern Narrative and Cultural Critique in the Age of Cloning.* Albany: SUNY Press, 2001.

Moss, Laura. "Between Fractals and Rainbows: Critiquing Canadian Criticism." *Tropes and Territories: Short Fiction, Postcolonial Readings, Canadian Writing in Context.* Ed. Marta Dvorák and W.H. New. Montreal: McGill-Queen's University Press, 2007. 17–32.

Mukherjee, Arun. *Oppositional Aesthetics: Readings from a Hyphenated Space.* Toronto: TSAR, 1994.

Munce, Alayna. *When I Was Young and in My Prime.* Roberts Creek, BC: Nightwood Editions, 2005.

Neufeld, Dietrich. *A Russian Dance of Death: Revolution and Civil War in the Ukraine.* 1921. Trans. Al Reimer. Winnipeg: Hyperion, 1977.

New, William H. *Encyclopedia of Literature in Canada.* Toronto: University of Toronto Press, 2002.

Nickel, John P. *Hope beyond the Horizon: Stories by Russian Mennonite Refugees Fleeing the Soviet Union.* Saskatoon: self-published, 1997.

Nishimura, Tomi, ed. *Maple: Poetry by Japanese Canadians with English Translations.* Trans. Kisaragi Poem Study Group. Toronto: Continental Times, 1975.

Nómez, Naín, ed. *Chilean Literature in Canada/Literatura Chilena en Canadá.* Ottawa: Ediciones Cordilera, 1982.

Oberle, Andre. "Arnold Dyck German Volume to Revive Interest in Writer's Work." Rev. of vol. 1 of *Arnold Dyck Collected Works. Mennonite Mirror* 15.3 (1985): 25.

Ostry, Bernard. *The Cultural Connection: An Essay on Culture and Government Policy in Canada.* Toronto: McClelland and Stewart, 1978.

Oyer, John S., and Robert S. Kreider. *Mirror of the Martyrs.* Intercourse, PA: Good Books, 1990.

Padolsky, Enoch. "Canadian Ethnic Minority Literature in English." *Ethnicity and Culture in Canada: The Research Landscape.* Ed. J.W. Berry and J.A. Laponce. Toronto: University of Toronto Press, 1994. 361–86.

Park, Noon. "Rebirth through Derision: Satire and the Anabaptist Discourse of Martyrdom in Miriam Toews' *A Complicated Kindness.*" *Journal of Mennonite Studies* 28 (2010): 55–68.

Pell, Barbara. *Faith and Fiction: A Theological Critique of the Narrative Strategies of Hugh MacLennan and Morley Callaghan.* Waterloo: Canadian Corporation for Studies in Religion, 1998.

Penner, Raylene Hinz. Rev. of *My Harp Is Turned to Mourning*, by Al Reimer. *Mennonite Life* 42.2 (1987): 29–30.

Peters, Victor. "With 'Koop enn Bua' on a Journey." *Mennonite Life* 14 (1959): 88.

Pier, John, and José Ángel García Landa, eds. *Theorizing Narrativity*. New York: Walter de Gruyter, 2008.

Pivato, Joseph. *Echo: Essays on Other Literatures*. 2nd ed. Toronto: Guernica Editions, 2003.

Polachic, Darlene. "Writers Approach Work from Christian Perspective." *Star-Phoenix* [Saskatoon] 28 June 2008: E15.

Pollock, Zailig. "*The Blue Mountains of China*: A Selective Annotated Genealogy." *Essays on Canadian Writing* 26 (1983): 70–73.

Prince, Gerald. "Narrative, Narrativeness, Narrativity, Narratability." Pier and Landa 19–28.

Quiring, Walter, and Helen Bartel. *In the Fullness of Time: 150 Years of Mennonite Sojourn in Russia*. Trans. Katherine Janzen. Ed. A. Klassen. Waterloo: Reeve Bean, 1974.

Redekop, Calvin. "The Mennonite Identity Crisis." *Journal of Mennonite Studies* 2 (1984): 87–103.

_____. "The Mennonite Romance with the Land." Loewen and Reimer 83–93.

_____. *Mennonite Society*. Baltimore: Johns Hopkins University Press, 1989.

_____. "The Sociology of Mennonite Identity: A Second Opinion." Redekop and Steiner 173–92.

Redekop, Calvin Wall, and Samuel J. Steiner, eds. *Mennonite Identity: Historical and Contemporary Perspectives*. Landham: University Press of America, 1988.

Redekop, John H. *A People Apart: Ethnicity and the Mennonite Brethren*. Winnipeg: Kindred Press, 1987.

_____. "The Roots of Nazi Support among Mennonites, 1930–1939: A Case Study Based on a Major Mennonite Paper." *Journal of Mennonite Studies* 14 (1996): 81–95.

Redekop, Magdalene. "Escape from the Bloody Theatre: The Making of Mennonite Stories." *Journal of Mennonite Studies* 11 (1993): 9–22.

Redekop, Magdalene Falk. "Translated into the Past: Language in *The Blue Mountains of China*." Keith, ed., 97–123.

Regehr, T.D. *Mennonites in Canada, 1939–1970: A People Transformed*. Toronto: University of Toronto Press, 1996.

Reimer, Al. "Arnold Dyck: Writer, Editor, Publisher, and Cultural Entrepreneur, 1889–1970." *Shepherds, Servants, and Prophets: Leadership among the Russian Mennonites (ca. 1880–1960)*. Ed. Harry Loewen. Kitchener: Pandora Press, 2003. 69–84.

_____. "Coming in Out of the Cold." Loewen, *Why* 254–67.

_____. "The Creation of Arnold Dyck's 'Koop enn Bua' Characters." Loewen, *Images* 256–66.

_____. "Foreword." *Kroeger Clocks*, by Arthur Kroeger. Steinbach: Mennonite Heritage Village (Canada), 2012. xix–xx.

_____. "Foreword." *Storm Tossed: The Personal Story of a Canadian Mennonite from Russia*, by Gerhard Lohrenz. Winnipeg: Christian Press, 1976. 7–9.

_____. *Mennonite Literary Voices Past and Present*. North Newton: Mennonite, 1993.

_____. *My Harp Is Turned to Mourning*. Winnipeg: Hyperion, 1985.

_____. "The Print Culture of the Russian Mennonites 1870–1920." *Mennonites in Russia: 1788–1988: Essays in Honor of Gerhard Lohrenz*. Ed. John Friesen. Winnipeg: CMBC Publications, 1989. 221–37.

_____. Rev. of *Hochfeld: Ein Steppendorf im Bürgerkrieg, Ukraine, 1918–19. Journal of Mennonite Studies* 17 (1999): 219–23.

_____. "The Role of Arnold Dyck in Canadian Mennonite Writing." Tiessen and Hinchcliffe 29–38.

_____. "The Russian-Mennonite Experience in Fiction." Loewen, *Images* 221–35.

_____. *When War Came to Kleindarp: And More Kleindarp Stories*. Winnipeg: Rosetta, 2008.

Reimer, Al, ed. *Collected Works of Arnold Dyck*. Vol. 2. Steinbach: Derksen, 1985.

_____. *Collected Works of Arnold Dyck*. Vol. 3. Steinbach: Derksen, 1988.

Reimer, Douglas. *Surplus at the Border: Mennonite Writing in Canada*. Winnipeg: Turnstone, 2002.

"Religion." Def. 4.a. *Oxford English Dictionary Online*. 2000. Web. 4 Oct. 2010.

Rempel, Peter Gerhard, John D. Rempel, and Paul Tiessen, eds. *Forever Summer, Forever Sunday: Peter Gerhard Rempel's Photographs of Mennonites in Russia, 1890–1917*. Trans. Hildegard E. Tiessen. St. Jacobs: Sand Hill, 1981.

Ricoeur, Paul. *Memory, History, Forgetting*. Chicago: University of Chicago Press, 2004.

_____. *Time and Narrative*. 2 vols. Trans. Kathleen McLaughlin and David Pellauer. Chicago: University of Chicago Press, 1983–85.

Rimland, Ingrid. *Lebensraum!* 3 vols. Toronto: Samisdat Publishers, 1998.

_____. *The Wanderers: The Saga of Three Women Who Survived*. St. Louis: Concordia, 1977.

Roth, John D. and Ervin Beck, eds. *Migrant Muses: Mennonite/s Writing in the U.S.* Goshen, IN: Mennonite Historical Society, 1998.

Royal Commission on Bilingualism and Biculturalism. *The Cultural Contributions of the Other Ethnic Groups*. Vol. 4 of the *Report of the Royal Commission on Bilingualism and Biculturalism*. Ottawa: Queen's Printer, 1970.

Royal Commission on National Development in the Arts, Letters, and Sciences. *Report of the Royal Commission on National Development in the Arts, Letters, and Sciences*. Ottawa: King's Printer, 1951.

Ruth, John L. *Mennonite Identity and Literary Art*. Kitchener: Herald, 1978.

Sarat, Austin, Nadav Davidovitch, and Michal Alberstein. "Trauma and Memory: Between Individual and Collective Experiences." *Trauma and Memory: Reading, Healing, and Making Law.* Ed. Austin Sarat, Nadav Davidovitch, and Michal Alberstein. Stanford: Stanford University Press, 2007. 3–18.

Saveson, Mary. Rev. of *Lost in the Steppe,* by Arnold Dyck. Trans. Harry Loewen. *Mennonite Mirror* 5.1 (1975): 17.

"Schleitheim Confession." 1527. *Global Anabaptist Mennonite Encyclopedia Online.* Web. 10 Feb. 2011. http://www.gameo.org/encyclopedia/contents/S345. html.

Shenk, Sara Wenger. "Remember Who You Are." *Mennonite Quarterly Review* 69, 3 (1995): 337–53.

Singer, Melina Baum. "Unhomely Moves: A.M. Klein, Jewish Diasporic Difference, Racialization, and Coercive Whiteness." Kim, McCall, and Singer 99–118.

Smith, Barbara Herrnstein. "Narrative Versions, Narrative Theories." *On Narrative.* Ed. W.J.T. Mitchell. Chicago: University of Chicago Press, 1981. 209–32.

Smucker, Barbara Claassen. *Days of Terror.* Toronto: Puffin, 1979.

_____. *Henry's Red Sea.* Scottdale, PA: Herald, 1955.

_____. *Underground to Canada.* Toronto: Clarke, Irwin and Company, 1977.

Sneath, Robyn. "Imagining a Mennonite Community: The *Mennonitische Post* and a People of Diaspora." *Journal of Mennonite Studies* 22 (2004): 205–20.

Snyder, Arnold. *Anabaptist History and Theology: An Introduction.* Kitchener: Pandora Press, 1995.

_____. "Anabaptist History and Theology: History or Heresy?" *Conrad Grebel Review* 16, 1 (1998): 53–59.

Sollors, Werner. "Ethnicity." *Critical Terms for Literary Study.* 2nd ed. Ed. Frank Lentricchia and Thomas McLaughlin. Chicago: University of Chicago Press, 2004. 288–304.

Spriet, Pierre. "Rudy Wiebe's *The Blue Mountains of China:* The Polyphony of a People or the Lonely Voice of the Fringe?" *Multiple Voices: Recent Canadian Fiction.* Ed. Jeanne Delbaere. Sydney: Dangaroo, 1990. 59–68.

"Strain." *Oxford English Dictionary Online.* 2000. Web. 5 Mar. 2001.

Symposium Planning and Findings Committee. "A Symposium on Faith and Ethnicity among the Mennonite Brethren: Summary and Findings Statement." *Journal of Mennonite Studies* 6 (1998): 51–59.

"Theology." Def. 1.b. *Oxford English Dictionary Online.* 2000. Web. 4 Oct. 2010.

Thiessen, Jack. "Canadian Mennonite Literature." *Canadian Literature* 51 (1972): 65–72.

Tiessen, Hildi Froese. "The Artist Rooted in a Traditional Community: Mennonite Writers Escape the Binary Paradigm." *The Strategic Smorgasbord of Postmodernity: Literature and the Christian Critic.* Ed. Deborah C. Bowen. New Castle: Cambridge Scholars, 2007. 225–37.

———. "Critical Thought and Mennonite Literature: Mennonite Studies Engages the Mennonite Literary Voice." *Journal of Mennonite Studies* 22 (2004): 237–46.

———. "Introduction: Mennonite Writing and the Post-Colonial Condition." Tiessen and Hinchcliffe 11–21.

———. "Mennonite/s Writing: State of the Art?" *Conrad Grebel Review* 26.1 (2008): 41–49.

———. "'Well Then, Eric Reimer, Where Are You Going?' Mennonites Writing Diaspora." Opening address at the Narrating Mennonite Canada: History and/as Literature Colloquium. TransCanada Institute, Guelph, 27 Feb. 2009. www.transcanadas.ca. Web. 9 Sept. 2010.

———. "What Remains of What Does Not Remain? A Mennonite Reader Reflects on Mennonites Leaving Home." *Rhubarb* 30 (2012): 12–15.

Tiessen, Hildi Froese, and Peter Hinchcliffe, eds. *Acts of Concealment: Mennonite/s Writing in Canada.* Waterloo: University of Waterloo Press, 1992.

Tiessen, Paul. "Putting Herself Forward: Naming and Performance in Sandra Birdsell's *The Russländer.*" *Mennonite Quarterly Review* 74.4 (2003): n. pag. Web. 13 Nov. 2009.

Toews, Aron A. *Mennonite Martyrs: People Who Suffered for Their Faith 1920–1940.* Winnipeg: Kindred Press, 1990.

Toews, Gerhard. *Die Heimat in Flammen.* Regina: Sonderabdruck aus *Der Courier*, 1932–33.

———. *Die Heimat in Trümmern.* Steinbach: Warte Verlag, 1936.

Toews, John B. "Compelled to Reflect Anew after Reading Reimer's Novel." Rev. of *My Harp Is Turned to Mourning,* by Al Reimer. *Mennonite Mirror* April 1986: 7.

———. *Lost Fatherland: The Story of the Mennonite Emigration from Soviet Russia, 1921–1927.* 1967. Vancouver: Regent College Publishing, 2003.

Toews, Miriam. *A Complicated Kindness.* Toronto: Knopf, 2004.

Twigg, Alan. "Rudy Wiebe." *Strong Voices: Conversations with 50 Canadian Authors.* Madeira Park: Harbour, 1988. 280–86.

Ty, Eleanor, and Christl Verduyn, eds. *Asian Canadian Writing beyond Autoethnography.* Waterloo: Wilfrid Laurier University Press, 2008.

Urry, James. "Fate, Hate, and Denial: Ingrid Rimland's *Lebensraum!*" *Mennonite Quarterly Review* 72.1 (1999): 107–27.

———. "Listing of Sources in the *Odessaer Zeitung* (1863–1914) Held on Microfilm in the Centre for MB Studies, Winnipeg, Canada." www.mbconf.ca/home.

———. "Memory: Monuments and the Marking of Pasts." *Conrad Grebel Review* 25.1 (2007): 33–62.

———. *Mennonites, Politics, and Peoplehood: Europe—Russia—Canada 1525–1980.* Winnipeg: University of Manitoba Press, 2006.

_____. "A *Mennostaat* for the *Mennovolk?* Mennonite Immigrant Fantasies in Canada in the 1930s." *Journal of Mennonite Studies* 14 (1996): 65–80.

_____. "The Reading Worlds of Russlaender and Kanadier Mennonites: Print, Libraries, and Readers in the Origins of Mennonite Creative Writing." *Journal of Mennonite Studies* 28 (2010): 129–49.

_____. "The Russian Mennonites, Nationalism, and the State 1789–1917." *Mennonites and the Challenge of Nationalism.* Ed. Abe J. Dyck. Winnipeg: Manitoba Mennonite Historical Society, 1994. 21–67.

_____. "Time and Memory: Secular and Sacred Aspects of the World of the Russian Mennonites and Their Descendants." *Conrad Grebel Review* 25.1 (2007): 4–32.

_____. "Truth and Fantasy: The Writing of Russian Mennonite Histories." *Mennonite Mirror* 18.6 (1990): 9–11.

van Braght, Thieleman J. *The Bloody Theater or Martyrs Mirror of the Defenseless Christians Who Baptized Only upon Confession of Faith, and Who Suffered and Died for the Testimony of Jesus, Their Saviour, from the Time of Christ to the Year A.D. 1600.* 1660. Trans. Joseph F. Sohm. Scottdale, PA: Herald, 1972.

Van Toorn, Penny. *Rudy Wiebe: Historicity of the Word.* Edmonton: University of Alberta Press, 1995.

Wah, Fred. *Faking It: Poetics and Hybridity.* Edmonton: NeWest, 2000.

Walcott, Rinaldo. *Black like Who? Writing Black Canada.* Toronto: Insomniac, 2003.

Walker, Morley. "In Country." Rev. of *The Time in Between,* by David Bergen. *Quill and Quire,* June 2005.

Waltner-Toews, David. *One Foot in Heaven.* Regina: Coteau Books, 2005.

Watson, Sheila. *The Double Hook.* 1959. Toronto: McClelland and Stewart, 1991.

Watt, Ian. "The Rise of the Novel Form." 1962. *The Novel: An Anthology of Criticism and Theory, 1900–2000.* Ed. Dorothy J. Hale. Malden: Blackwell, 2006: 462–80.

Weaver, Alain Epp. *States of Exile: Visions of Diaspora, Witness, and Return.* Waterloo: Herald Press, 2008.

Weaver, J. Denny. "Reading Sixteenth-Century Anabaptism Theologically: Implications for Modern Mennonites as a Peace Church." *Conrad Grebel Review* 16.1 (1998): 37–51.

Weaver, Laura H. "Mennonites' Minority Vision and the Outsider: Rudy Wiebe's *Peace Shall Destroy Many* and *The Blue Mountains of China.*" *MELUS* 13.3–4 (1986): 15–26.

Weier, John. *Steppe: A Novel.* Saskatoon: Thistledown, 1995.

White, Hayden. *The Content of the Form: Narrative Discourse and Historical Representation.* Baltimore: Johns Hopkins University Press, 1987.

White Paper. *Announcement of Implementation of Policy of Multiculturalism within Bilingual Framework.* House of Commons, Canada, 8 Oct. 1971.

Whitehead, Anne. *Trauma Fiction*. Edinburgh: Edinburgh University Press, 2004.

Wiebe, Armin. *The Salvation of Yasch Siemens*. Winnipeg: Turnstone Press, 1984.

Wiebe, Natasha G. "Miriam Toews' *A Complicated Kindness:* Restorying the Russian Mennonite Diaspora." *Journal of Mennonite Studies* 28 (2010): 33–54.

———. "Restorying in Mennonite Canadian Writing: Implications for Narrative Inquiry." PhD diss., University of Western Ontario, 2010.

Wiebe, Rudy. "The Artist as a Critic and a Witness." 1965. Keith, ed., 39–47.

———. "The Blindman River Contradictions: An Interview with Rudy Wiebe." 1984. *Rudy Wiebe: Collected Stories, 1955–2010*. Edmonton: University of Alberta Press, 2010. 346–56.

———. *The Blue Mountains of China*. 1970. Toronto: McClelland and Stewart, 1995.

———. "Finally, the Frozen Ocean." *Rudy Wiebe: Collected Stories, 1955–2010*. Edmonton: University of Alberta Press, 2010. 485–512.

———. "Origins." *Blue Mountains of China*. 1970. New Canadian Library. Toronto: McClelland and Stewart, 2008. 289–98.

———. *Peace Shall Destroy Many*. Toronto: McClelland and Stewart, 1962.

———. *Sweeter than All the World*. Toronto: Knopf, 2001.

———. "Walking Where His Feet Can Walk." Interview. *Speaking in the Past Tense: Canadian Novelists on Writing Historical Fiction*. Ed. Herb Wyile. Waterloo: Wilfrid Laurier University Press, 2007. 53–77.

Wiens, Gerhard. "Arnold Dyck at Seventy." *Mennonite Life* 14 (1959): 80–84.

———. "Arnold Dyck in Translation." *Mennonite Mirror* Mar. 1974: 7–8.

Wonneberger, Astrid. "The Invention of History in the Irish-American Diaspora: Myths of the Great Famine." *Diaspora, Identity, and Religion: New Directions in Theory and Research*. Ed. Waltraud Kokot, Khachig Tölölyan, and Carolin Alfonso. London: Routledge, 2004. 223–61.

"Write Speaking Mennonites." Dialogue among Sandra Birdsell, Di Brandt, Rudy Wiebe, and Patrick Friesen. *Border Crossings* 5.4 (1986): 21–28.

Wyile, Herb. *Speculative Fictions: Contemporary Canadian Novelists and the Writing of History*. Montreal: McGill-Queen's University Press, 2002.

Young, Judy. "Canadian Literature in the Non-Official Languages: A Review of Recent Publications and Work in Progress." *Canadian Ethnic Studies* 14.1 (1982): 138–49.

Zacharias, Robert. "'And Yet': Derrida on Benjamin's Divine Violence." *Mosaic: A Journal for the Interdisciplinary Study of Literature* 40.2 (2007): 103–16.

———. "'Some Great Crisis': Vimy as Originary Violence." Kamboureli and Zacharias 125–46.

———. "'What Else Have We to Remember?': Mennonite Canadian Literature and the Strains of Diaspora." *Embracing Otherness: Canadian Minority*

Discourses in Transcultural Perspective. Ed. Eugenia Sojka and Tomasz Sikora. Torun, Poland: Wydawnictwo Adam Marszałek, 2010. 186–209.

Zerubavel, Yael. *Recovered Roots: Collective Memory and the Making of Israeli National Tradition*. Chicago: University of Chicago Press, 1995.

Index

813.54 ZAC
33292013309178
wpa
Zacharias, Robert.
Rewriting the break event :